# MARKETS, T...
## and
# THE ENVIRONMENT
### *Towards Integration*

D1092902

LIVERPOOL JMU LIBRARY

3 1111 00675 0580

# MARKETS, THE STATE
## and
# THE ENVIRONMENT

## *Towards Integration*

Edited by
**ROBYN ECKERSLEY**
*Graduate School of Government*
*Monash University, Australia*

© Robyn Eckersley and contributors 1995

All rights reserved. No reproduction, copy or transmission of
this publication may be made without written permission.

No paragraph of this publication may be reproduced, copied or
transmitted save with written permission or in accordance with
the provisions of the Copyright, Designs and Patents Act 1988,
or under the terms of any licence permitting limited copying
issued by the Copyright Licensing Agency, 90 Tottenham Court
Road, London W1P 9HE.

Any person who does any unauthorised act in relation to this
publication may be liable to criminal prosecution and civil
claims for damages.

First published in Australia 1995 by
MACMILLAN EDUCATION AUSTRALIA PTY LTD

First published in Great Britain 1996 by
MACMILLAN PRESS LTD
Houndmills, Basingstoke, Hampshire RG21 2XS
and London
Companies and representatives
throughout the world.

ISBN 0-333-65750-0 paperback

A catalogue record of this book is available
from the British Library.

10   9   8   7   6   5   4   3   2   1
05   04   03   02   01   00   99   98   97   96

Printed in Hong Kong

Cover design by Raul Diche

# Contents

# List of Tables

# Preface

This book grew out of a one day workshop on 'Bureaucracy, Markets and the Environment' held at Monash University in October 1992. The workshop gathered together an inter-disciplinary group of distinguished academics, consultants, activists and government officers from the environmental policy community to conduct a wide ranging, critical examination and review of the various environmental policy instruments available to governments.

The workshop proved to be an outstanding success and two generous grants enabled the momentum to be carried forward and to materialise in the form of this edited collection. In particular, I am grateful to the Victorian Office of the Environment (now part of the Department of Conservation and Natural Resources) and the Commonwealth Department of the Environment, Sport and Territories for their interest in the workshop and for their financial assistance towards the publication costs of this book.

The majority of the chapters in this collection are revised versions of a selection of the original papers presented at the workshop. However, three previously published papers have also been enlisted (and revised) to round out the volume. In particular, the chapter by Robert Hahn is a reworked and updated version of 'Economic Prescriptions for Environmental Problems: How the Patient Followed the Doctor's Orders', which appeared in the *Journal of Economic Perspectives* 3(2), Spring 1989: 95–114; the chapter by Peter Grabosky is a revised version of 'Green Markets: Environmental Regulation by the Private Sector', which will appear in a forthcoming issue of *Law and Policy*; and the chapter by Gordon Clark is a revised and updated version of 'Global Competition and the Environmental Performance of Australian Mineral Companies: Is the "Race to the Bottom" Inevitable?', which appeared in *International Environmental Affairs*, 5(3), Summer 1993: 147–72. I am grateful to the respective publishers of these three journals for their permission to publish revised versions of the articles in this collection.

I convened the workshop on 'Bureaucracy, Markets and the Environment' in my capacity as Program Director for Environment and Development with the Institute of Ethics and Public Policy at Monash. The Institute is the brainchild of Gordon Clark, who served as Director from 1991 until 1994, and who has since taken up an appointment as the Halford Mackinder Professor of Geography at the University of Oxford. I am indebted to Gordon for his advice and strong support in relation to the various projects of the Institute, including this one.

I am also indebted to all the contributors to this volume for their cooperation and excellent contributions. Finally, it has been a pleasure to work with Peter Debus from Macmillan and I would especially like to thank him for his patience and support.

Robyn Eckersley
Melbourne, December 1994

# Notes on Contributors

*Peter Christoff* is an environmental policy consultant and currently a research student in the Politics Department at the University of Melbourne. Formerly the Assistant to the Commissioner for the Environment in Victoria, he was responsible for establishing and managing the State of the Environment (SOE) Reporting Program in Victoria. His recent consultancy work includes the Australian Conservation Foundation's 1994 and 1995 federal budget submissions and reports for the federal Department of the Environment on National SOE Reporting, National Environmental Indicators and the Use of Economic Instruments for Environmental Protection in the Netherlands.

*Gordon L. Clark* is the Halford Mackinder Professor of Geography at the University of Oxford and Professorial Fellow at St Peter's College. Prior to his appointment at Oxford, he was Professor of Geography and Environmental Science, Professor of Government in the Graduate School of Government, and Director of the Institute of Ethics and Public Policy at Monash University. Author of many books and articles, he is the co-editor of an ethics case book *Management Ethics: Cases and Materials* published by HarperCollins and author of *Pensions and Corporate Restructuring in American Industry* published by The Johns Hopkins University Press.

*John S. Dryzek*, formerly of the University of Oregon, is Professor of Political Science at the University of Melbourne. He is the author of *Rational Ecology: Environment and Political Economy* (Basil Blackwell 1987), and *Discursive Democracy: Politics, Policy and Political Science* (Cambridge University Press 1990). His articles on environmental politics, political theory, policy analysis and the history and philosophy of social science have appeared in journals such as the *American Political Science Review*, *Journal of Politics* and *British Journal of Political Science*.

*Robyn Eckersley* is program director for environment and development at the Institute of Ethics and Public Policy, Graduate School of Government, Monash University and a senior lecturer in the Politics Department at Monash University. Formerly a constitutional lawyer, she has specialised in environmental politics since 1986 and has taught courses in environmental law, environmental politics and green political theory. She has also published extensively in environmental politics, ethics and public policy, including *Environmentalism and Political Theory* (State University of New York Press and UCL Press 1992).

*Peter N. Grabosky* is a Visiting Fellow in the Administration, Compliance and Governability Program, Research School of Social Sciences, Australian National University. Formerly an Associate Professor of Political Science at the University of Vermont, he has held a senior position in the South Australian Attorney-General's Department and was Director of Research at the Australian Institute of Criminology. His writings on regulatory systems include (with John Braithwaite) *Of Manners Gentle: Enforcement Strategies of Australian Business Regulatory Agencies* (Oxford University Press 1986).

*Robert W. Hahn* is a Resident Scholar at the American Enterprise Institute and an Adjunct Research Fellow, John F. Kennedy School of Government, Harvard University. He recently served as Co-Chair of the US Alternative Fuels Council. Prior to that, Dr Hahn worked for two years as a senior staff member of the President's Council of Economic Advisers, where he focused on issues concerning energy policy, the environment and science policy. He also served as a member of the White House Drafting Team for the President's *Clean Air Act.* Dr Hahn is one of the architects of the innovative market-based approach for reducing acid rain.

*Michael Jacobs* is a Research Fellow at the Centre for the Study of Environmental Change, Lancaster University. Formerly a lecturer in the Department of Adult Education at the University of Southampton, he spent four years working as a consultant on sustainable development policy and environmental management systems, working principally for the UK central and local governments and environmental NGOs. He is author of *The Green Economy: Environment, Sustainable Development and the Politics of the Future* (Pluto Press 1991), together with a number of papers on valuation, macro-economic planning, and other aspects of environmental economics.

*Peter Kinrade* is currently the sustainable energy and transport campaign convenor with the Australian Conservation Foundation (ACF) after working as a policy analyst with the Ecologically Sustainable Development (ESD) Unit of the ACF and the World Wide Fund for Nature. Peter has undertaken a diverse range of environmental policy work for the ACF and he has published numerous reports. He has also represented the ACF on a number of national environmental committees, including the Energy Use and Energy Production Working Groups of the Federal Government's ESD process. He is currently a member of the National Greenhouse Advisory Panel.

*Alan Moran* is an economist and Deputy Secretary of Energy in the Department of Energy and Minerals in Victoria. He is the author of many articles on the environment, regulation and industry policy. He has co-edited three books on the environment, including *The Price of Preservation* (Tasman Institute 1993) and *Markets, Resources and the Environment* (Allen and Unwin 1991). Dr Moran was formerly the Research Director of the Melbourne-based 'think tank', the Tasman Institute, and has also served as the Director of the Australian Government's Office of Regulation Review and a senior official in the Industry Commission.

*Susan L. Smith* is Associate Professor at the Willamette University College of Law. Before joining the Faculty at Willamette, Professor Smith served as Assistant Chief, Environmental Defence Section, Land and Natural Resources Division, US Department of Justice. In that capacity, she supervised federal enforcement actions against persons accused of wetlands destruction under the *Clean Water Act* and the *Rivers and Harbors Act*. She also supervised all federal environmental litigation against federal facilities accused of pollution control violations.

*Janna Thompson* is a senior lecturer in the School of Philosophy at La Trobe University in Melbourne. She has taught courses and written articles in the areas of environmental ethics and politics, womens studies, peace studies and social and political philosophy. Her main research interests are discourse ethics and the ethics of international society. She has recently published *Justice and World Order: A Philosophical Inquiry* (Routledge 1992).

# Introduction

## Robyn Eckersley

One of the enduring legacies of the sustainable development debate of the 1980s has been a quest for greater integration of the economy and the environment. A significant by-product of this quest has been growing interest in the potential of market-based instruments of environmental policy as a supplement, or in some cases an alternative, to the traditional approach of setting environmental standards by direct legal regulation.

This book seeks to advance the quest for economy–environment integration by providing a critical, interdisciplinary review of the case for a more market-based approach to environmental policy, taking stock of key theoretical debates and recent policy developments in Australia, the United States and Europe. The phrase 'market-based instrument' has been interpreted broadly in this collection to include not only new economic instruments such as environmental taxes, charges, subsidies and tradable emission permits but also other policy tools that directly or indirectly structure the market place in ways that make commercial decisions more compatible with environmental public policy objectives.[1] Although the primary focus of the collection is on market-based approaches, consideration is also given to the traditional regulatory approach, which has often served as a convenient foil for those wishing to caricature the 'old' in order to extol the virtues of the 'new'.

As the debate about sustainable development broadens, and in some cases shifts, from a general debate about broad policy objectives to a specialist debate about policy tools, many hitherto contentious political questions have been recast as technical questions to be solved by specialists such as economists, lawyers and bureaucrats at several removes from the 'centre stage' of the political process. Yet the task of evaluating and choosing the 'technologies of governance' in relation to particular problems has never been merely a technical matter (although it usually requires technical expertise). As the contributors to this collection demonstrate, the choice of policy instruments can have significant implications not only for the environment and the economy but also for social justice and democracy. Indeed, in some circumstances, a particular configuration of policy instruments may be seen to 'summon' particular social relationships or embody particular visions of the social order; in other cases, they may simply produce consequences that may be unintended and unforeseen by policy makers.

The characterisation of the choice of policy tools as a 'technical' question is but one manifestation of what Habermas long ago described as the 'scientisation of politics' — the process whereby the lay public is expected to cede ever greater areas of 'system steering' to technocratic elites.[2] However, this tendency has been countered by the increasing 'politicisation of science': critical reflection on (as distinct from the simplistic debunking of) the assumptions, methodologies and norms embedded in particular specialist disciplines, whether in the natural sciences or the social sciences. Many of the recommendations for market-based instruments for environmental protection have been based on the theoretical models of economic textbooks rather than detailed empirical studies of the actual behaviour of economic actors or state agencies in the context of specific cultural and institutional frameworks.[3] A key objective of this book is to provide a more rounded analysis of the case for market-based instruments by reviewing both economic theory *and* practice while also offering a broader range of critical perspectives from other disciplines in the social sciences, notably political science, law and social philosophy.

One of the significant findings to emerge from this inquiry is that, despite the many wide-ranging arguments in favour of market-based environmental policy tools, most governments have been rather slow to respond and the traditional regulatory approach still remains dominant. This collection offers a range of explanations as to why this might be so, whether such a cautious response remains justifiable and whether the response is likely to change in the future.

Part I provides a general background and introduction to the key terms, themes and arguments of the book. Chapter 1 provides a broad overview of the theoretical debates and practical experience concerning new environmental policy instruments, incorporating and building on the general lessons emerging from the anthology. Michael Jacobs' chapter provides an enlightening taxonomy of environmental economics that challenges the usefulness of the conventional dichotomy between 'command-and-control' and 'market-based' instruments.

Part II juxtaposes Alan Moran's neoclassical economic defence of market-based instruments with a critical examination of the role and limits of market instruments from the perspective of a key campaign researcher in the Australian environment movement, Peter Kinrade. The chapters by Michael Jacobs, Robert Hahn and Peter Christoff in Part III then put the economic theory to the political test by providing a critical review and analysis of the recent practical experience of market-based instruments in Britain, USA (and, selectively, Continental Europe) and Australia.

Part IV examines the broader question of the relationship between competition and environmental performance. Peter Grabosky explores the more subtle and indirect ways in which the state may 'govern at a distance' by facilitating self-regulating green markets while Gordon Clark examines the international competitive conditions that give rise to both upward and downward pressures on environmental performance through a case study of the Australian minerals industry.

Finally, Part V explores the questions of enforcement, social and global justice, and democracy in relation to the choice of environmental policy tools. Susan Smith examines the deterrent and symbolic effects of imposing criminal sanctions on corporate directors in relation to violations of environmental law and argues, more generally, that monitoring and enforcement problems are not necessarily any easier under market-based schemes. Janna Thompson explores the distributive implications of environmental policy tools in the context of a broader examination of policy goals and moral obligations concerning the social burden of environmental protection vis-a-vis rich and poor classes and nations. John Dryzek provides both a macro-level analysis of the liberal democratic state's commitment to environmental policy and a micro-level analysis of the democratic implications of different environmental policy tools.

The various contributors to this collection by no means all share the same theoretical analysis or political perspective in relation to market-based instruments. Together, however, they provide a rounded mix of different disciplinary and normative perspectives in the environmental policy debates and thereby shed considerable light on one of the most complex and urgent challenges of our time: how to approach the *political* task of integrating economic activity and environmental protection.

## Endnotes

1. Included in the latter category are (i) the privatisation of publicly owned, or unowned, environmental assets and (ii) other policy instruments for 'governing at a distance' such as the provision of government information and advice; research and development; government purchasing policies; ecolabelling; recognition (e.g. awards) and the certification of management practices; and the facilitation of self-regulation through third-party commercial activity.
2. See 'The Scientization of Politics and Public Opinion' in Habermas (1971), 62–80.
3. Notable exceptions include the extensive work of Hahn (listed in the bibliography to Hahn's chapter in this volume) and the recent work of Skou Andersen (1994).

# Part I

# *Anchoring the Debate*

# 1

# Markets, the State and the Environment: An Overview

## Robyn Eckersley

### Growing Pressure for Change: To Market, to Market?

Although the emergence of widespread popular concern over environmental problems is typically dated from the 1960s, the 1980s decade is more likely to be remembered as the period during which environmentalism rose to prominence in terms of the degree of media saturation, public concern and national and international political debate given over to environmental problems. This was also the decade that saw the emergence of Green parties as a new minority political force — a symptom of increasing frustration and disillusionment with the capacity of established political parties and the policy-making process to address ecological problems. The mounting popular concern and political agitation over the environment have exerted pressure on governments around the world to move from a piecemeal and largely reactive response towards a more integrated and anticipatory strategy.

By the end of the 1980s many governments had endorsed the concept of sustainable development as providing the integrating framework for future environmental policy making. This concept was brought to international prominence by the report of the influential World Commission on Environment and Development (the Brundtland Report, WECD 1990) in 1987 and officially endorsed by the international community at the Earth Summit in 1992. Although sustainable development remains a highly contested concept, it has nonetheless provided a basis for a critical confrontation with the intellectual premises, time horizons and instruments of traditional environmental policy.

The traditional — and still dominant — approach of government has been to regard economic policy as central and environmental policy as peripheral to, and largely in tension with, economic policy. Indeed, economic development and environmental protection have been widely interpreted as essentially antagonistic goals: more development has been understood to mean less environmental protection (or more degradation) and vice-versa. According to this characterisation, the task of government is to manage the environment in ways that strike an acceptable 'balance' or 'trade-off' between environmental protection and economic growth — a politically volatile strategy that has proved to be highly responsive to cyclical swings in the economy. The compartmentalised, hierarchical and (often) competitive structure and character of bureaucratic agencies has kept at bay the promise of more constructive communication between environment and development (including Treasury) departments.

The Brundtland Report played a major role in directing attention to the many interdependencies between economic and environmental administration: instead of allocating responsibility for 'after the fact' environmental damage to sectoral ministries and agencies, the report urged nations to anticipate and prevent environmental damage by integrating environmental policy with economic, trade, energy and agricultural policy (WCED 1990, 83). To this end, the Brundtland Report recommended that governments make more effective use of economic instruments to promote 'clean production' (i.e. production that uses less energy and resources and generates less pollution and waste) (1990, 264–66).

Traditionally, sectoral environmental agencies have generally followed a direct regulatory approach by prescribing standards and licensing schemes, backed by monitoring and sanctions for non-compliance. However, these traditional tools of environmental policy had already come under increasing critical scrutiny well before the publication of the Brundtland Report. As Albert Weale has shown, by the early 1980s traditional regulation was increasingly seen as lacking in both *efficiency* and *legitimacy* (Weale 1992, chapter 6). As to the efficiency question, environmental economists had pointed to the potential of market-based instruments to achieve the same emission reductions at much lower costs than traditional regulatory tools while also providing greater incentives for ongoing technical innovation. As to the legitimacy question, environmentalists had long complained of the less than vigilant monitoring and enforcement of environmental regulations.

The new discourse on economy–environment integration has also been one of the features of what Weale (1992) has dubbed 'the new politics of pollution', which emerged in the 1980s. According to Weale, the new approach — also known in Europe as 'ecological modernisation' — pointed to the longer term limitations of 'end-of-pipe' solutions to pollution and the economic and environmental advantages of undertaking a longer term assessment of costs and benefits and a more cautious approach to risk assessment and scientific uncertainty. The traditional discourse of balance, which pulled back from charging producers and consumers the full environmental costs of their activities, came under challenge for not avoiding costs but rather merely passing them on in space and time. Moreover, it was pointed out that such costs would mount dramatically over time, with an increasing proportion being required for restoration or damage limitation rather than problem prevention. In short, the new environmental policy discourse of the 1980s highlighted *the longer term social, ecological and economic costs of failing to act* as much as the immediate economic costs of taking action. The growing consumer demand for environmentally friendly products and services indicated that the short-term costs incurred by firms in improving environmental performance could bring longer term competitive advantages, new investment opportunities and significant commercial rewards.

Ever since the establishment of the OECD Environment Committee in 1970, the OECD has consistently promoted greater use of economic instruments in environmental policy. For example, the Polluter Pays Principle — endorsed by the OECD and the European Community — provides an official recognition of the environmental welfare economists' case for the internalisation of negative ecological externalities (OECD 1975). This principle, primarily designed as a 'no-subsidy' principle to prevent distortions in trade and investment, requires that the costs of environmental protection should be imposed on the polluter (rather than subsidised by government) to enable the incorporation of environmental costs into prices and markets.[1] Although such costs may be imposed by a number of means (standard setting, issuing permits, as well as market-based instruments such as taxes and charges), the OECD has recommended that more attention be given to the use of market-based instruments as a means of implementing the Polluter Pays Principle (OECD 1989, 3).

Indeed, OECD economists have suggested that 'Direct regulation of societal processes seems to have reached its effectiveness frontier, or even to have gone beyond that, which calls for deregulation, or at least "regulatory reform"' (1989, 25).[2] The OECD has recently published a set of common guidelines to assist member countries in implementing market-based instruments (OECD 1991).

By the early 1990s, the case for greater use of economic instruments had captured the attention of many policy advisers and governments and had received official endorsement at the regional and international levels. For example, the European Community's Fifth Action Plan on the Environment placed greater emphasis on the use of fiscal instruments such as taxes to achieve environmental protection goals rather than relying on regulation (*International Environmental Reporter* 1993b, 755). Internationally, market-based instruments have been promoted in Agenda 21 and in many international environmental treaties.

Yet the growing appeal of economic instruments should not be attributed simply to a new-found political commitment to 'account' for the environment in response to growing public environmental concern. According to Weale (1992, 160-61), the neoclassical economic framework provided the rhetorical veneer, not the driving force, for the new environmental policy debates. For most OECD countries, the 1980s was a period of economic instability, low levels of growth, increasing capital and labour mobility and high government budget deficits. It should hardly be surprising that policy advisers should show increasing interest in experimenting with new tools of environmental policy that promised greater efficiency at a time of shrinking revenue, especially when set against the climate of deregulation in many OECD countries. Moreover, the mounting news of serious ecological degradation in Eastern Europe, which reached the West following the collapse of the Soviet Union at the end of the 1980s, has been interpreted by critics of Big Government as providing an historical vindication of the virtues of the decentralised price mechanism vis-a-vis centralised planning in relation to both economic performance *and* environmental protection.

Despite these broad developments, however, the growing official interest in market-based instruments has not been matched with a proliferation of new environmental policy designs that have employed economic instruments. Apart from several significant exceptions (reviewed in Part III), caution and modesty in new policy design have been the order of the day, although Hahn suggests in chapter 6 that the situation may change in the future in the wake of the 'demonstration effect'. To date, the most prevalent economic instruments are modest charges, which are used to fund environmental programs.[3] Meanwhile, the traditional regulatory approach remains dominant. Indeed, the practice of many governments has been to replace regulations not with economic instruments but with voluntary agreements or covenants with industry (Verbruggen 1993, 8).

Why, then, has there not been a more concerted implementation of market-based regimes, given the growing consensus among many of the major stakeholders in the environmental policy community (including bureaucrats, economic consultants, some sections of industry and many sections of the environment movement) that the traditional forms of environmental regulation and administration are 'suboptimal'? In examining this question, it is important to separate out the arguments for better economy–environment integration and environmental protection from the arguments for market-based measures. The latter do not necessarily flow from the former. That is, better integration and protection might just as easily be achieved by a range of bureaucratic reforms as by the introduction of new market-based measures. For example, many observers have attributed the 'suboptimality' of administrative regulation to weak political commitment and accountability, inadequate resourcing and staffing, poor policy design and/or weak monitoring and enforcement. Market-based measures are likely to reproduce many of these problems if they are introduced without a careful evaluation of the reasons for bureaucratic failure. Given that market-based and state-based steering systems have never been mutually exclusive regulatory domains, there is little to be learned from contrasting the ideal theory of one regulatory domain (whether market or state) with the highly imperfect practice of the other. Yet it is surprising how many economists and public choice theorists have committed this kind of category error in the course of defending their favoured model.

Indeed, neither the Brundtland Report nor the 'ecological modernisers' sought to foreclose the debate about regulatory reform; rather, they simply recommended that more *emphasis* be given to market-based instruments. While such instruments might provide a means of overcoming the inefficiencies of traditional environmental administration, they do not necessarily provide an appropriate response to the legitimacy problems. These problems have been attributed, in part, to the relatively closed and elitist nature of the traditional environmental policy community, which has often allowed compliance to be 'negotiated' between regulatory agencies and the industry 'clientele' rather than strictly enforced (e.g. Yeager 1991). Of course, improving the cost-effectiveness of environmental administration may go some way towards redressing these general legitimacy problems. However, lasting community confidence in environmental administration is more likely to come about through a range of 'process' reforms that widen and deepen the opportunities for community participation in policy formulation and strengthen the lines of responsibility and accountability in relation to policy implementation and monitoring.

As we shall see, the growing disillusionment with traditional environmental regulation has not been matched by a general consensus over problem analysis, policy goals or the circumstances in which new, market-based instruments should be employed. Not all advocates of market-based instruments have defended them with the same degree of enthusiasm or for the same reasons. Indeed, the case for market-based instruments has generated some strange alliances and shifting positions throughout the 1980s and early 1990s, and it has been pursued on both pragmatic and theoretical grounds to promote radical, moderate and conservative environmental causes.

## State versus Market: Competing 'Failure Theories'

The discipline of environmental economics has played a key role in shaping the economy–environment integration debate, and in putting market-based instruments on the environmental policy agenda. Although by no means new, environmental economics has certainly been reinvigorated and popularised in the past decade, especially since the publication of the influential Pearce Report (Pearce, Markandya and Barbier 1989).[4] Yet environmental economics by no means exhausts the range of economic and institutional analyses regarding the lack of integration between environmental and economic policy. Indeed, one of the most interesting features of the general environmental policy debates is the proliferation of different theoretical analyses of the 'failure' of society's two major steering systems — the market and the state — to manage environmental problems. Here the economic analysis of 'market failure' by neoclassical environmental welfare economics (e.g. Pearce et al. 1989) is shadowed by a more radical critique of market rationality by the emerging discipline of ecological economics, exemplified in the work of Herman Daly (1991). (Indeed, ecological economists have sought to highlight not only the failure of the market but also the 'paradigm failure' of neoclassical economics.) Similarly, the analysis of 'bureaucratic failure' in relation to environmental problems offered by public choice theorists, such as Anderson and Leal (1991), finds a much more radical counterpart in the critique of 'state failure' offered by defenders of ecological modernisation and discursive democracy, such as John Dryzek (1987, 1990 and in this volume), Martin Jänicke (1990), Albert Weale (1992) and Peter Christoff (1995). Ulrich Beck's (1992) influential analysis of 'the risk society' and his defence of 'reflexive modernisation' might also be included in this latter general category.

What is noteworthy about these different economic, political and sociological 'failure' theories is that they provide different analyses of *problem displacement* in relation to environmental decision making — whether as 'negative ecological externalities'; bureaucratic competition, 'buck-passing' and corruption; a break down between political accountability and control; or an asymmetry between the production and distribution of ecological risks. Beyond these general similarities, however, there remain significant differences in analysis concerning the institutions, processes and mechanisms that might be enlisted to prevent 'problem displacement'. Behind these different institutional analyses lie competing ethical principles concerning how, and to what extent, environmental costs should be avoided and/or allocated in relation to geographical regions, nations, social classes, non-human species and future generations. Understanding these competing analytical and normative approaches (together with the conflicting responses of the key political stakeholders) is crucial to understanding why there remains so much disagreement within the environmental policy community concerning how, and to what extent, market-based instruments may be enlisted as tools of environmental policy. Environmental economists may have opened the debate about the potential of market-base instruments, but they by no means have the 'last word'.

*Environmental (Welfare) Economics*
According to the standard analysis of neoclassical welfare economics, markets 'fail' to take into account the full environmental costs and benefits of economic activity because environmental assets and services (many of which are 'public goods') have not been properly valued. In many cases, the environment has been exploited as a 'free resource' or has been chronically undervalued. In other cases, exploitation has been intensified through government subsidies that 'distort' markets (e.g. tax relief for land-clearing or subsidies on the commercial use of fertiliser and energy). Yet environmental goods and services are essential 'factors of production', serving important economic and welfare functions.

Environmental costs and benefits are therefore seen by environmental welfare economists as representing 'incomplete or missing markets' (Helm and Pearce 1991, 2). To address this problem, such economists have recommended that governments 'correct' market failure by imposing taxes or charges (or removing subsidies) on polluters and other environmental degraders to enable the 'environmental factors of production' to be 'internalised' by the market so that prices reflect the 'full costs of production' (i.e. the marginal private cost of production as well as the marginal social costs). According to this standard analysis, it is only when all relevant factors of production are properly priced that an efficient use and allocation of resources will be achieved. However, the questions of how such taxes and charges should be calculated, and how the revenue should be spent, remain theoretically and politically contentious.

According to Pigou's early analysis (Pigou 1932), such externality taxes (or Pigouvian taxes) should be based on the estimated damage to the environment caused by pollution emissions (including the damage to future generations). While the theory is elegant, the practical task of calculating such a tax remains methodologically contentious, especially bearing in mind the scientific uncertainties associated with many environmental problems. Aside from these technical problems, there remain even more significant political hurdles impeding the imposition of full externality taxes on producers and consumers; such taxes would be massive in relation to many polluting activities and therefore likely to be most unwelcome by industry. These problems have prompted some economists to recommend a more pragmatic standards-tax approach whereby the pollution tax is merely imposed as an incentive to reach certain politically agreed standards set by the government (e.g. Baumol and Oates 1988). As Martinez-Alier (1993) observes, no-one really knows how to 'correct' the market; taxes are merely technical instruments based on scientific/political compromises, not economic theory. In this respect, prices can be 'ecologically corrected' without necessarily being 'ecologically correct' in the Pigouvian sense (1993, 105). As the chapters in Part III demonstrate, the majority of the environmental charges and fees that have thus far been imposed in different countries have been based on neither damage costs nor special environmental quality targets (see also Turner, Pearce and Bateman 1994, 150). In a recent empirical study of the use of economic instruments to control water pollution in four European countries, Skou Andersen (1994a) points out that economic theory has to date paid insufficient attention to the economic and environmental implications of how the revenue is spent (i.e.

whether it is earmarked or paid directly into consolidated revenue).

In addition to green taxes, charges and fees, environmental welfare economists have also pointed to the efficiency gains to be enjoyed from other market-based instruments, such as deposit–refund schemes and tradable resource and pollution permits, which have been shown to enable pollution reduction to take place at least cost. Indeed, we have seen that this is the general defence of all market-based measures: that they provide a more efficient *alternative* to direct legal regulation because they allow the individual polluter the freedom to adjust production to that point where the marginal costs of pollution reduction equal the marginal costs of the damage caused by pollution. However, most of the economic instruments that have been applied to date have been grafted onto existing regulatory regimes rather than introduced as an alternative to such regimes.

*Free Market Environmentalism*
Whereas welfare environmental economists have directed their attention to the problem of 'market failure', self-styled 'free market environmentalists' (such as Anderson and Leal 1991) have approached the problem of environmental degradation through a critique of the 'command-and-control' approach to environmental policy. In drawing on the public choice critique of bureaucratic decision making, Anderson and Leal offer an analysis that is much closer to Coase (1960) than Pigou (1932), although they do not specifically enlist Coase. That is, environmental externalities are attributed to the *absence* of markets and property rights in relation to the environment; if property rights over the environment are well defined, then the problem can be addressed through voluntary transactions among those causing environmental degradation and those suffering such degradation.[5] The ideal solution to the 'tragedy of the commons', then, is neither regulation nor a new regime of eco-taxes and charges but rather the conversion of the commons (e.g. rivers, national parks, wildlife) into private property rights.

The decentralised private choice of the market is defended as being inherently superior to the centralised public choice of bureaucracy (which includes setting taxes). Bureaucratic regulation is characterised as necessarily inefficient, liable to 'regulatory capture' and undue influence by special interest lobby groups, and liable to corruption by self-seeking officials. Indeed, free market environmentalists have exposed numerous cases of maladministration, regulatory capture and gross inefficiency in many environmental regulatory regimes concerned with the management of forests, water rights and public lands. However, while they argue for the removal of distorting government subsidies, they do not recommend further government intervention in the form of externality taxes to correct 'market failure'. Instead, they recommend slimming the state and 'liberating' market forces wherever possible by decentralising and 'depoliticising' resource allocation decisions. Unlike bureaucrats, private property holders are believed to possess the necessary information and incentives to take responsibility for environmental resources by bargaining among themselves and, where necessary, settling disputes in the courts in accordance with the common law rules regulating the use of private property.

One obvious objection to free market environmentalism is that full-scale privatisation of the commons is not possible. After all, many environmental assets (e.g. clean air) are public goods, which, by definition, are not amenable to being captured, commodified and bought and sold (i.e. they are non-excludable and able to withstand non-rival consumption). However, free market environmentalists respond by pointing out that 'property rights are not static' (Anderson and Leal 1991, 33). Indeed, they cite numerous examples of how entrepreneurial creativity and new technologies are able to convert public goods into private goods in response to the market opportunities created by rising environmental demand. The development of barbed-wire fences, radio collars for animals and satellite tracking for migrating wildlife are offered as examples of how new technologies have facilitated the creation of new 'property rights on the environmental frontier' (1991, 34). Similarly, automobile congestion and pollution may be dealt with by privatising public highways and charging a toll that varies according to emission levels and peak traffic flow periods (1991, 165). Indeed, they point out that while 'fencing' of the atmosphere may seem fanciful today, technological change may make the idea commonplace tomorrow (1991, 165).

Ideally, then, free market environmentalists argue that entrepreneurial initiative will respond to rising environmental demand by generating new property defining technologies that will enable the internalisation of external costs. However, there still remain many cases where the creation of property rights is not presently feasible (either because the technologies have not been developed or because the transaction costs are too high). In view of such problems, Moran (1991, 256–58) has recommended a hierarchy of actions to minimise the inefficiencies of command-and-control: allocate property rights wherever possible; then regulate by granting tradable emission/use rights; then adjust or establish taxation levels to reduce the output of the externality; then specify standards or particular technologies to reduce the externality; and, lastly, impose an outright ban (1991, 256–58). As Bennett explains, the general objective should be 'to integrate more environmental goods with the market economy, rely on government intervention only when transaction costs are extreme and then make most use of market forces when designing intervention mechanisms' (Bennett 1991, 9).

## Ecological Economics or 'Constrained Market Environmentalism'

Ecological economists support the use of economic instruments such as taxes, charges and tradable emission permits, but they do so on the basis of a different set of arguments from those of Pigouvian or Coasian environmental economists. According to Herman Daly, ecological economics (which includes Daly's own 'steady-state economics') proceeds on the basis of a different 'preanalytic vision' from that of environmental economics. As Daly explains, '[f]or steady-state economics, the preanalytic vision is that the economy is an open subsystem of a finite and non-growing ecosystem (the environment)' (Daly 1991, xiii).[6] Whereas environmental economics is limited to ensuring an optimal *allocation* of resources (an efficiency issue), ecological economics *also* seeks an optimal ecological *scale* of resource use. The added requirement of scale is considered essential because Pareto optimality can be achieved irrespective of whether or not the scale of material-energy throughput in the economy is sustainable in relation to the ecosystems in which the economy operates. According to the model of ecological economics, economy–environment integration is only achieved when the economy operates within the carrying capacity of the parent ecosystem. This point is reached when the use of natural resources (e.g. forests, fisheries) does not exceed regenerative capacity and the production of wastes does not exceed the assimilation capacity of ecosystems or otherwise jeopardise the maintenance of bio-diversity. Ecological economists argue that the environmental renovations that have been made to the neoclassical economic paradigm cannot vouchsafe ecosystem integrity; the economically optimal solution is not necessarily the ecologically optimal one.

Not surprisingly, the arguments of ecological economists have been enthusiastically endorsed by many environmental organisations and Green parties, which look to the state as the vehicle for the democratic, collective determination of 'sustainability parameters' within which both the market and the state must operate. Jacobs (1991, 120) refers to this as 'sustainability planning', which requires the development of primary indicators measuring environmental capacity (e.g. soil, water and air quality, atmospheric carbon dioxide concentrations, species diversity) and secondary indicators measuring the economic activities that cause changes in the primary indicators (e.g. emissions, chemical use, resource exploitation). On the basis of such information, the state is then in a position to determine what are likely to be the most effective instruments to curtail environmentally degrading activities to levels that are compatible with maintaining ecosystem integrity and biodiversity. The appropriate role of the state, then, is to introduce ceilings, bottom lines, minimal standards and general sustainability limits to *contain and channel* market transactions in ways that limit the rate of material-energy throughput so that the economy operates safely within the carrying capacity of ecosystems. Market-based instruments are included among a wide range of available instruments that may be used to achieve such goals. Indeed, Daly is particularly enthusiastic about tradable permit schemes because they are able to blend collective control of *optimal scale* (e.g. airshed protection) with the private incentives to achieve *optimal allocation* of scarce resources within the airshed. Daly (1992, 176–77) calls this approach '*constrained* market environmentalism' (as distinct from free market environmentalism). The chapter by Peter Kinrade in this volume provides a practical application of these principles to a selection of key environmental policy areas: pollution control, the protection of biodiversity and the reduction of greenhouse gas emissions.

*Discursive Democracy*
A number of political theorists (Dryzek 1987; Jänicke 1990; Weale 1992) have reworked elements of the public choice analysis of bureaucratic/regulatory failure in relation to environmental management into a more critical and overarching theory of 'state failure'. Unlike public choice theorists, these 'state failure' theorists accept the proposition that 'the state is bound to intervene to correct market failure' (Jänicke 1990, 32). As Jänicke explains, the state, in its attempts to address environmental (including inter-related health, energy or transport) problems, has generally compounded rather than alleviated them. Thus the problem is not state intervention *per se*, but rather *inappropriate* intervention. Moreover, Jänicke not only questions the cost-effectiveness and quality of the environmental public goods produced or protected by the state; he also points to a failure of democratic account-ability and control in relation to environmental management both within and outside the state sector (1990, 32).

    Foreshadowing Weale's characterisation and analysis of the 'old politics of pollution', Jänicke argues that most state responses to environmental problems have been *post facto* rather than anticipatory. Consequently, such responses have turned out to be far more expensive, politically troublesome and inefficient than they might have been. Jänicke has argued that the expensive, symptom-combatting regulatory and fiscal responses of the state have generally failed to *restructure* the outmoded post-war pattern of industrialism along ecologically sustainable lines. Moreover, the more money the state spends on addressing problems that have already appeared (by, for example, prescribing end-of-pipe pollution abatement), the more it institutionalises a lack of interest in taking preventative action (1990, 35). So, for example, the state's response to growing traffic congestion is to continue to build more roads rather than ecologically restructure public and private transport or reduce the need for the movement of people and goods; the response to rising environmental health problems is to build more hospitals rather than convert the 'toxic environment' into a healthy one.

According to Jänicke (1990), the persistence of environmental degradation is attributable not simply to the functional inter-relationships and special alliances that develop between the regulatory agencies and their 'clientele', the regulated industry sectors (a symbiosis that Jänicke calls 'bureaucratic–industrial complexes'). Nor is it attributed simply to the relatively greater bargaining power of industry vis-a-vis what he calls the 'counter-vailing power of the weakly organised public interest' represented by new social movements such as the environment movement (28–30). Rather, he identifies the major source of state failure to be the breakdown in the linkages between those who negotiate, decide and implement environmental policy (the bureaucracy) and those who seek to legitimate and carry responsibility for the process in relation to the public (the 'scapegoat' politicians). Jänicke identifies the accumulated power of the 'bureaucratic–industrial complex' — which looks to routine, predictable and standardised Band-aid solutions — as providing one of the major obstacles to innovative social learning in relation to ecological problems.

Similarly, John Dryzek has provided a critical study of the incapacity of traditional bureaucratic administration to deal with ecological problems. Such problems, Dryzek points out, are *inherently complex, non-reducible, variable, uncertain, spontaneous, and collective in nature* (1987, 26–33). Traditional bureaucratic systems are ill-suited to dealing with such problems because they do not allow for sufficient communication and integration across the boundaries of administrative agencies, which often leads either to deliberate buck-passing or unwitting problem displacement. (The standard forms of inter-agency communication and coordination, such as Cabinet discussions, interdepartmental committees and informal liaison among civil servants, are too overloaded or *ad hoc* to systematically anticipate and prevent problem displacement.)

Both Jänicke and Dryzek reach broadly similar conclusions. According to Jänicke, the solution to the pervasive state mismanagement of the environment is not necessarily to move away from command-and-control towards a market-based approach (although there is certainly scope for greater use of more flexible and cost-effective market-based measures). Rather, the essential task is to arrest 'the steady deterioration in the *control ratio* between politics and the machinery of government' (Janicke 1990, 27). Following Schumacher, he praises the virtues of smaller, decentralised units of decision making and, following Montesquieu, he emphasises the importance of the separation of powers; both are considered crucial to making bureaucracy less powerful, more responsive and more accountable. Accordingly, Jänicke recommends breaking down the power of the bureaucratic–industrial complex by strengthening or developing new institutional forms of 'countervailing power' from above ('consensual planning' initiated by the government), from below (citizens), from outside (market innovators) and from within (institutional reform within bureaucratic agencies) (1990, 131–34). Although Jänicke looks to many forms of countervailing power, he attaches particular importance to citizen participation in consensual planning concerning environmental policy goals and tools. This has also been a central preoccupation in the work of John Dryzek (1987, 1991, 1992 and this volume), who has strongly defended 'the construction and maintenance of *autonomous* public spheres, whose confrontation with the state is unremitting' (1992, 35).

The foregoing general 'failure' theories by no means exhaust the range of theoretical analyses of environmental problems. However, they provide an indication of the range of approaches to economy–environment integration; understanding these competing frameworks is logically prior to understanding how and why market-based instruments may be enlisted. However, it should also be pointed out that, despite their significant differences, these 'failure' theories are not mutually exclusive. For example, environmental welfare economists and free market environmentalists both employ partial equilibrium theory in defending the price mechanism as the most efficient mechanism for the allocation of resources. Moreover, ecological economists and the defenders of discursive democracy may be seen as offering a broadly complementary economic and political analysis of the market and the state respectively.

# The Politics of Taxonomies

Despite the wide variety of different theoretical analyses of the role of the state in environmental management, the debate about environmental policy tools has been officially framed in terms of a narrow choice between bureaucratic regulation (or the more pejorative, military term 'command-and-control') versus market-based instruments. This dichotomy, widely used by environmental economists, corresponds to a 'coercion versus choice' polarity, constructed from the point of view of economic actors. According to this dichotomy, command-and-control regulations leave no room for manoeuvre on the part of economic actors; failure to comply renders offenders liable to face judicial or administrative proceedings and penalties. In contrast, market-based instruments merely alter the set of costs and benefits facing economic actors, leaving 'actors free to respond to certain stimuli in a way they themselves think most beneficial' (OECD 1989, 12–13). Implicit in this characterisation is a judgment that command and control instruments are coercive and undesirable whereas market-based instruments permit greater freedom and choice and are therefore to be preferred.

Indeed, the basic regulation versus incentive dichotomy does register some very important arguments concerning flexibility, efficiency and ongoing innovation. The chapter by Alan Moran on 'Tools of Environmental Policy: Market Instruments versus Command and Control' provides a succinct outline of the general economic advantages of market-based instruments over direct legal prescription. As Moran explains, it is precisely the extra flexibility afforded by market-based instruments that enables polluters to choose their own least-cost solution to meeting public environmental objectives. By comparison, regulatory regimes that prescribe uniform technologies or performance standards are much less sensitive to the variations in the abatement cost differences between firms. Market-based instruments also provide incentives for ongoing technical innovation whereas direct legal regulation usually offers little incentive for firms to perform beyond the legally prescribed standards. In some cases, rigid standards may keep newer and cleaner technologies from entering the market.

Market-based mechanisms have rarely been introduced in their textbook form; accordingly, the actual level of savings achieved has been much lower than the potential savings. Nonetheless, as Hahn shows in chapter 6, the practical performance of charges and tradable permits in the US and charges in Continental Europe has been broadly consistent with economic theory:

environmental objectives have indeed been achieved at much lower cost.

Yet the command-and-control versus economic incentive dichotomy by no means exhausts the ways in which environmental policy instruments may be classified and understood. Much depends on the relevant standpoint that is adopted and the way in which problems and objectives are framed. Indeed, it is always possible to devise a range of different policy instrument taxonomies constructed from different vantage points that may be linked to some of the alternative 'failure theories' introduced above, such as the degree of democratic accountability of environmental decision making (this forms the basis of Dryzek's assessment of policy instruments in chapter 12, which leads him to a very different conclusion regarding the 'appropriateness' of market-based instruments). Clearly, vocabularies and taxonomies are not socially innocent or neutral — they all embody explicit or implicit standpoints, analyses and evaluative criteria.

In his chapter on 'Sustainability and "the Market"' in Part I of this volume, Michael Jacobs has challenged the usefulness of the simple regulation/incentive distinction in the environmental policy instrument discourse, at least in terms of its relevance to achieving the goal of environmental protection (which he takes to be fundamental). According to Jacobs, the crucial question is not whether economic actors are compelled or merely induced or invited to behave in certain environmentally beneficial ways. Rather, the question ought to be whether the government has maintained or relinquished control over the overall levels of environmental protection. According to this classificatory schema, there is a much more fundamental cleavage between environmental regulation (broadly conceived to include law *and* taxation) and the property rights approach known as 'free market environmentalism' than there is between legal and fiscal policy measures.

Jacobs' taxonomy is designed not only to clarify the relationship between objectives, decision-making institutions and instruments in environmental policy but also to defend an explicit ethic of sustainability and a particular version of deliberative democracy that is broadly sympathetic with the 'discursive democracy' defended by Dryzek in chapter 12 (although Dryzek has a stronger 'in principle' objection to market-based instruments). Jacobs argues in favour of the maintenance of government control over the general levels of environmental protection in ways that maximise participatory democracy. Provided such citizen control is maintained, Jacobs argues that the question as to what is the best instrument or combination of instruments to achieve socially determined environmental objectives is ultimately an *empirical* one. In other words, there are no reasons to favour, a priori, incentives over prescriptions. The question of choice or flexibility from the point of view of economic actors only becomes relevant when it can be shown to further the pursuit of environmental objectives, or at least not impair them. A similar position is defended by Kinrade and Christoff in chapters 4 and 7.

Jacobs is not the only observer who has doubted both the comprehensiveness and usefulness of the widely used regulation versus incentive distinction (even when stripped of the pejorative language of command-and-control). Indeed, many environmental economists concede that the distinction cannot always be sharply made (OECD 1989, 13; James 1993, 3). For example, should non-compliance fees and performance bonds be classified as market-based instruments or regulatory instruments? Moreover, the conditions and context in which particular instruments operate may work to alter the character of the instrument.

For example, if regulatory sanctions are weak and/or poorly enforced, then regulation loses its 'coercive' character in terms of forcing certain kinds of behaviour. That is, economic actors may choose not to comply with environmental regulations in the belief that they are unlikely to be detected, or because they can afford the fine, which effectively becomes an additional cost of production for the firm and an additional form of revenue for the state, rather than a means of reducing pollution. Moreover, while market-based instruments are defended as increasing the flexibility and efficiency of firms, in some cases firms prefer the certainty and predictability of direct legal regulation.

There are also different ways in which the choice/coercion distinction may be applied, depending on the way in which the question 'whose freedom and whose coercion?' is applied. To declare baldly that 'regulation is a restriction of freedom' (HMSO 1993, 1) is to avoid asking whether there are circumstances in which one agent's freedom becomes someone else's 'unfreedom'. For example, the decision to apply a tradable emission scheme rather than prescriptive regulations may enhance the freedom of the polluters but not necessarily the freedom of third parties living in 'hotspots' within the airshed. More generally, at what point do high taxes and charges become coercive when those on whom the taxes are levied have no reasonable means of adjusting their behaviour to avoid or minimise the taxation?

As many contributors to this volume point out, a more useful way of understanding legal and fiscal instruments is to regard them simply as different kinds of environmental regulation by the state. After all, both instruments require the passing of laws and the monitoring of compliance by the state; both involve a bureaucratic agency to administer and enforce the scheme; both alter the price incentives facing individual actors, albeit in different ways; and both seek to alter behaviour in pursuance of particular policy objectives. Viewed in this broader context, the distinction between coercive commands and optional incentives takes on a fluid character; particular policy instruments take their meaning from the particular ensemble of social relations in which they are embedded and from the objectives that guide their use.

What remains crucial, however, at least from the point of view of achieving environmental policy objectives, is the degree to which the state maintains or relinquishes ultimate control and/or influence over decisions and practices that carry actual or potential environmental consequences. As Peter Grabosky demonstrates in his chapter on 'Governing at a Distance', such control and influence may be exerted by a range of means that extend well beyond formal legal and fiscal policy. Indeed, control and influence may also be exerted at several removes from the targeted problem or the relevant decision makers, even to the point where those whose behaviour is being influenced are not even aware of any government 'presence'.

Like Jacobs, Grabosky argues that the legal command versus economic incentive dichotomy conceals as much as it reveals. He points out that, in any given regulatory domain or policy space, the law is but one stratum of a complex layer of quasi-legal rules and forms of social control and conflict resolution. There are also many microcosms of power — constellations of interests, institutions and interpersonal relations — that lie at many removes from direct state control (although never entirely 'beyond' the state since the state and civil society are deeply enmeshed). Grabosky also highlights the many indirect ways in which non-government institutions may be articulated into the activity of government. For example, the state may work not only as a commander but also as a facilitator and broker by structuring mechanisms for self-regulation (or 'regulated autonomy') largely based on private orderings. These more discrete 'technologies of governance' include the encouragement of self-help environmental initiatives by local communities, the provision of environmental education and the encouragement of self-regulation by providing technical advice, accreditation and support for voluntary codes of practice.

Voluntary codes of practice are usually criticised by environmental organisations for being little more than public relations exercises that lack effective sanctions. However, there are ways in which a government or a particular state agency might enforce 'voluntary' codes of practice without resorting to legislation. They may, for example, develop government procurement policies that 'black-ban' firms that fail to conform to industry codes of practice, or they may withdraw other government services or support. Clearly, there are many subtle means, beyond law and taxation, by which the state may structure and influence commercial decisions to conform with particular environmental goals.

## The Stakeholder Response: General Lessons in the Politics of Economic Instruments

The taxonomical debate partly foreshadows some of the conflicting interests of the key stakeholders in the policy instrument debate. As the chapters in this collection show, the response of the key non-government protagonists — the environment movement and industry — towards a more market-oriented approach to environmental policy has been mixed, ranging from outright hostility to enthusiastic support, depending on the nature of the instrument and the institutional setting. Moreover, many of these stakeholder responses vary on a country by country basis. As Hahn notes, in the Netherlands environmental groups tend to prefer charges while employer groups tend to prefer regulatory instruments. In the US, however, environmentalists generally prefer regulatory instruments over both charges and marketable permit systems. These national differences reinforce the insight that particular policy instruments take their meaning from the particular legal, social and cultural context in which they operate. Despite these interesting national differences, it is nonetheless possible to proffer several generalisations concerning policy tool preferences among the key political stakeholders.

*The Environment Movement's Response*
Environmentalists have tended to be rather hostile towards the case for the privatisation of public assets such as national parks, beaches and wildlife advanced by free market environmentalists, largely for the reasons outlined by Jacobs, Kinrade and Dryzek in this volume: it signals a relinquishment of public control over environmental assets. This is considered bad for democracy and bad for the environment. It is bad for democracy because citizens are denied the opportunity to participate in, or otherwise call to account, decisions made by private property managers, other than through common law actions. For example, when state property (such as a national park) is privatised, the new owners/managers are exempt from Freedom of Information legislation. Citizens are therefore denied access to information that may affect general environmental welfare or the welfare of other species. Priva-

tisation can be bad for the environment because private property holders cannot be counted on to maintain the environmental integrity of their property. The environmental success of the property rights approach is a function of opportunity costs, information and preferences; changes in one or more of these variables may lead to environmental values being outbid by competing uses. Not all property holders are likely to be altruistically or ecologically motivated; most act as profit-seeking entrepreneurs. In this respect, the free market environmentalist's in-principle preference for private choice over public choice may be seen as a refusal to countenance the distinction between entrepreneurship and citizenship (Eckersley 1995, 10).

Nonetheless, many environmental organisations have sought the sanctity of private property rights in relation to threatened habitats or heritage areas. The US Nature Conservancy, for example, has a long history of raising money to buy and maintain private land for the purposes of protecting wilderness or indigenous flora and fauna. While this practice has been interpreted, somewhat disingenuously, as 'an excellent example of how free market environmentalism works' (Anderson and Leal 1991, 3), a more likely interpretation is that it signals a lack of trust in the state to discharge properly its responsibility of protecting environmental public goods such as biodiversity.

The response of environmental organisations to other market-based measures has been highly variable. As Dryzek points out in chapter 12, tradable emissions permits and environmental charges have often been criticised for effectively sanctioning the right to pollute.[7] Indeed, Goodin (1992) has likened the selling of pollution rights to the selling of indulgences by the medieval Catholic church. In both cases, the authority is selling something it has no right to sell. Long established industries, on the other hand, generally regard their pollution permits as a quasi-property right and are hostile towards any 'encroachment' on such 'rights'. As Hahn points out in chapter 6, regulators in the US have sought to play down the property rights aspect of the new emission trading regimes under the *Clean Air Act*.

Yet the environment movement's objections to marketable permits are sometimes misplaced; the crucial question from the point of view of the environment is not the creation of new, tradable property rights *per se* but rather the adequacy of the total emissions ceiling in the airshed (which is divided into individual tradable quotas) and the regional ecological effects of particular trades (whether particular 'hotspots' develop following trading). Moreover, the medieval indulgence argument has much less force in relation to those cases where tradable rights are allocated as part of an emissions *reduction* program, because the right to pollute is not entrenched. Such reduction programs also alleviate the problem of 'hotspots' developing in particular localities. Moreover, we have seen that the emergence of the new discipline of ecological economics has provided the environment movement with a new, ecologically inspired theoretical model within which to locate and justify a range of market-based measures, including tradable permits. We have seen how Daly, in particular, has defended tradable permit systems as providing an ideal combination of collective control over optimal scale with the private incentives necessary to achieve optimal allocation of scarce resources. Appropriately scaled charges can also provide significant incentives for continuing improvements to environmental performance.

Indeed, environmental charges and taxes now serve as the centre-piece of the fiscal policies promoted by Green parties and many environmental organisations. In particular, green economists have long advocated a shift in the burden of taxation away from 'goods' (profits, income, employment, savings) towards environmental 'bads' (pollution, waste, congestion) or environmentally significant inputs (energy, natural resources) (e.g. Kembal-Cooke, Baker and Mattingly 1991; von Weizsacker and Jesinghaus 1992; Repetto et al. 1992; Repetto 1993). Environmental taxes and charges are generally more cost-effective than direct regulation, especially in those cases where environmental problems are changing, or where the sources of pollution are numerous, diverse and dispersed (Repetto 1993, 3). There are also advantages to business and labour, such as potentially increased profits and employment from lower company and payroll taxation and increased productivity from reductions in energy-material inputs. A study carried out by the World Resources Institute (WRI) has estimated that the US economy could 'easily shift $100 to $150 billion in federal, state and local revenues from taxes on the "goods" of work and investment to charges on the "bads" of waste, pollution, and congestion'. The WRI estimates that 'The [US] economy would reap dividends of $50 to $80 billion per year, in the form of reduced environmental damage and greater economic productivity. And other opportunities abound' (Repetto 1993, 4).

The macro-economic effects of such a shift in the burden of taxation would depend on how much revenue is earned and how it is redirected. For example, the shift might be revenue neutral (that is, taxes on profits and income would be correspondingly reduced), or it might be applied to decrease or increase the general taxation burden. Most of the studies that have been carried out have been based on fiscally neutral regimes (e.g. von Weizsacker and Jesinghaus 1992) — a politically appealing approach given general political hostility towards any increase in taxation. However, from an environmental perspective, the greater the taxation shift towards environmentally degrading activities, the more radical the ecological restructuring of the economy is likely to be.

One common objection to environmental taxes is the fear (usually expressed by Treasuries) that the taxation base may shrink as firms respond positively to environmental incentives by adopting environmentally benign technologies and practices to the point of avoiding payment. However, environmental tax advocates usually point out that there will always be other environmental 'bads' to tax and that, in any event, it is impossible to achieve 100 per cent efficiency in energy and resource use. Moreover, the shift towards environmental taxes and charges is not intended to be total; that is, considerable revenue will still be derived from traditional sources.

### The Response from Industry

For its part, industry has generally supported new economic instruments (such as tradable emission permits) that offer greater flexibility and efficiency for firms. However, as the chapters in Part III show, industry has been much more reticent, and in some cases openly hostile, towards new proposals for environmental taxes — a stance that has proved fatal to the success of many of the broad-based carbon tax proposals that have been mooted at the national, regional and international levels. The basis of industry's objection is that such taxes would raise the costs of production and reduce international competitiveness. The proposal of the Commission of the European Community (EC) to introduce an EC-wide carbon/energy tax as a means of fulfilling its Earth Summit pledge of stabilising carbon dioxide emission levels at 1990 levels by the year 2000 now appears to have fallen by the wayside, notwithstanding burden-sharing proposals designed to protect the poorer Southern European countries. In addition to the implacable opposition from Britain, strong resistance has also come from the European Community finance and economic ministers. The current signs are that the EC will scrap the broad-based carbon/energy tax proposal and settle instead for a modest increase in the excise duties on oil products within the existing framework of duties in the EC (*Global Environmental Change Report* 1994, 3). Although the matter is not yet settled, a more modest approach is likely to prevail given that unanimous agreement is necessary to make taxation decisions at the European Union level.

It has been argued by Buchanan and Tullock (1975) that setting emission standards via direct regulation is more suited to the needs of established industry than economic instruments such as taxes and charges because regulation provides specific forms of market protection to established firms (e.g. by creating entry barriers to new firms). However, as both Moran and Hahn point out in this volume, whether standards are preferred to economic instruments by industry will depend on the instrument in question and the extent to which the industry status quo is affected (including the distribution of property rights). For example, industry has tended to be less hostile towards modest charges, especially where the revenue from charges is recycled back to industry to assist in pollution control. The practical experience with effluent charges shows a pattern of initial opposition followed by gradual acceptance, especially if charges are relatively low, increases are gradual and abatement activity is subsidised from the revenue raised. From an environmental perspective, however, the primary objective of green charges is to reduce environmentally degrading activity and restructure the economy; earning revenue is but a means to this larger end, not an end in itself. However, to bring about the desired change in behaviour often requires very high taxes and charges — a move that is likely to encounter very strong opposition from industry and not much sympathy from governments in view of the likely inflationary effects.

As Jacobs shows in chapter 5 in his review of the British experience with economic instruments, the proposals contained in the highly publicised Pearce Report (Pearce et al. 1989) evoked a powerful opposition from Treasury (mainly due to the inflationary consequences). Such proposals also evoked inter-agency conflict over how to spend the revenue. As Jacobs points out, Treasuries seek to protect consolidated revenue whereas environmental agencies prefer to earmark the earnings to offset the higher costs of compliance by industry.

Despite these conflicts, governments are likely to remain interested in new sources of revenue, and a broader range of modest green taxes may not be long in coming. According to Jacobs, although the Liberal Democrats and Labour Party publicly opposed the Conservative government's fuel tax in Britain, they are busily exploring new tax options behind the scenes. The Danish coalition government has already (June 1993) introduced a comprehensive income tax reform package that includes a range of new environmental taxes (on gasoline, water, electricity, automobiles and packaging) designed to finance reductions in the marginal income tax rate and help stimulate environmentally sound economic growth (*International Environmental Reporter* 1993a, 519). As Skou Andersen (1994b, 140) observes, 'Green taxes are indeed a potential asset for a welfare state suffering from financial shortages'. Nonetheless, the scope and degree of Denmark's green taxes have been carefully tailored with a close eye on tax and price differentials in neighbouring Germany and therefore fall well below full ecological costs.[8]

Some general lessons can also be gleaned from the experience with tradable emissions schemes. As the chapter by Hahn shows, established industry generally regards its current claims on the environment as akin to a quasi-property right and it is generally hostile towards any new scheme that seeks to 'appropriate' such 'rights'. Predictably, industry has tended to be more supportive of new tradable emission schemes that allocate permits on the basis of the status quo — a response that discriminates against new firms. However, as with most forms of environmental law and taxation, much will depend on the degree of stringency of the relevant standard. The more standards, charges and taxes are increased, the higher the marginal abatement costs and the greater the likelihood of political opposition from industry.

## Competition, Trade and Investment: Moving Beyond Compliance

Choice of instruments can have different impacts on international competitiveness and on trade and investment patterns. Regulatory instruments and modest charges that are recycled back to industry have been shown to have a negligible impact on competitiveness (except for pollution-intensive sectors), largely because firms are not made to bear the full costs of environmental protection and such costs that are imposed provide a very small increment to the operating costs of firms (Verbruggen 1993, 13). According to Verbruggen, '[t]his largely explains the revealed preferences in OECD countries for the regulatory approach' (17).

Of course, these 'revealed preferences' for regulation are contrary to the Polluter Pays Principle and to orthodox trade theory: both argue that trade policies should seek to improve the efficiency of resource use. As we have seen, the Polluter Pays Principle is a 'no-subsidy' principle, which requires that the costs of environmental protection be incorporated into the prices of traded goods and services (rather than subsidised by governments) to avoid trade distortions. From this particular trade perspective, economic instruments are generally less distorting, more transparent and more efficient than regulatory instruments.

However, in those cases where governments seek to change domestic behaviour in order to reach strict environmental targets (such as greenhouse gas emission targets), and where polluting industries are not sheltered or compensated, then significant effects on competitiveness can be expected to the point where affected firms may even consider relocating to less environmentally stringent jurisdictions or to 'pollution-havens'. Such consequences may arise irrespective of whether legal or fiscal instruments are employed. However, few governments have been prepared to push environmental policy to such lengths; the general concern to avoid any policies that may adversely affect industry competitiveness stands out as one of the major constraints on the scope, reach and stringency of environmental policies. Moreover, any unilateral attempt by governments to introduce restrictions on imports to ensure that foreign producers incur the same environmental *production costs* as domestic producers runs the risk of being classified as a 'non-tariff barrier' and therefore a trade restriction under the General Agreement on Tariffs and Trade (GATT), unless the restrictions can be brought within the narrow General Exemptions in Article XX of the GATT.[9] In short, certain kinds of environmental protection measures may be struck down as a disguised or unwarranted form of protectionism. The GATT Secretariat has recently confirmed that while contracting parties to the GATT may take reasonable and necessary measures to protect their own environment from damage arising from the *domestic consumption* of imported goods, they may not determine the environmental and health protection policies of other nations by making access to their domestic market conditional on the environmental policies, practices and manufacturing processes of the exporting country (Hartwell and Bergkamp 1994, 10113–14).

Environmentalists have increasingly complained that international trade rules discriminate against the environment. Environmentalists point out that the failure of governments presiding over pollution havens to impose domestic environmental taxes or regulations has never been interpreted as an *unwarranted subsidy* in international trade law (Shrybman 1990, 31). Trading in goods that have been 'environmentally subsidised' in this way has been characterised as 'ecological dumping' (Martinez-Alier 1993, 106) or 'dirty trade'. However, proposals to amend the GATT to redress this problem are likely to engender strong opposition from developing countries and the former Eastern bloc.[10] The control of transboundary environmental problems largely falls to international environmental treaties, some of which impose trade restraints on environmental grounds.

However, such trade restraints are potentially liable to be challenged, as being contrary to the GATT, by affected nations who are not parties to the relevant treaty. In any event, the vast bulk of world trade is not subject to environmental treaties. (And as the volume of world trade continues to grow, so too does the energy use and pollution arising from the transport and refrigeration of traded goods.) International harmonisation through specific multilateral treaties has generally been the favoured official response to environmental problems. The growth of regional trading blocs may also give rise to stronger and more harmonised environmental standards in those trading regions where members have relatively similar economic conditions, such as the European Community.

However, as the chapters by Grabosky and Clark in Part IV demonstrate, under certain conditions, there can be a virtuous relationship between markets, international competition and environmental performance that can set off a 'race to the top' rather than 'a race to the bottom' (or a 'race to the middle'). This virtuous relationship has yet to be fully appreciated and explored by governments and industry alike. As Clark demonstrates in chapter 9, many globally competitive, transnational companies maintain their competitive edge by setting the pace in environmental technologies, processes and management practices in anticipation of rising environmental demand. Under these circumstances, the particular environmental standards and requirements imposed by the state (whether through law or taxation) in any given 'operating jurisdiction' will often be well behind (and therefore largely irrelevant to) the longer term, strategic environmental investment decisions of such 'big players'.

Grabosky carries this theme further by pointing to many examples of how the influence of 'naturally occurring market responses' (or market responses occurring as indirect by-products of direct legal regulation) can often lead to the adoption of environmental standards and management practices that are far in excess of those prescribed or recommended by governments. More generally, it has been shown how 'moving beyond compliance' and adopting a proactive response to environmental risk can provide the basis for establishing and maintaining a competitive advantage for firms (Gunningham 1994); or, as Grabosky puts it in more prosaic terms, 'where there's muck there's money'.

The ecological demands on business from sources other than direct legal regulation are certainly intensifying. In particular, increasing pressure from the community; from green consumers (along with green suppliers and retailers); from 'ethical investors';

from the insurance and banking sector (in response to growing environmental damage claims and strict liability rules for hazardous sites) and from international environmental management standards all point to inexorably rising environmental expectations. Notwithstanding the green adage that 'small is beautiful', however, it is usually the larger companies that are less constrained by short-term pressures and better able to build a competitive advantage by moving beyond compliance. It is noteworthy that Martin Jänicke includes market innovators as one of the forms of countervailing power to the 'bureaucratic–industrial complex'. Moreover, his preference for smallness and decentralisation overlooks the fact that most innovative environmental strategies in the private sector tend to emerge from the very large, globally competitive companies rather than the local firm.[11]

One key lesson emerging from the chapters by Clark and Grabosky is that effective environmental governance by the state requires the development of a mix of different strategies that are sensitive to whether or not business has a self-interest in avoiding, limiting or 'going beyond compliance' (see also Gunningham 1994). Grabosky concludes that, ideally, the imperfections in politics and markets will be cross-cutting to enable the strengths of one to compensate for the weaknesses of the other. He suggests that in between the 'commanding state' and the 'minimalist state' lies the 'facilitating state', which seeks to enhance individual and commercial autonomy in ways that promote community environmental goals.

## Securing Compliance Through the Criminal Law

It is often assumed that the problems of monitoring and enforcement are unique to regulatory schemes, but not to market-based schemes. However, as Susan Smith's chapter makes clear, securing compliance will not necessarily be any easier, and may in some cases be harder, under market-based schemes such as tradable permits and emission fees. To be effective, both regimes require continuous monitoring and prompt enforcement of violations. One of the standard criticisms of the traditional regulatory approach is that it confers too much bureaucratic discretion regarding the monitoring, negotiation and enforcement of emissions permits. Such discretion can lead to the familiar problems of agency capture, and sometimes to corruption. Yet, as Smith shows, market-based approaches sometimes raise additional enforcement problems that are not encountered under traditional schemes, such as anti-trust claims and disputes over the details of particular contractual bargains concerning the trading of pollution credits.

However, there are some cases where market-based schemes are much easier to enforce. This applies especially in relation to non-point sources of pollution that are diffuse, variable and hard to monitor (such as fertiliser run-off from farms, greenhouse gas emissions and the congestion of landfills). In these cases, it is much easier to secure compliance by imposing taxes or fees on the purchase or use of fertiliser, petrol, or waste disposal than by imposing a licensing regime.

There are also different symbolic and deterrent considerations associated with the choice of sanctions. We have seen that one of the criticisms of emission fees is that they tend to sever the social disapprobation attached to non-compliance. As Smith demonstrates, one of the simplest and most effective ways of redressing the 'implementation deficit' in environmental law is to turn pollution into a serious criminal offence. Smith shows how compliance has dramatically improved in the United States following the imposition of prison sanctions on corporate managers and directors for violations of environmental laws. She also shows how the potential for bureaucratic co-optation can be dramatically reduced by maintaining a well resourced, highly trained and specialised prosecution branch and ensuring that criminal investigation and prosecution responsibilities do not fall on field inspectors, who need to maintain a working relationship with the regulated parties. The criminal prosecutions of corporate directors in the US has had a dramatic deterrent effect on polluters and has led to the development of strong internal compliance and auditing systems on the part of affected companies. Such criminal prosecutions need not be confined to regulatory systems; they may also be extended to market-based systems. Following this criminal sanction path, of course, is dependent on there being sufficient consensus within the relevant jurisdiction that pollution — especially the release of hazardous substances — is a serious matter.

However, as Thompson argues in chapter 11, the decision to apply criminal sanctions should only be made in relation to behaviour that is avoidable. There is no point punishing people or firms who have no practical alternative; it is better to pay them to change their ways. If criminal sanctions are to be applied, it is also necessary to create the appropriate infrastructure to provide feasible alternatives.

*Environmental Progress — Social Regression?*

Just as there is no point in punishing people or firms for degrading the environment when they have no practical alternative, there is no point in introducing environmental fiscal measures as an inducement to behavioural change if people or firms have no practical alternative. One of the problems of environmental taxes and charges is they are often socially regressive (i.e. they take an increasing proportion of income as the taxpayer's income falls). In those cases where the demand for certain products and services is relatively inelastic (such as petrol, which for many people is a daily necessity for which there are no, or only very poor, substitutes), low income earners have little choice but to pay the tax or charge. Environmental taxes and charges on goods such as petrol may be lucrative revenue earners for governments, but they are weak instruments for inducing modifications in behaviour (unless they are imposed at very high levels). This, of course, explains why attempts to impose environmental taxes on price-inelastic goods have attracted so much political opposition from social justice groups and why they have been condemned as opportunistic revenue raisers, thinly disguised behind an environmental facade. As Christoff shows in chapter 7, such was the response of the social justice lobby in Australia following the differential increase in excise duties on both leaded and unleaded petrol in the 1993/94 budget. Similarly, in chapter 5 Jacobs documents the uproar that followed the British government's decision in 1993 to introduce a VAT (sales tax) on domestic fuel (at 8 per cent in the first year, and then 17.5 per cent from the second). Such increases were 'cold comfort' for pensioners and others suffering from 'fuel poverty'. Similar distributive problems have also beset proposals for carbon/energy taxes.

In her chapter on 'Sustainability, Justice and Market Relations', Janna Thompson defends a Rawlsian approach as the basis for deciding how to allocate the burden of environmental protection. That is, the only justifiable departure from equal treatment in environmental policy is when the departure can be shown to increase the well-being of the least well off more than any other alternative measure. This general principle, Thompson argues, is logically prior to, and should condition, the choice of particular policies and instruments. In this respect, environmental justice is not simply one more consideration to take into account in choosing environmental policies; whether we should depart from the principles of justice is itself a question of justice.

The socially regressive consequences of many green taxes should not be taken as a reason for dismissing entirely any green tax on price-inelastic goods. (As Kinrade points out in relation to carbon/energy taxes, the importance of energy prices to long-term trends in energy consumption remains significant.) Rather, Thompson, together with Jacobs, Kinrade and Christoff, all argue the case for complementary measures that compensate low income earners and provide attractive and effective alternatives for everyone (such as efficient, reliable and affordable public transport). Indeed, it is the very provision of alternatives that serves to increase the price elasticity of the taxed good and thereby reduce the regressivity of green taxes (Jacobs 1991, 163–77). Revenue earned in the short term (while inelasticity remains relatively high) can be used to finance environmentally appropriate alternatives for the medium and longer term. In the case of carbon taxes, Kinrade has argued that the removal of energy market distortions through a carefully targeted and integrated package of policy measures should serve as the initial policy focus.

However, as Thompson points out, not all economic instruments are regressive if changes in behaviour can occur at little or no cost to producers and consumers. So, for example, charging households for the amount of garbage generated may impact more severely on the poor than the rich. However, it is a relatively easy matter for all households to change their disposal practices to avoid or minimise the charge; what is required is information and advice from local councils and a little more effort on the part of households, rather than increased expenditure.

Thompson also extends the Rawlsian-based principle of justice beyond the nation state to the world society. She concludes that a regulated international economy provides greater opportunities for global justice than a free international market with no or limited restrictions on the movement of goods, services, capital and labour. The inevitable implication of this argument is that greater reliance must be placed on international regulatory bodies equipped with the power to make and enforce environmental policies. This is consistent with her defence of a cosmopolitan (rather than communitarian) world society, which enables the development of affiliations and concerns beyond the immediate community.

The North/South gap looms large in most discussions of global environmental justice. Under the current international market economy, developing countries face declining commodity prices, weak terms of trade, crippling external debt, and onerous structural adjustment programs. Despite these dire constraints, such countries are being asked to avoid many of the ecological mistakes that have *already been committed* by the developed world. It is against this background that Martinez-Alier has argued that global environmental justice demands that the 'distributional obstacles to environmental policy should be removed by redistribution rather than growth' (1993). In relation to global problems such as the enhanced greenhouse effect, Martinez-Alier has defended the creative use of tradable property rights on behalf of the poor. Instead of seeking a proportional reduction of emissions from all nations via an environmental treaty, Martinez-Alier defends the proposal put forward by Anil Agarwal and Sunita Narain (1991) from the Centre for Science and Environment in Delhi for an international market in tradable permits for carbon dioxide emissions. According to this proposal, the total emission quota would, ideally, be determined on the basis of the global absorption capacity for carbon dioxide and tradable emission quotas would be allocated to nations on the basis of *per capita* emissions. Given the vast disparity in energy consumption patterns between North and South, such a scheme would effectively transfer the majority of emission credits to developing nations. The upshot would be that rich nations seeking to go beyond their allowable quota would be required to pay poor nations for the privilege. The scheme recognises an equal claim on the part of all peoples of the world to the Earth's carbon dioxide absorption facilities and effectively provides a redistributive mechanism whereby the rich are made to pay their Ecological Debt to the poor as an admission of their responsibility for past greenhouse gas emissions (1993, 120). Of course, such schemes are not without their own special problems. For example, they would need to be carefully designed to avoid the scenario of poor countries quickly cashing in their unused quotas to rich countries only to be forced to buy them back again at a later stage at very high prices when most of the cheap abatement options had been exhausted. Moreover, in order to counteract the effect of population growth, Martinez-Alier suggests that emission quotas could be pegged at today's population (1993, 107). In principle, however, the tradable permit concept does have considerable scope for operating under the umbrella of an international agreement on greenhouse gases. In a review of international policy options for curbing greenhouse gas emissions, Bertram, Stephens and Wallace (1990) concluded that the tradable permit concept offered the greatest scope for successful application at the international level than the two instruments usually found in national regulatory systems — direct legal restrictions on individual emissions and carbon taxes. According to these authors (whose favoured scheme varies in detail but not in substance from the one defended by Martinez-Alier):

> A regime which legitimated a set of internationally-tradeable emission entitlements to restrict gross emissions, while at the same time driving pollution prices to levels sufficient to induce large-scale substitution towards energy-saving and renewable energy

systems, could open the way to solving other pressing international issues of poverty and indebtedness

(1990, 23).

Not surprisingly, as Martinez-Alier notes, such schemes have touched some very raw nerves in the developed world and it is difficult to envisage such a proposal receiving an enthusiastic reception on the part of rich nations, especially the G7. Indeed, Pearce believes that the developed world is unlikely to come to the negotiating table unless the initial emission allowances are 'grandfathered' (i.e. allocated on the basis of current emissions), although they might consider a modification of allowances over time (Pearce 1992, 82–83). Nonetheless, such proposals demonstrate that market-based schemes such as tradable permits can, with ingenuity, be tailored not only to enhance efficiency but also to promote environmental justice on a global scale.

## Democracy and the State

The last chapter in this collection, by Dryzek, addresses two questions: can *any* more effective shaping of environmental policy be undertaken by democratic means in liberal capitalist societies? And can the choice of environmental policy instruments affect the prospects for democratic control?

It is clear that popular concern over environmental degradation is a necessary but by no means a sufficient condition for the state to redress the prevailing contradictions between economic and environmental policy. Indeed, Dryzek suggests that there is an enduring conflict between democratic pressures and the structural constraints faced by the modern state. Indeed, he regards the rhetoric about sustainable development and the integration of environment and economy as, for the most part, just that — rhetoric. Certainly, the over-riding imperatives — to maintain order, economic stability and growth in the context of a global economy — do not augur well for the kinds of radical economic restructuring required to alleviate environmental stresses, although the prospects for more limited kinds of ecological modernisation in the form of cleaner production remain more hopeful.[12] The uncanny waxing and waning of government commitment to environmental protection in accordance with economic booms and recessions is telling evidence of the priority of economic policy. What is more surprising, however, is the pervasive failure of so many governments to capitalise on the competitive advantages promised by cleaner production — a failure Dryzek attributes to the narrow horizons embedded in political and economic systems.

A common theme in many of the contributions to this anthology is that the comfortable accommodation reached between industry and government under traditional (and poorly enforced) regulatory systems is likely to impede not only environmental performance but also the long-term competitiveness of industry (see also Gunningham 1994). A related theme is that regulatory capture is not only bad for economic innovation, it is also bad for democracy.

Does this suggest that market-based instruments hold out better prospects for democracy and public confidence in environmental administration than regulatory instruments? Dryzek concludes that while there is nothing intrinsically democratic in regulation, it nonetheless carries far more potential for democratic innovation than market-based instruments (which are usually set centrally and provide fewer formal channels for political participation and public review). Such a conclusion applies, *a fortiori*, to bureaucratic regulation when compared with privatisation, which involves a relinquishment of state control.

In support of this argument, Dryzek points to a range of process innovations, or 'discursive designs', such as public hearings, impact assessment, the right to know, the right to seek review, environmental mediation, policy dialogue and regulatory negotiation, which have been introduced in response to community environmental concern and conflict. In Dryzek's estimation, as a general rule, it is better to build on the islands of democratic control that already exist than to embrace market-based alternatives that may subtly undermine democratic control. In short, we should look to those instruments that summon *homo civicus* rather than *homo economicus*. More generally, Dryzek has consistently argued that deliberative, or 'communicatively rationalised', forms of social choice are more likely than conventional liberal democratic bargaining practices to lead to better environmental protection in the particular local territorial space of deliberation, with possibly fewer spill-over effects to neighbouring regions (1987, 1990).

## Coda

Despite the wide ranging arguments in favour of greater use of market-based instruments, such arguments have not yet managed to congeal with sufficient political strength to prompt concerted action on the part of governments in OECD countries. Many environmental groups remain suspicious of any new policy measures that appear to sanction the right to pollute (such as tradable permits or low charges). All but the globally competitive businesses are likely to remain hostile towards new policy measures, such as green taxes and 'unfunded' charges, that are likely to raise internal costs without compensation. And social welfare lobbies stand ready to condemn any new fiscal move that is socially regressive. Meanwhile, governments have shown a reluctance to impose new green fiscal (or legal) measures that might jeopardise the international competitiveness of industry or impose inflationary pressure domestically. For all the inefficiencies and rigidities attributed to the traditional regulatory approach, it appears to have suited the key players — industry and government — more than the more proactive, market-based alternatives.

But it would be wrong to conclude from this general evaluation that all environmental regulations necessarily take the form of rigid technology or performance specifications or that alternative, market-based schemes are necessarily more efficient. In some cases, the transactions costs of establishing market-based schemes are simply too high, or the industry configuration is inappropriate (i.e. too large, too small, or uncompetitive), to warrant the effort. We have also seen that regulatory schemes carry greater potential for ongoing democratic participation in environmental policy formulation and implementation.

More generally, the experience to date suggests that it is better to understand regulatory and market-based schemes as complementary rather than mutually exclusive options. As Grabosky notes, one very neglected area of policy analysis is the study of the *interaction* between different policy instruments. To this end, Grabosky outlines in his chapter a taxonomy of possible forms of interaction between different environmental policy instruments: neutralisation, catalysis, inhibition, activation, redundancy, synergy and complementarity. Understanding these different forms of interaction is crucial if the challenge of policy coordination is to be met.

It should also be clear from the foregoing overview that no single policy instrument can provide an 'optimal outcome' for the simple reason that there is no single notion of 'optimality'. Herman Daly has called for the analytical separation of three independent environmental policy goals that relate to the *efficiency* of resource allocation, the *equity* of social distribution and the ecological *sustainability* of the overall scale and rate of material-energy throughput and waste production of the economy (Daly 1992, 177). Following the lead from John Dryzek, we might also add the further goal of *openness* to democratic participation by citizens. It is highly unlikely that one policy instrument can provide an 'optimal outcome' in respect of all of these goals. In most cases, a combination of different instruments will need to be applied to maximise these four objectives. Although the discipline of environmental economics has dominated the 'new policy' agenda, this analysis cautions against 'disciplinary overreach' and suggests that environmental economics should be neutral in relation to all but the first of these objectives, at least if it is to remain a 'positive science'.

However, from an environmental perspective, the debate over policy instruments is of less significance than the more general debate concerning the overall targets and timetables of environmental policy. Yet it is here that strategic considerations and competitive pressures have dominated the policy landscape. Even before the world recession of the late 1990s began to take hold, environmental protection was increasingly regarded in many jurisdictions as a 'luxury item' on the political agenda, confirming the belief that industry is more likely to be attracted (or to remain) by maintaining or lowering taxes and charges, fast tracking environmental planning and approval processes, minimising 'green tape' and offering less onerous (or minimally enforced) environmental regulations. It is therefore of no great surprise (though certainly lamentable) that very few countries are on track to achieve their greenhouse gas emission reductions. Although a regulated international economy may, as Thompson argues, provide greater opportunities for global justice and environmental protection than a thoroughly liberalised international market, at present there is no world government or democratic coordinating agency that is able to oversee, manage, implement and enforce such a regime. The state system remains vulnerable to defection and free riding, and uncertainties and disputes about the costs and benefits of reform abound.

Although the much lauded potential of market-based instruments remains unfulfilled, there are some modest signs that the tide may be gradually turning. Europe currently leads the way in environmental taxes and charges whereas the US remains in the forefront of tradable permits (although there are some new experiments afoot in Australia, particularly in the state of New South Wales). Indeed, one significant prompt for more concerted use of market-based instruments is likely to be what Hahn calls the 'demonstration effect' of the existing schemes. The same arguments might be extended to the case for ecological modernisation, for moving 'beyond compliance' in anticipation of rising environmental expectations and for cultivating a virtuous relationship between markets, international competition and environmental performance. The irony for firms and nations alike, however, is that waiting for the 'demonstration effect' may mean losing the race.

# Endnotes

1. The OECD recognises certain exceptions to the 'no-subsidy principle' to ease the transition period towards stricter pollution control regimes, to stimulate investment in new technologies and to counter regional imbalances. For a discussion, see Stevens (1993, 608–11).
2. A more recent OECD report has urged developing countries to place greater emphasis on market instruments as a complement to the dominant regulatory approach (OECD 1993).
3. An OECD survey of 14 member countries found a total of 150 cases of different market-based instruments already in operation, with charges proving to be the most commonly applied instrument (1989, 111).
4. By environmental economics, I am referring to the extension of the theory of neoclassical welfare economics to environmental problems. However, this model of analysis, which may be traced to the work of Pigou (1932), has been challenged by a rival approach towards the internalisation of externalities, which stems from the work of Coase (1960). Although both approaches employ partial equilibrium theory in defending the price mechanism as the most efficient means of allocating 'environmental resources', they proceed from different starting points and generate markedly different environmental policy prescriptions (externality taxes and charges versus a clearer specification of property rights in relation to the environment).
5. According to the Coasian analysis, the question of who pays and who suffers is a function of the distribution of property rights and the common law rules of liability (thus the Polluter Pays Principle would not necessarily always apply).
6. Ecological economics builds on the pioneering work of Nicholas Georgescu-Roegen (1971). The growing interest in this new area of inquiry has now manifested in the form of the International Society for Ecological Economics and the Society's new quarterly journal *Ecological Economics*, published by Elsevier.
7. Strictly speaking, this argument would also apply to traditional regulatory schemes, which issue pollution licences.
8. Skou Andersen (1994b, 144) estimates that a tax would need to raise petrol prices to around 12 Danish kroner (DKK) per litre to reflect all externalities; however, the price cannot exceed 6–7 DKK/litre at the present German price level. Moreover, the new suite of green taxes are mainly directed towards households and consumers rather than manufacturers (143).

9. The GATT allows trade restrictions that can be shown to be 'necessary to protect human, animal or plant life or health' (Article XX [b]) as well as measures 'relating to the conservation of exhaustible natural resources if such measures are made effective in conjunction with restrictions on domestic production or consumption' (Article XX [g]). Such restrictions must be shown to be non-discriminatory, legitimate, proportional to the problem addressed, and necessary (i.e. the least restrictive measure necessary to achieve the environmental objective).

10. For a discussion of recent proposals to amend the GATT to address ecological dumping, see Hartwell and Bergkamp (1994, 10114–5).

11. Jänicke's discussion of market innovation is somewhat sketchy (and not reconciled with his critique of bureaucratic–industrial sclerosis).

12. For a discussion of 'weak' versus 'strong' forms of ecological modernisation, see Christoff (1995).

# References

Agarwal, A. and Narain, S. (1991) *Global Warming: A Case of Environmental Colonialism*, Centre for Science and Environment, New Delhi.

Anderson, T. and Leal. D. (1991) *Free Market Environmentalism*, Pacific Research Institute for Public Policy, San Francisco.

Baumol, W. and Oates, W. (1988) *The Theory of Environmental Policy*, 2nd edn, Cambridge University Press, Cambridge.

Beck, U. (1992) *The Risk Society: Towards a New Modernity*, Sage, London.

Bennett, J. (1991) 'Introduction' in J. Bennett and W. Block (eds), *Reconciling Economics and the Environment*, Australian Institute for Public Policy, Perth.

Bertram, J., Stephens, R. and Wallace, C. (1990) *Economic Instruments and the Greenhouse Effect*, Working Paper Series 3/90, Graduate School of Business and Government Management, Victoria University of Wellington.

Buchanan, J. and Tullock, G. (1975) 'Polluters' Profits and Political Response: Direct Controls Versus Taxes', *American Economic Review* 65, 139–47.

Christoff, P. (1995) 'Exploring Ecological Modernisation' in S. Young and J. van der Straaten (eds), *Ecological Modernisation*, Routledge, London, forthcoming.

Coase, R.H. (1960) 'The Problem of Social Cost', *Journal of Law and Economics* 3: 1–44.

Daly, H. (1991) *Steady-State Economics*, 2nd edn, Island Press, Washington.

Daly H. (1992) 'Free Market Environmentalism: Turning a Good Servant into a Bad Master', *Critical Review* 6(2–3): 171–83.

Dryzek, J. (1987) *Rational Ecology: Environment and Political Economy*, Basil Blackwell, Oxford.

Dryzek, J. S. (1990) *Discursive Democracy: Politics, Policy, and Political Science*, Cambridge University Press, Cambridge.

Dryzek, J. S. (1992) 'Ecology and Discursive Democracy: Beyond Liberal Capitalism and the Administrative State', *Capitalism, Nature, Socialism* 3(20): 18–42.

Eckersley, R. (1995) 'Disciplining the Market, Calling in the State: The Politics of Economy–Environment Integration' in S. Young and J. van der Straaten (eds), *Ecological Modernisation*, Routledge, London, forthcoming.

Georgescu-Roegen, N. (1971) *The Entropy Law and the Economic Process*, Harvard University Press, Cambridge, Massachusetts.

*Global Environmental Change Report.* (1994) 6(15), 12 August, 3.

Goodin, R.E. (1992) 'The Ethics of Selling Environmental Indulgences', Paper presented to the Australasian Philosophical Association Annual Conference, University of Queensland.

Gunningham, N. (1994) 'Moving Beyond Compliance: Management of Environmental Risk' in B. Boer, R. Fowler and N. Gunningham (eds), *Environmental Outlook: Law and Policy*, Federation Press, Sydney.

Habermas, J. (1971) *Toward a Rational Society*, translated by J. Shapiro, Heinemann, London.

Hartwell, R.V. and Bergkamp, L. (1994) 'Environmental Trade Barriers and International Competitiveness', *ELR* 24(3) 10109–15.

Helm, D. and Pearce, D. (1991) 'Economic Policy Towards the Environment: An Overview' in D. Helm (ed.), *Economic Policy Towards the Enviroment*, Blackwell, Oxford.

HMSO, (1993) *Making Markets Work for the Environment*, Department of the Environment, HMSO, London.

*Intrernational Environmental Reporter* (1993a) 16(14), 14 July, 519.

*International Environmental Reporter* (1993b) 16(21), 20 October, 755.

Jacobs, M. (1991) *The Green Economy*, Pluto Press, London.

James, D. (1993) *Using Economic Instruments for Meeting Environmental Objectives: Australia's Experience*, Environmental Economics Research Paper No. 1, Department of the Environment, Sport and Territories, Canberra.

Jänicke, M. (1990) *State Failure*, Polity Press, Cambridge.

Kemball-Cooke, D., Baker, M. and Mattingly, C. (1991) *The Green Budget*, Greenprint, London.

Martinez-Alier, J. (1993) 'Distributional Obstacles to International Environmental Policy: The Failures at Rio and Prospects after Rio', *Environmental Values* 2(2), 97–124.

Moran, A. (1991) 'Addressing the Limits of Market Solutions' in J. Bennett and W. Block (eds), *Reconciling Economics and the Environment*, Australian Institute for Public Policy, Perth.

OECD. (1975) *The Polluter Pays Principle: Definition, Analysis, Implementation*, OECD, Paris.

OECD. (1989) *Economic Instruments for Environmental Protection*, OECD, Paris.

OECD. (1991) *Environmental Policy: How to Apply Economic Instruments*, OECD, Paris.

OECD. (1993) *Economic Instruments for Environmental Management in Developing Countries*, OECD, Paris.

Pearce, D., Markandya, A. and Barbier, E. (1989) *Blueprint for a Green Economy*, Earthscan, London.

Pearce, D. (1992) 'Economics and the Global Environmental Challenge' in I. Rowlands and M. Greene (eds), *Global Environmental Change and International Relations*, Macmillan, London.

Pigou, A.C. (1932) *The Economics of Welfare*, Macmillan, London (first published in 1920).

Repetto, R., Dower, R.C., Jenkins, R. and Goeghagen, J. (1992) *Green Fees: How A Tax Shift Can Work for the Environment and the Economy*, World Resources Institute, Washington DC.

Repetto, R. (1993) 'Green Taxes: Their Environmental and Economic Benefits', Occasional Paper Number 5, Institute of Ethics and Public Policy, Monash University, November.

Shrybman, S. (1990) 'International Trade and the Environment: An Environmental Assessment of the General Agreement on Tariffs and Trade, *The Ecologist* 20(1), 30–34.

Skou Andersen, M. (1994a) *Governance by Green Taxes: Making Pollution Prevention Pay*, Manchester University Press, Manchester.

Skou Andersen, M. (1994b) 'Green Tax Reform in Denmark', *Environmental Politics* 3(1), 139–45.

Stevens, C. (1993) 'The OECD Guiding Principles Revisited', *Environmental Law* 23(2), 607–19.

Turner, R.K., Pearce, D. and Bateman, I. (1994) *Environmental Economics: An Elementary Introduction*, Harvester Wheatsheaf, New York.

Verbruggen, H. (1993) 'The Trade Effects of Economic Instruments', Paper prepared for the OECD Environment Directorate/NACEPT Trade and Environment Committee, Informal Experts' Workshop 'Environmental Policies and Industry Competitiveness', 28–29 January.

von Weizsacker, E.U. and Jesinghaus, J. (1992) *Ecological Tax Reform*, Zed Books, London.

Weale, A. (1992) *The New Politics of Pollution*, Manchester University Press, Manchester.

World Commission on Environment and Development (WCED). (1990) *Our Common Future*, Australian edition, Oxford University Press, Melbourne.

Yeager, P. (1991) *The Limits of the Law*, Cambridge University Press, Cambridge.

## 2

# *Sustainability and 'the Market': A Typology of Environmental Economics*

## Michael Jacobs

### Introduction

Since the subject of environmental economics first began to arouse public debate at the end of the 1980s, attention has focused on what are widely described as 'market' solutions to environmental problems. Predisposed as they are to market-based analysis, and to the abstract concept of 'optimality', the majority of environmental economists have been engaged either in studying 'market-based mechanisms' of environmental control, such as green taxes and tradable quotas, or in devising hypothetical markets by which to value environmental goods. Needing snappy headlines and uncomplicated arguments, media commentators have eagerly seized on the apparent Left–Right conflict in environmental policy, with the Left said to favour old-fashioned 'regulation', the Right the new solutions of the 'free market'. Meanwhile real free market solutions, grounded in other policy areas, have been cheerfully applied to environmental issues by those with a genuinely ideological axe to grind.

In this chapter I shall try to show why the conventional understanding of these arguments in environmental economics is seriously misleading. I shall argue that the problem lies in the use of the word 'market', which is used to describe many things that are not at all similar, but are then taken as being similar because of their common epithet. I shall offer an alternative typology of environmental economics, which in my view better describes what the subject is about — and the real ideological divisions it provokes.

I shall then offer some arguments, arising from these divisions, for one specific approach to the subject, combining both a method of making environmental policy and a substantive environmental objective.

## The Four Questions

The key to understanding what environmental economists are doing lies in separating out four questions that they seek to answer.

(I should say at once that these observations apply only to those who might be called micro-environmental economists. These are people working on solutions to individual environmental problems in the fields of pollution, resource and land use. They constitute the vast majority of scholars within the discipline, but not all. Environmental economics also encompasses extremely interesting 'macro-level' work looking at issues such as how damage to the environment should be measured in the national income accounts, how environmental variables should be incorporated into economic models, and what structure of economies and economic institutions can best achieve environmental protection. These latter fields have not, unfortunately, received so much public attention, and I am not concerned with them here.)

The four questions are:

1.  What level of environmental protection should society choose? (We might call this the question of the *ethics of environmental objective setting.*)
2.  How should this level be chosen? (The question of the *institutions of environmental objective setting.*)
3.  How should this level be achieved? (The question of *instruments.*)
4.  How should the costs and benefits associated with this level be distributed among different groups in society? (The question of *distribution.*)

Question 4 is something of a rogue here: it is not really true to say that environmental economists have sought to answer this, or even to analyse it. Because of its roots in neoclassical welfare economics, which has traditionally emphasised the *allocation* of resources rather than their distribution, very little attention has been devoted to this question.[1] It has certainly not substantially divided economists themselves. But it is a very important one politically, and I shall discuss it further later.

Note that these questions are concerned with separate, distinguishable environmental problems. Such problems might be particular types of air or water pollution, particular natural resources such as forests or minerals, or particular types of land use such as natural habitats or landscapes. The first three questions are applied to these individually in turn, as it were: on each issue, it is asked how much protection should be given, how this should be decided, and how it should be achieved.

This dependence of micro-environmental economics on the divisibility of environmental problems is an important limitation. Most economists will acknowledge that environmental problems are inter-linked, but this is either dealt with through the joint specification of objectives (for example for air and water pollution together), which makes appropriate solutions more complex but is conceptually straightforward; or it is assumed that inter-related problems can be analysed in their component parts without significant loss of understanding. It is pointed out that environmental policy, towards which the discipline is oriented, also tends, and perhaps has, to treat problems separately. Where natural scientists insist on the indivisibility of large and multi-faceted environmental problems (as ecologists frequently do in relation to biodiversity, and climatologists may yet do with respect to the greenhouse effect) micro-environmental economics is ill-equipped to deal with them.

The distinction between the first two questions is not always recognised — this is indeed a part of the argument I wish to make. But their conceptual differences are very important. Asking, for any given environmental issue, what level of protection society should choose, is not the same as specifying the institution that should make that choice. In the end, of course, specifying the institution may make one's own choice of objective academic, but this does not undermine one's ability to make that choice. Schooled in the 'positive', non-normative tradition of economics, many environmental economists will claim that they have no business answering question 1 at all — this is a matter for politicians or philosophers. But it is not so easy to escape answering it, if only by default, as we shall show below. Moreover, there is one school of environmental economics that *has* wanted to answer it, using the widely advocated concept of 'sustainability'. So it cannot be ignored.

The difference between questions 1 and 2 and question 3 should be less controversial, though it is surprising how often they are confused. Questions 1 and 2 are concerned with *objectives* — the end point that policy is trying to achieve. Question 3 is concerned with *instruments* — the means by which this end point is reached. Regulations, taxes and charges, subsidies, tradable quotas and so on are all instruments — they are the means of achieving environmental objectives. They do not in themselves specify such objectives, which is a prior question, as again we discuss below.


## The Typology

Armed with these four questions, we can now set out a typology of approaches in environmental economics (Table 2.1). Initially we shall concentrate on the first three questions, where the major disagreements lie. Because of the paucity of answers to question 4, these will all be discussed together in a subsequent section.

### The Traditional Approach
Column A in Table 2.1 represents what I have called, for want of a better term, the 'traditional' approach. This is broadly speaking the way in which environmental policy was thought about, and made, before modern environmental economics entered the scene. (It is in fact still largely the way policy is made.) In the traditional approach the objectives of environmental policy (question 1) can be characterised as the protection of health and amenity at safe and decent levels, in so far as this can be done without excessive cost to economic growth. In question 2, the traditional approach argues that these levels should be decided in practice by public authorities. Scientific evidence should be used to determine safe levels of environmental hazards, and these weighed against the economic costs of achieving them. The normal political processes of public opinion, lobbying and so on should determine appropriate levels of amenity. To question 3, the traditional approach applies the use of law. Legal regulations allow firms to discharge certain levels of pollutants or prescribe particular standards for technologies or products. Land use is controlled by a law-based planning system. All this is familiar.

### The Neoclassical School
Columns B to D represent different aspects of the neoclassical school in environmental economics — effectively, different groups of practitioners, all of whom share the same basic assumptions. The distinction between columns B and C is not fundamental: we shall discuss the reasons for drawing it below. The difference between these two columns and column D, however, is very important. Columns B and C represent those economists working on *instruments*, that is, on question 3. Specifically, they are concerned with financial incentives: tradable quotas, green taxes and charges, subsidies, deposit refund schemes and so on.

**Table 2.1** A taxonomy of environmental economics

| Question | | Approach | | | | |
|---|---|---|---|---|---|---|
| | A<br>'Traditional' | B<br>Neoclassical I:<br>Financial<br>incentives<br>(tradable quotas) | C<br>Neoclassical II:<br>Financial<br>incentives<br>(taxes, etc.) | D<br>Neoclassical III:<br>Monetary<br>valuation<br>('pure' form*) | E<br>Property<br>rights | F<br>Environmental<br>democracy |
| 1: Ethics of environmental objective setting | Health and amenity at reasonable cost | ? | ? | Whatever results from the CBA | Whatever results from the market bargain | Sustainability |
| 2: Institutions of environmental objective setting | Government decision making† | ? | ? | Social cost–benefit analysis (CBA) | Market bargain | Government decision making after open, participatory public debate |
| 3: Instruments | Legal regulation | Tradable quotas | Taxes, charges, subsidies, etc. | ? | Privatisation | Legal regulations, financial incentives, public expenditure, etc. |
| 4: Distribution | ? | ? | ? | ? (likely to favour better off) | Not relevant (likely to favour better off) | Equitable (intention) |

* The 'pure' form of the neoclassical method seeks to create a supply and demand curve for the environmental good. Some neoclassical economists acknowledge that cost–benefit analysis should be one contribution to public decision making, which can also consider other criteria.
† Government decision–making methods are unspecified.

Column D represents the branch of the subject interested in the monetary valuation of environmental goods and services. People working in this field are concerned with *objectives*: with how much of a particular environmental feature should be protected (question 2). Contingent valuation and the other techniques of monetary valuation aim to determine the benefit side of a social cost–benefit calculation: that is, how much an environmental feature (such as an area of landscape or a particular level of water quality in a river) is valued by its users and others who care about it. By measuring this value against the financial costs of protecting the feature in question, the cost–benefit calculation can determine whether or not public policy should protect it. In theory at least, a range of such calculations can determine the 'optimal' level of environmental protection at which marginal benefit equals marginal cost. At this level, any more protection will not be worth its costs, while any less will undervalue the benefits the environment provides. In this way, the neoclassical economists represented in column D believe they can (help to) discover the level of environmental protection that society should choose.

Note that these economists do not say that this is the *right* level of environmental protection. Like all neoclassical economists, they argue that this ethical question (question 1) is not for an economist — at least, in his or her role *as* an economist — to answer. As a positive not a normative science, economics is concerned only with discovering what people prefer, and then identifying how society can most efficiently achieve it. Monetary valuation and social cost–benefit analysis (CBA) are institutions designed to reveal social objectives, not means of ethical judgment. A similar agnosticism on the appropriate level of environmental protection is offered by economists in columns B and C, though with an important difference, to which we shall return a little later.

For now, the important point to note is that columns B and C are *only* concerned with instruments, and column D *only* with objectives. Conceptually, it is possible to link them: the ideal 'Pigouvian' tax on an externality is based on the measured size of the 'market failure' it is correcting. Thus the level of environmental protection that the instruments in B and C are designed to achieve can be set by the methods of monetary valuation and CBA used in column D. But this is not necessary, and in fact it is by no means always done. Economists working on energy taxes, pollution charges and tradable permits, deposit-refund schemes for products, and so on, do not necessarily start off by trying to work out the 'optimal' level of environmental protection in the field under question. Frequently, they assume that public authorities will set the objective through some 'non-economic' process, probably of the kind described under the traditional approach above. Their role (as they see it) is then to take whatever has been decided is the objective, and find the most efficient way of achieving it: in other words the way that generates the least total cost to society.

An examination of work in this field reveals this lack of concern for how objectives are set. Many of the economists working on energy taxes, for example, *assume* a carbon dioxide emissions target, taking whatever has been proposed by international conferences or climatology experts (Brinner et al. 1991; Karadeloglou 1992; Barker, Baylis and Madsen 1993). (There *are* economists trying to do cost-benefit analyses of global warming, to be sure; but most of these are not particularly concerned with the detail of the necessary carbon tax or other measures. They are working in column D (e.g. Nordhaus 1991; Cline 1992).

Similarly, those working on tradable permits for air pollution do not try to work out the optimal level of air quality by finding out people's willingness to pay for it. (There are other economists, in column D, doing this.) They say, 'Give me whatever level of air quality you want, and I can show that a tradable pollution system will reach or exceed it more cheaply and reliably than any other method' (e.g. Tietenberg 1985 and 1990).

A similar single-mindedness exists among those working on monetary valuation of the environment. In suggesting suitable objectives of environmental policy they do not assume that these must be achieved by applying a tax or tradable permit or other financial incentive. On the contrary, they are often working in fields, such as land use and species protection, where legal regulation is the preferred instrument. If a contingent valuation exercise reveals that the public's 'willingness to pay' for a National Park is greater than its value to mining companies, the neoclassical economist does not then propose to tax mining there or offer tradable mining permits. Mining is forbidden by law.

This separation between columns B/C and D is not just a product of academic specialisation. It represents a genuine conceptual break between the activity of setting objectives and that of identifying instruments to achieve them. It is important to recognise this, because much criticism of financial incentives in the environmental movement has derived from the mistaken belief that they depend on giving the environment a monetary value. They do not.

## The Property Rights School
Column E represents the 'property rights' school of environmental economics. It is based on the theory of public choice first

developed by Coase (1960) and since applied in many fields inside and outside economics. In recent years its advocates have turned their attention to the environment (e.g. Anderson and Leal 1991; Bennett and Block 1991; Moran, Chisholm and Porter 1991).

The defining characteristic of the property rights school is its proposal that all environmental decisions should be made through bargains struck between actors in markets. To do this it argues that environmental goods and services should be privatised, and markets thereby created in their use. This use can be preservation or exploitation — this is not for public policy to decide. (Its advocates tend to regard question 1 as illegitimate, as we shall show below.) Rather, environmental objectives should be determined (question 2) through the market bargain. The objective is whatever happens to emerge when people concerned to protect the environment have to bargain with those who wish to exploit it in some way or other.

For example, the property rights economist argues that a National Park should be auctioned off to the highest bidder. If environmental organisations can bid more than the mining companies, they can have the park and it will be protected. If not, the reverse result will occur. Of course, the process can be more sophisticated than this: once either side owns the park they can then decide to sell or lease parts of it to others, which they will do if they feel the benefits (as they see them) are worth the costs. The park need not be auctioned off, either; it can be given away if need be, so long as it ends up as private property subject to market transactions. Thereafter the state has no role (beyond the upholding of private property rights in law); its only instrument (question 3) is the act of privatisation itself.

## The 'Environmental Democracy' School

The final column, F, represents what I have called the 'environmental democracy' position. This column does not represent a 'school' or subset of environmental economics; it is overtly a political position. But because of the way in which the other five columns are used to represent political positions also, it is useful to include it.

'Environmental democracy' is characterised, first, by its substantive answer to question 1: the concept of 'sustainability' is proposed (and defined) as the objective of environmental policy. Second, it is argued that in practice public authorities should determine environmental objectives (question 2): they should do this specifically through open and participatory methods of public debate. Finally, this school is agnostic on the use of instruments, advocating that all kinds of instruments, including both legal regulations and financial incentives, should be used as appropriate, and that all are equally worthy of economic study.

I should declare an interest here, since column F represents my own position. Exercising author's prerogative, I therefore intend to explain it further in the course of my analysis of the other five positions. (This also explains its semi-detached status in Table 2.1. Whereas there is a logic to the order in which the other five columns are placed, column F has no particular position and its location to the right of column E has no significance.)

## The Fallacy of 'The Market'

The public debate about environmental economics has drawn the positions identified in the first five columns of Table 2.1 into a simple dichotomy. This is between the traditional approach in column A, which existed before modern environmental economics and is concerned entirely with the political and legal activities of the state, and the remaining columns, which are all about markets and their use for environmental purposes. As anything to do with markets is assumed to be Rightward leaning, and anything to do with the state the province of the Left, a major cleavage has been assumed between column A and the rest of the table.

This is an unfortunate and possibly dangerous mistake. In fact the intellectual cleavage in the table is between columns C and D. The fact that all the columns B to E can be described using the term 'market' does *not* mean that they are similar; it merely shows how misleading the term 'market' is. The crucial distinction is between those fields of environmental economics that seek to use the market to determine environmental objectives (columns D and E) and those that are concerned only with instruments (columns A to C).

I say 'intellectual cleavage' because many practitioners working on monetary valuation techniques and CBA do not argue that the results of cost–benefit analyses should in themselves determine the objective of environmental policy. Many will acknowledge that other factors ought also to be considered — distributional concerns, moral and cultural arguments, and so on. Nevertheless the intellectual basis of monetary valuation techniques — the reason such techniques are used — is clearly the belief that they can establish the 'optimal' objective of environmental protection, whether or not disclaimers are subsequently issued that 'optimal' does not actually mean the one society should choose. This makes the intellectual division between column D and columns A to C (which are not concerned with objectives at all) unequivocal.

## Regulations and Financial Incentives

Let us start with columns A to C: those concerned with instruments. My argument is that there is not nearly as much difference between the regulatory instruments represented by column A and the 'market-based' ones of columns B and C as is usually claimed. In the first place we should be very careful not to obscure the issues by use of language: the common practice of calling regulatory instruments 'command and control', with its pejorative connotations, is simply propaganda.

Equally (though more subtly) misleading is the term 'economic instruments' for columns B and C. This suggests that regulation is somehow 'not economic'; that it is not what economists are or should be concerned with. But how could this be? *All* tools that change the behaviour of firms and consumers are economic, since economics is the study of the behaviour of those agents. Behaviour is changed as much by regulation as by taxes and subsidies: if economists do not study how, they do not understand what is going on in the economy. (Consider employment protection laws and their influence on the labour market.) Responses to regulation are by no means uncomplicated: for example, as Susan Smith shows in this anthology, the severity of punishment may have a crucial effect on responses to pollution laws. Since regulations and market-based mechanisms are often presented as alternatives, it seems odd that economists show so little interest in how the many different kinds of regulations do and could work — to the point of not calling them economic instruments at all.

I am not particularly happy even about the use of the term 'market-based', though I think we are stuck with this. This suggests that regulatory instruments somehow do not operate in markets — a misconception that has reinforced the idea that there is a Left–Right division in this field. Of course regulations operate in markets. Employment protection laws have not abolished the labour market; consumer protection laws haven't given us a command economy. Neither have the thousands of existing environmental regulations. Regulations shape and influence markets, just as taxes and subsidies do. My own preferred term for 'market-based mechanisms' — those that attempt to influence behavioural change rather than requiring it — is 'financial incentives', which seems to me to capture their key characteristics without unnecessary accompanying baggage.

The key point here is that *all* kinds of instruments, whether regulatory, financial or of other kinds, attempt to change behaviour. They do so in different ways — I am not suggesting that there is no difference between them. But as behaviour-changers, they share the common characteristic of being *government interventions in markets*. This is why the idea that 'green taxes' and similar financial incentives are somehow a 'free market' response to environmental problems is so strange. Taxes are imposed by governments, and their purpose (in the environmental case) and result is to change behaviour. They no more allow a 'free market' — whatever that is — than legal regulations do. It is true, of course, that agents in the market can react in different ways to financial instruments, whereas with regulations they generally have only one (legal) option. But that hardly creates a 'free market': if a sufficient number of agents do not react in the required way to change the environmental result, the theory argues that the tax should be increased until they do! It is odd that this limited freedom of response to financial instruments has led people to believe that in some way such instruments are Right-wing, whereas regulations are Left-wing. Both require the state to intervene in the economy; in the classical sense, both are a form of economic 'regulation'. Anyone who has tried to set a tax knows just how interventionist an instrument it is!

Tradable quotas are particularly interesting in this regard. They have been heralded as a new and innovative form of financial incentive. They have even been given the name 'market creation' because new markets are created in pollution or resource permits. Since the property rights instrument of privatisation in column E is also described as 'market creation', this has led some people, including some property rights economists themselves, to suppose that the two approaches are essentially the same.[2] But they are not at all. Privatisation creates *permanent* markets in *the environmental goods themselves*. It does this by abstracting government from the arena altogether: the state has no say in the eventual environmental result. Tradable quotas, by contrast, bring the state further into the market, determining specifically how much of the environment will be used and protected. The quotas merely create *temporary* markets in permits to *use* the environment.

This difference is absolutely crucial. What matters for the environment is how much of the environment is used and how much is preserved: that is, the level of environmental protection achieved. In the 'true' property rights approach represented by column E, this is not determined by government. It is determined by the market transaction of buyers and sellers. No particular level of environmental protection can therefore be guaranteed; from the environment's point of view, the result is uncertain and arbitrary.

This is not what happens with tradable permits. Here governments set the overall level of environmental protection, such as the ambient pollution level or resource extraction rate. All the tradable permits do is allow different allocations within that total. But from the environment's point of view it is the total that matters, and that is socially determined and (if the policy works) certain.

Tradable quotas are in this sense very similar to traditional regulatory instruments (which is why they have been placed next to column A in Table 2.1). Take the example of air or water pollution. Traditionally, firms have been given permits or 'consents' to emit or discharge a certain volume of pollutants. This is exactly what tradable quotas do, with the one difference that the firms may then trade their permits, either with other companies or with themselves over time. In effect, quotas are just the old regulatory system with the added lubricant of trading attached. This is not exactly a 'free market', incidentally, either: in the United States, where tradable quotas for air pollution have been operating for some time, *every trade* must be approved by the Environmental Protection Agency.

### *The Superiority of Financial Incentives?*
Seeing all the instruments in columns A to C as government interventions in the market should help to dispel the myth of ideological difference. There really should be no reason why, a priori, any type of instrument should be favoured by any particular political position. (It should not be thought that taxes have necessarily or uniquely regressive distributional effects, for example. Environmental taxes, such as on fuel, can be progressive in effect, particularly when the use of the tax revenues is included in the analysis. Taxing petrol and using the revenues to subsidise public transport, for example, would clearly benefit the poorest sections of the population, who do not own or have access to cars. Regulations also generally raise prices, and so also have distributional effects, which can equally be regressive or progressive.)

Even more importantly, we should be careful about glib assertions, often made, that financial incentives are always superior to regulatory instruments. They are more efficient, it is argued; they provide a constant motivation to environmental improvement; and they are less bureaucratic.

The efficiency argument is most often put, and the least often examined. It is easy to show the greater efficiency of a tax over a regulatory standard in theory, where markets are perfectly competitive and firms — but not regulators! — have perfect information. But in the real world the arguments often do not hold. In Britain a rise of 400 per cent in sewerage charges failed to change firms' behaviour, even though it was shown that small investments in pollution control would pay back in under a year.

The charging system was not understood by the firms affected; it was dealt with by the finance department, not the engineers; and the firms did not know the technological options available. A regulation requiring them to install the better technology would almost certainly have been more efficient — that is, cost less overall — than the huge price hike that would have been required to get the same changes made (Rees 1988).

The energy market provides similar lessons. Energy costs are too small for most firms to devote management time to their reduction; borrowing for new equipment is expensive and competes with other investment options; information about more efficient technologies is difficult to obtain and assess. So even where payback periods are relatively short, energy price rises (i.e. taxes, the financial incentive instrument) do not have the required effect. Or rather, because elasticities are so low, it would take enormous and very costly price increases to make it happen. If by contrast building and appliance efficiency standards were raised by law, and if electricity supply companies (who can afford to borrow money) were required to offer energy conservation measures to their consumers, energy consumption would almost certainly fall *at less total cost to society*; that is, more efficiently (Jackson and Jacobs 1991).

Of course, in some circumstances financial incentives *are* more efficient than regulations. But the general argument is of little value. Each case must be examined, in the real world, not in theory, and policy formulated on that issue, not on all. The same goes for the arguments concerning continuing motivation and bureaucracy. It is true that financial incentives do generally provide a continuing motivation to reduce environmental damage. This can often be a strong argument in their favour. But in some cases it may be more important to stop the activity altogether, in which case regulations are more effective.

As for bureaucracy, there is little evidence that regulation requires more of it than taxation. Any system of environmental control needs inspectors to check whether claimed emissions, discharges or resource extractions are correct: they are not less 'bureaucratic' because they are tax inspectors rather than regulatory ones. Taxation requires the additional structure of revenue collection, which regulation does not, while not dispensing with the legal framework: tax avoidance, like flouting regulations, is an offence.

The foregoing suggests that the supposed great divide between regulatory and financial instruments is unhelpful and should be abandoned. Hence my own agnostic position represented in column F. I believe that all the possible instruments at our disposal should be considered on their merits in achieving our policy objectives, without neoclassically inspired theoretical prejudgment. For some environmental problems it seems likely that regulatory instruments will be preferable, particularly those, such as over land uses, where there are binary choices to be made (we either protect it or we do not). For others, different kinds of financial incentives will prove more effective. Often a combination of instruments will be required, as almost every country that has tried financial incentives has found.

## Environmental Objectives

*Procedural and Outcome-based Ethics*

I say that instruments should be considered 'on their merits in achieving our policy objectives'. This is really the heart of the matter. What are these objectives and how are they chosen? Policy makers can have a number of possible objectives, including efficiency (least total cost), administrative simplicity, flexibility, equity in distributional effects, and so on. But I am concerned here with the primary objective, namely the level of environmental protection that the policy is designed to achieve. How much 'environment' should we have? And how is this decided?

It is when these questions are asked — questions 1 and 2 in Table 2.1 — that the real divisions between the approaches are revealed. Columns A to C give very little role to economics. In the 'traditional' approach economists are required to calculate how much different possible levels of protection would cost; but they are not then expected to say whether the benefits in terms of amenity and health are worth those costs. That is left to the judgment of the legislators. The neoclassical positions concerned with financial instruments do not say even this much: in themselves they do not have any particular view on what the level of environmental protection should be or how it should be chosen.

Contrast this with the positions represented by columns D and E. Here there is a very specific answer to question 2, and this leads to an answer to question 1. The institution that society should use to determine the appropriate level of environmental protection is the market, either real or hypothetical. In the market, consumers and firms are free to express their preferences. And when they do so the market will generate the optimal result, namely, the level of environmental protection that maximises the net total benefit of the agents taking part.

This basic position is common to columns D and E. But its expression is different. Property rights theorists believe in real markets: privatising the environment generates real transactions between the environment's owners and those who wish to use it. Neoclassicists favour hypothetical markets: contingent valuation is designed to discover how people *would* behave *if* there were markets in environmental goods and such goods had to be paid for. The results should be used by governments to determine society's environmental objectives.

By specifying the market as the institution through which objectives should be set in question 2, both these schools render question 1 redundant, if not actually illegitimate. They argue that there is no separate question to answer: the morally best result *is* that which arises from the market process, whatever it is. This is because the ethical issue of concern to these schools is not the (environmental) *outcome* of decision making but its *procedure*. The highest ethical goal of both property rights theorists and (implicitly) of ideal-type neoclassicists is individual liberty, and this is best served, they argue, by market processes. Only in such processes can individual preferences be freely expressed and properly taken into account. The substantive outcome that results from the exercise of procedural liberty — in this case, the environmental outcome — has no *independent* ethical standing; its morality is judged entirely by the procedure that generated it.

In fact property rights theorists would go further than this. They would argue that it is politically dangerous for question 1 to be asked independently of question 2, for to do so implies that individual preferences are not sovereign. If the morally best outcome is determined substantively, who is to do this? If it is not the result of individual preferences, it must be chosen by government. But governments never act on 'neutral' ethical concerns; they always represent the interests of powerful groups in society. To the advocate of column E, the ethical importance of markets is precisely their decentralised character, allowing the expression of individual preferences without the interest-based interference of governments. Markets are thus seen as the guarantor of individual liberty.

But of course the unwillingness of property rights theorists and valuation-oriented neoclassicists to answer question 1 independently of question 2 does not mean that the question, 'what level of environmental protection should society choose?' cannot be asked. In any political process it is possible to apply ethical judgments to outcomes as well as to procedures. We do not suspend our belief that racism is wrong, for example, simply because in some instances it is supported by democratic majorities. Similarly, it is perfectly legitimate to argue that environmental outcomes are right or wrong, whatever the ethical virtues — or otherwise — of the political procedure that generated them. If there is a conflict between outcome-based and procedure-based moral judgments, it is true that we may have to choose which we value more highly. It may also be that the institution (say, government) that is theoretically able to generate the morally best outcome is *in practice* likely to produce a bad one, so providing an argument for a second-best solution (say, a market procedure). But neither of these arguments mean that outcomes raise no ethical questions in their own right, as the advocates of columns D and E claim. They clearly do.

*Sustainability*
There is, in fact, a specific environmental ethic against which outcomes can be judged. This is the concept of 'sustainability'. Understood as an economic objective, sustainability is the requirement that the 'natural capital stock' — the amount or level of environmental assets and services — should be maintained over time. As such, sustainability is essentially an ethical principle, concerned with intergenerational equity. Society should allow future generations to enjoy the same opportunities provided by the natural environment as those available to the present generation.[3]

There are a number of different ways of defining and measuring the natural capital stock. But however this is done, the concept of sustainability provides a substantive answer to question 1. The level of environmental protection that society should choose is that which maintains the natural capital stock over time. Sustainability thus specifies a particular level of environmental protection as the ethically right one. It is a different level from the one proposed in the 'traditional' approach of column A, which is not (explicitly) concerned with future generations. But both are substantive, in the sense that, at least in theory, both can say, for any proposed level of environmental protection (a particular ambient pollution standard, for example, or a particular land-use decision), 'this is enough', or 'this is not enough'. Neither reduces the issue of environmental objective (question 1) to whatever outcome emerges from a specified institution (question 2). These are regarded as independent questions. One can prescribe an institution and still criticise the environmental result it produces.

Judged against the objective of sustainability, the market-based institutions of the property rights and 'pure' neoclassical schools do not fare well. Neither a real nor a hypothetical market is likely to generate sustainable outcomes. This is because in markets both households and firms tend to discount the future, an entirely rational procedure for self-interested agents acting in ignorance of others' actions (i.e. in decentralised markets) where there are positive interest rates and time preference. Sustainability, on the other hand, requires that the future is not (or is only marginally) discounted. Not being represented in current markets, the interests of future generations are unlikely to be taken into account. It would be surprising indeed — and quite contrary to current experience — if the sum total of market decisions led to environmental results that provided for intergenerational equity. (If this were likely to happen, it could be argued, we would not be facing an environmental crisis.)

This conflict between the institutions favoured by the property rights and 'pure' neoclassical schools and the sustainability objective might be represented simply as a conflict between procedural and outcome-based ethics. Perhaps these schools value the individual liberty provided by markets more highly than the environmental objective of sustainability. But the conflict is in fact more serious than this. The ethic of sustainability actually undermines the ethic of individual liberty as expressed in markets. For this is based on the notion that individual preferences should be sovereign in societal decision making. But markets do not make all individual preferences sovereign. The preferences of future generations are excluded, since unborn people (indeed, to a considerable extent present children too) are not represented in current markets. It is precisely such preferences (or at least, interests) that sustainability seeks to protect. There is therefore ostensibly an internal contradiction in the position of property rights and pure neoclassical theorists: their chosen institution of the market does not have the procedural virtue ascribed to it.

This flaw can be overcome in a number of ways. Logical consistency can be preserved by making a distinction between the ethical standing of present and future people: effectively, to argue that future people's preferences count less. This might be either because we cannot know what such preferences will be, or because they are subject to circularity. The people who will exist in the future will be different if we take action A from those who would exist if we took action B. Therefore we cannot act now on the basis of future people's preferences: such preferences will be formed (in part) by our actions (this argument is made in Parfit 1984). This argument removes the internal contradiction, but in doing so reinforces rather than answers the case for sustainability: what many will assume are the likely interests of future generations are simply believed not to count very much.

Alternatively, a more practical line may be taken. It could be argued that discounting is not an inevitable result of market behaviour. If present people care about the future they can make non-self-interested choices in their consumption and production decisions, as many 'green consumers' and 'ethical investors' are already doing. But this is barely tenable. In markets, people do not know how other people are behaving, and their choices cannot be enforced on others. They therefore face the equivalent of a multi-person prisoner's dilemma. If they act ethically, but no-one else does, the result will be their loss and (since the effect on the environment of each person's actions is minuscule) no environmental gain. Everyone is in this position, ignorant of others' intentions: the rational choice for each person is therefore to act in private self-interest. Even if a majority wants to act for sustainability, a minority can still wreck the outcome, either by continuing with environmentally damaging behaviour or by undercutting 'ethical' firms and driving them out of business — or both. In most cases sustainable behaviour is not achievable unless (nearly) everyone practises it. This requires mutual coercion, of which the market by itself is incapable.

It is notable in this regard that when creating hypothetical markets for contingent valuation exercises neoclassical environmental economists have specifically ruled out any communication between participants. Such communication would overcome the prisoner's dilemma, but would not replicate market conditions.[4] Direct communication is a feature of democratic decision-making arenas, not market ones. Researchers have now begun to try contingent valuation-type exercises in which respondents are allowed to talk to one another, in which ethical goals are discussed and progressive taxes rather than private spending are used as payment vehicles. But such exercises precisely do *not* generate hypothetical markets: they are a form of opinion survey, in which respondents are asked to make social not individualistic choices, and not therefore to reproduce market behaviour at all.[5]

There is a third, 'negative', defence of the property rights and pure neoclassical positions. This is that, while market-based institutions may not guarantee sustainability, they are likely to generate better environmental outcomes than any other available institutions, particularly those involving governments (Anderson and Leal 1991). With this argument, the onus of proof shifts onto those who oppose market-based institutions for setting environmental objectives. Can public decision-making processes achieve sustainability?

*Deliberative Democracy*
In column F of Table 2.1, the 'environmental democracy' school argues for governments to set environmental objectives through open, participatory processes of public debate. The best

institutions and methods through which to conduct such a debate are open to question, but its purpose is clear: to arrive at a socially agreed answer to the question, 'What level of environmental protection should society choose?'. The concept of 'social agreement' here stands in contrast to the decision-making process represented by the market (real or hypothetical). The process does *not* aim simply to aggregate individual preferences and so arrive at a collective result. Rather, it is concerned to ask individuals in society a different type of question: not, 'What do you (personally) want?', but 'What should society do?'. Of course, part of what society should do is to fulfil individuals' preferences, and the fulfilling of my own private preferences is likely to be part of my answer to the question of what society should do. But it is unlikely to be the whole answer. In social decisions, many people will argue that there are non-self-interested — perhaps even explicitly 'ethical' — concerns that should be taken into account too, such as the rights of other people or species, or they may simply acknowledge the claims of other individuals' preferences, which in fairness cannot be distinguished from their own, and which therefore deserve equal standing.

Public debate of this kind, and the political decisions that are its outcomes, are manifestations of a 'deliberative' or 'discursive' democracy (Cohen 1989; Dryzek 1990; Miller 1992). There is no suggestion that conflict can somehow be eliminated in such a process — that millions of people will eventually agree on environmental or any other objectives. Governments will still have to take decisions that will disappoint some and please others, and there are no easy decision rules in such circumstances. But whatever decisions are made they will reflect not just individual preferences but the conclusions of the debate on what should be done; and these are unlikely to be the same.

Two features of the deliberative democratic ideal suggest this unlikelihood. The first is a conception of the individual person. The market model assumes (and to a considerable extent requires) individuals to be simply bundles of preferences seeking satisfaction. By contrast, the deliberative model holds that people are able to understand the interests of others and are capable of non-self-interested concern. Second, the market model assumes that preferences are fixed; in the decision-making process, all individuals do is reveal them. The deliberative model sees people's views as transformable, particularly through rational persuasion about what is socially (and also perhaps personally) desirable. It is such persuasion and transformation that is the function of public debate.

The conception of the person underlying the deliberative ideal has an interesting effect on the notion of 'individual liberty'. It was argued earlier, conceding the claim of property rights theorists and pure neoclassicists, that markets are the best guarantors of individual liberty, since they allow the sovereign expression of individual preferences. But if individuals do not simply have preferences, this argument may no longer hold. If people also have non-self-interested ideals, and if these ideals may change through argument, markets may not guarantee individual liberty. If, as we have suggested, individuals are not able in markets to express these ideals, or to develop them through argument, their liberty may be equally (though differently) safe-guarded by participative democratic institutions in which they can do these things.

And what of sustainability? It should be said at once that the institutions of a deliberative democracy do not guarantee that sustainable outcomes will be chosen. The future can be dis-counted in the process of public debate as in a market. There can be ethical and non-self-interested arguments for consuming the natural capital stock as well as preference-driven ones: not least, the interests of the poor living today. It is possible that the institutions of deliberative democracy fail to elicit the hoped-for responses in terms of human behaviour, and little rational or ethical debate occurs. Interest-group politics may prevail, as the property rights theorists predict.

But this is simply an acknowledgment that there will always be a gap between questions 1 and 2. No institution of itself, certainly no democratic institution, can be designed to guarantee sustain-ability, or any other specific environmental outcome. The results that emerge from institutions are always uncertain; and hence always open to ethical criticism, even from those who have de-signed the institution. This is the inherent dilemma of 'democratic sustainability'. But some institutions are more likely than others to generate specific results. In the case of deliberative democracy and sustainability, the reason is clear. Deliberative democratic institutions — media discussion, public enquiries, Royal Com-missions, legislative debate — *allow the question of sustainability to be explicitly put.* Environmental organisations (and others) can take part in the debate and argue that the interests of future generations should be taken into account, specifically as an ethical principle. Most crucially, governments can make collective decisions that require, and enforce, environmentally acceptable behaviour. In the knowledge that this can occur, environmental concerns can be expressed and argued for in a way that the atomism of the market precludes. Deliberative democracy thus offers both the forum, and the means of implementation, absent in the market models.

# The Question of Distribution

As noted earlier, environmental economists have not been particularly concerned with question 4, which asks how the benefits and costs of environmental policies are distributed among different groups in society. The traditional approach and the neoclassical schools concerned with instruments (columns A to C) have not generally sought to answer this question. They have not regarded it as important, despite the obvious distributional implications of both regulatory and financial incentive policies. The neoclassical school concerned with monetary valuation (column D) has had to address it, since one of the criticisms of monetary valuation is its inegalitarian nature. 'Willingness to pay' is clearly dependent on ability to pay, which means that the objectives derived by this school tend to be weighted in favour of those with greater income. It is possible to 'correct' valuations for income effects, but this is in fact rarely done.[6]

The property rights school has been bolder. Following in the Coasian tradition, economists in this school have argued that distribution does not matter. Arguing for privatisation of environmental assets, they have been concerned only with the allocatory efficiency of the market bargain, and have explicitly regarded the question of *to whom* the assets should be privatised as political and therefore illegitimate (Ackroyd and Hide 1991). As many critics have pointed out, this is essentially a defence of the status quo: those who currently have property rights and higher incomes are favoured. But although this defence is more blatant, it is in fact no different from the effective position taken by both the regulatory and neoclassical schools represented in columns A to D. All assume no change in the current distribution of property rights and incomes.

This position is exposed more starkly when the favoured instruments specifically allocate new 'rights' to use the environment to particular actors (as occurs with both tradable permits and privatisation), but it is just the same in the other cases. Legal regulations, charges and taxes and monetary valuation also assume that existing polluters or resource extractors have rights to use the environment. Indeed it can be argued that tradable permits and privatisation at least offer the option, which the other approaches do not, of *changing* the allocation of property rights, by giving permits or environmental property to new, perhaps poorer, groups. (If permits and assets are auctioned, of course, this is specifically inegalitarian, since it reinforces unequal distributions of income.)

The point here is that equity of distribution is an objective that cuts across all the approaches represented in columns A to E. In theory at least, none of them *require* an inegalitarian outcome. But all of them may result in such an outcome, either through specific types of policies (such as auctioning of permits) or if the issue of distribution is simply ignored, in which case the current distribution of property rights and income is likely to be reinforced.

## Conclusion: Environmental Democracy

Column F in Table 2.1 represents an alternative (political) position to those generally perceived in the environmental economics debate. It starts with an ethical objective, sustainability: a clear statement that what society should be seeking is equity between generations through the maintenance of the natural capital stock. It seeks a second objective of policy in answer to question 4, namely that the environmental outcome should also result in greater equity between rich and poor, particularly between North and South. In specifying its objectives in these substantive ways it differs both from those positions that have no inherently preferred outcomes (columns B and C) and from those whose interest lies solely in institutions (columns D and E), not in the consequent environmental results.

The decision-making institution favoured by environmental democracy — democratic government, using open, participatory public debate — is that which seems most likely to deliver these objectives. Much more needs to be said about the details of this institution — it is a common failing of critics of CBA, such as Sagoff (1988), to leave their alternative arrangements vague — but its justification is clear. Only through such a 'deliberative democracy' can the interests of future and poorer people be properly represented, and taken into account in decision making. Underlying this ideal is a conception of human beings as social agents capable of ethical and non-self-interested judgments about societal decisions. People, it is argued, are not simply the 'rational' bundles of preferences assumed by the property rights and neoclassical schools.

The setting of objectives is the first stage of environmental policy making in practice.[7] The second is the choice of instruments to achieve these objectives. Although the concept of 'market failure' does allow for a link between these two stages (via the pricing of an externality and the imposition of an equivalent tax or charge), they are conceptually separate. The environmental democratic approach argues that once society has chosen its environmental objectives, governments should use all the possible instruments at their disposal to achieve them. This should include not just regulation and financial incentives, but government expenditures, the creation of civil liabilities, educational activities and even measures to encourage cultural change. All such instruments are interventions in markets, and their use should be based on what will work to achieve the objectives, not ideological prejudgment.

A final point, which runs throughout the foregoing analysis, should be noted. The term 'market' is apt to mislead. Not everything that can be labelled 'market' belongs in the same category. Perhaps most importantly, the market makes a good servant but a bad master. It can be used, through a variety of financial incentives, to help society achieve its objectives. But those objectives should be chosen through a public, democratic process, not a private, market one. The environment is (most of the time) a public good; its protection or consumption should therefore be a matter of social concern, and collective action.

## Endnotes

1. An exception is Johnson, McKay, and Smith (1990). See also Dorfman (1977) and Peskin (1977). Distributional issues are discussed in Jacobs (1991, chapter 14).
2. This mistake appears in Anderson and Leal (1991), Bennett and Block (1991) and Moran, Chisholm and Porter (1991). Critics, such as Eckersley (1993), have also failed to make the distinction.
3. The economic concept of sustainability is defined and elaborated in (among others) Jacobs (1991, chapters 7 and 8); Goodland et al. (1991); Pezzey (1992). For the sake of clarity in the argument, I shall assume that sustainability is simply a concern for the interests of future generations and requires some sacrifice on the part of the present generation. In fact many (though not all) policies for sustainability are likely to have present benefits too.
4. Advocates of contingent valuation, such as Mitchell and Carson (1989), specifically rule out communication between their subjects.
5. These issues are interestingly explored in Lockwood and DeLacy (1992).
6. See, for example, Hanley (1988). An exception in which hypothetical incomes were used was the study by the Australian Resource Assessment Commission of Coronation Hill, Kakadu National Park (Imber, Wilks and Stevenson 1990).
7. This position is defended in Jacobs (1991).

## References

Ackroyd P. and Hide, R. (1991) 'A Case Study — Establishing Property Rights to Chatham Islands' Abalone (Paua)' in A. Moran, A.

Chisholm and M. Porter (eds), *Markets, Resources and the Environment*, Allen and Unwin, North Sydney.

Anderson, T.L. and Leal, D.R. (1991) *Free Market Environmentalism*, Pacific Research Institute for Public Policy, San Francisco.

Barker, T., Baylis S. and Madsen P. (1993) 'A UK Carbon/Energy Tax: The Macroeconomic Effects', *Energy Policy* 21(3), 296–308.

Bennett J. and Block, W. (eds) (1991) *Reconcilling Economics and the Environment*, Australian Institute for Public Policy, Perth.

Brinner, R.E., et al. (1991) 'Optimizing Tax Strategies to Reduce Greenhouse Gases without Curtailing Growth', *Energy Journal* 12(4), 1–14.

Cline, W.R. (1992) *The Economics of Global Warming*, Institute for International Economics, Washington DC.

Cohen, J. (1989) 'Deliberation and Democratic Legitimacy' in A. Hamlin and P. Pettit (eds), *The Good Polity*, Basil Blackwell, Oxford.

Dorfman, R. (1977) 'Incidence of the Benefits and Costs of Environmental Programmes', *American Economic Review*, Papers and Proceedings, 333–40.

Dryzek, J. (1990) *Discursive Democracy*, Cambridge University Press, Cambridge.

Eckersley, R. (1993) 'Free Market Environmentalism: Friend or Foe?', *Environmental Politics* 2(2), 1–19.

Goodland, R., Daly, H., El Serafy, S. and van Droste, B. (eds) (1991) *Environmentally Sustainable Economic Development: Building on Brundtland*, UNESCO, Paris.

Hanley, N.D. (1988) 'Using Contingent Valuation to Value Environmental Improvements', *Applied Economics* 20(4), 541–50.

Imber D., Wilks, L. and Stevenson, G. (1990) *A Contigent Valuation of the Kakadu Conservation Zone*, Resource Assessment Commission, Canberra.

Jackson T. and Jacobs, M. (1991) 'Carbon Taxes and the Assumptions of Environmental Economics' in T. Barker (ed.), *Green Futures for Economic Growth*, Cambridge Econometrics, Cambridge.

Jacobs, M. (1991) *The Green Economy*, Pluto Press, London.

Johnson, P., McKay S. and Smith, S. (1990) *The Distributional Consequences of Environmental Taxes*, Institute for Fiscal Studies, London.

Karadeloglou, P. (1992) 'Energy Tax Versus Carbon Tax: A Quantitative Macroeconomic Analysis with the HERMES/Midas Models' in Commission of the European Communities, *The Economics of Limiting $CO_2$ Emissions*, Special Edition No 1, Luxembourg.

Lockwood M. and DeLacy T. (eds) (1992) *Valuing Natural Areas: Applications and Problems of the Contingent Valuation Method*, The Johnstone Centre of Parks, Recreation and Heritage, Charles Sturt University, Albury, NSW.

Miller, D. (1992) 'Deliberative Democracy and Social Choice', *Political Studies* 40: 54–67.

Mitchell R.C. and Carson, R.T. (1989) *Using Surveys to Value Public Goods*, Resources for the Future, Washington DC.

Moran A., Chisholm A. and Porter M. (eds) (1991) *Markets, Resources and the Environment*, Allen and Unwin, North Sydney.

Nordhaus, W.D. (1991) 'To Slow or Not To Slow: The Economics of the Greenhouse Effect', *Economic Journal* 101(407), 920–37.

Parfit, D. (1984) *Reasons and Persons*, Oxford University Press, Oxford.

Peskin, H.M. (1977) 'Environmental Policy and the Distribution of Benefits and Costs' in P.R. Portney (ed.), *Current Issues in US Environmental Policy*, Johns Hopkins University Press, Baltimore.

Pezzy, J. (1992) 'Sustainability: An Interdisciplinary Guide', *Environmental Values* 1(4), 321–62.

Rees, J. (1988) 'Pollution Control Objectives and the Regulatory Framework' in R.K. Turner (ed.), *Sustainable Environmental Management: Principles and Practice*, Belhaven Press, London.

Sagoff, M. (1988) *The Economy of the Earth*, Cambridge University Press, Cambridge.

Tietenberg, T. (1985) *Emissions Trading: An Exercise in Reforming Pollution Policy*, Resources for the Future, Washington DC.

Tietenberg, T. (1990) 'Economic Instruments for Environmental Regulation, *Oxford Review of Economic Policy* 6(1), 17–33.

Part II

# *Market-based Instruments versus Regulation*

# 3

# *Tools of Environmental Policy: Market Instruments versus Command-and-control*

## Alan Moran

## The Nature of Pollution and Alternative Control Instruments

Pollution is an inevitable by-product of living. It is of concern where someone uses something and fails to take the costs resulting from that use into account. Normally this is due to the absence of a feedback mechanism to sheet home to producers and consumers the full costs of their decisions. Thus the operator of a steel mill emitting smoke may cause considerable harm in terms of respiratory aggravation, increased cleaning costs and so on. But in the absence of markets, the mill owner has no accurate information on the extent of that harm and certainly has no price incentive to do anything about it.

The issue of which sort of pollution control to use turns on the perception of government as an actor in the economy. Command-and-control refers to government stipulated measures that firms must follow. Economic instruments apply a tax or tradable right to emit, leaving the solution to the firms themselves. Both command-and-control and economic instruments bring increased costs. The policy problem is how to minimise these costs.

# Economic Instruments versus Command-and-control

## *Command-and-control*

Conventional command-and-control measures involve the authorities determining the optimal trade-off between the costs of abating pollution and the consequent benefits to those adversely affected by the pollution. With perfect information, and total impartiality, government command-and-control will be a more successful approach than any that the market can devise.

Empirical observation has, however, heavily discredited the command-and-control approach in recent years. The long journey from the 1930s when von Mises and others debated the merits of central planning — even of an indicative nature — with Socialist economists is now over. Central planning has been examined and has failed every test. This is not to say that where spillovers — externalities — are dominant, as is clearly the case with many environmental matters, laissez-faire will always offer the best results.

But even where externalities are dominant, market approaches may allow the lowest cost means of reaching the desired solution. In such cases, markets involving individual decision making can be galvanised to central determinations about a tolerable overall community cost or level of emissions.

There is no single notion of command-and-control. Its most extreme form dictates every aspect of an activity. In this form, command-and-control may require that particular inputs be used, that specific production technologies be employed, that defined operational and maintenance schedules be used, that predetermined output mixes be produced and so on. Clearly, the more comprehensive the command-and-control stipulations, the less likely it is that government will have the necessary detailed information on what parameters to use and the greater the risk of arbitrary decisions. In short, the more intricate the command-and-control, the less likely it is to reach an efficient outcome.

## *Entering the Shadow of Economic Instruments*

Where direct controls specify an aggregate level of emissions for a polluting facility, they leave it to the firm to find the lowest cost means of staying within the level. This method is likely to be more cost-effective than if the regulator, who has highly imperfect knowledge of the options confronting the firm, were to specify the detail of the emission control procedures. Producers are left to determine for themselves the lowest cost means of meeting the requirements.

Furthermore, for every requirement to undertake particular expenditures, there must, if only implicitly, be a goal being targeted. For manufacturing emissions, this might be expressed in terms of the aggregate level of pollutants or pollutants per unit of finished product. That being the case, it would be preferable to specify such limits and install measuring equipment to monitor the level of residues being combated rather than to require that this be undertaken in particular ways. This would allow the firm, which is itself most likely to have the greatest expertise on how to reduce its pollutants most cheaply, to decide how to achieve the goals set for it. Arguably, Greenpeace adopted this philosophy in its demands regarding Tasmanian pulp mills, where it was calling for specific, albeit very stringent, levels of emission to be met.

*Economic Instruments*
Taxes and marketable permits take this efficiency generating approach further. They leave individual emitters free to decide their output and emissions levels, within a framework set for the community as a whole. Not only do they offer scope for producers to meet production levels at lowest cost but they extend this to allow scope for the output to be produced by those producers that can do so most cheaply.

It follows that further economies to those available intra-firm are available from allowing trading of pollutants between different sources. Crandell (1983), for example, found that the cost of controlling emissions from paper mills was threefold that of controlling similar ones from metal-working factories — fewer pollutants could be achieved at the same social cost by concentrating on the latter.

Levin (1985) quotes some specific examples where these approaches have allowed gains to be made. Dupont, facing a requirement to reduce emissions by 85 per cent in each of 119 stacks, negotiated to reduce 99 per cent of emissions in seven stacks, which proved faster and over-achieved the aggregate goal at a saving of US$12 million in capital cost and US$4 million a year in operating costs. General Electric was allowed to forego US$1.5 million in capital expenditure and US$300 000 in operating costs required to meet emission controls in Louisville by negotiating with International Harvester, which was able to exceed mandatory requirements relatively cheaply.

The effect brought about by imposing taxes follows a different route but arrives at the same end point. Emitters weigh up the costs of foregoing emissions in terms of lost revenues or additional clean-up bills, against the tax penalty they face from avoiding those costs. They have every incentive to find the lowest net cost solution through a combination of:

- reducing output or changing the output mix;
- changing the input mix used in production, that is, the production process, so that the ratio of emissions to product is reduced;
- adding emissions controls at the end of the production process, relocating production to an alternative site or varying the timing of emissions.

The choice between 'carrots' (tradable rights), and 'sticks' (taxes) is mainly a matter of ethical and distributional judgment, rather than of efficiency in pollution control. The difference is that with a tax the government implicitly determines the price at which the total level of emissions will be reduced and the costs involved be just counterbalanced by the benefits of reduced pollution. For tradable rights, the government determines the aggregate level of emissions that it considers are tolerable (or that it considers firms can abate at a cost that just balances the improvement in benefits of lower pollution).

In both cases, the flexibility that is introduced is designed to bring about lower costs in the achievement of the emission abatement (or a greater level of abatement at the prevailing costs). If the government correctly estimates the appropriate tax rate, on the one hand, or the price at which emission rights would trade, on the other hand, there would be no difference in outcomes.

### Reasons for the Superiority of Economic Instruments
The preference for economic measures follows the renewed faith in the superiority of markets over government direction. Whereas it is always conceivable to construct a perfect regulatory framework for environmental spillovers, just as it is conceivable to construct a perfect centrally planned economy, practical considerations rule this out.

The reasons for this fall into two categories: information and incentives. Both pollution taxes and marketable pollution permits rely on monetary signals and incentives for emitters to reduce the costs they impose on others. Market systems are formidable processors of information. They operate by allowing individuals to assemble information selectively and to do so in a way that allows great economy. The outcome is, of course, far from unblemished but alternatives to markets are generally much worse.

Economic instruments, then, involve the design of processes that *signal* to emitters the costs imposed on recipients, and create *incentives* for emitters to take account of those costs in their use of natural resources. Individuals process information by focusing on those things of major interest to themselves. The outcome of decisions based on many different such foci gives us efficient market solutions. This occurs because individuals have the incentives to search for such solutions. It is individuals, rather than government agencies, who understand how much a particular course of action is worth and how much it will cost them. And individuals or firms are unlikely to reveal their true costs to a government agency. The practical knowledge of firms and individuals, married to their self-interest in minimising costs, leads them to seek out innovative ways of meeting the required emission levels. They are likely to be more heavily motivated in these directions than government officials.

Economic instruments encourage those firms able to do so to constantly seek out ways of improving on their abatement situations — they enjoy lower taxes or the ability to sell rights to pollute to the extent that they are successful in achieving reductions in emissions. Under command-and-control, there is never an incentive for a firm to do better than the stipulated measure, even if this could be achieved at very low cost. A system that allows market-based instruments recruits the self-interest of the emitter to finding the lowest cost solution.

The command-and-control solution, in opting for particular means of abatement, faces an impossible task of achieving abatement efficiently. Firms have a vast number of options in terms of their abatement equipment, its maintenance, the inputs they use and the quantity, quality and mix of their outputs. With direct controls, the regulatory authority needs to know the technological and other adjustment alternatives open to individual emitting firms in order to specify individual emission levels and technologies. Far less information is required for the implementation of taxes or marketable permits because individual emitters make their own decisions about output and emissions.

Furthermore, observations and experience have shown that the political/bureaucratic process does not provide regulatory structures that are economically optimal. Politicians and bureaucrats have their own interests, which are far from being consistently in accord with economic efficiency. Moreover, governments like to focus on high-profile aspects of a solution, to demonstrate that they are hitting the problem in the solar plexus. And in doing so, they will often engender increased costs. Thus, the phase-outs of CFCs involved some interventionist measures, such as banning aerosols, to which CFCs generally add little value. Such policies are ill conceived. Market approaches would automatically phase down the least valued usages without requiring the considerable administrative resources that command-and-control policies need. This is especially pertinent in the case of CFCs in aerosols where specialist medical applications rule out 'blanket' bans.

By and large, however, CFCs have been phased out without the use of command-and-control mechanisms. In Australia's case, the use of tradable rights plus a tax, while forcing the required reductions in the use of CFCs, has also encouraged conservation and recycling. This approach to a greater or lesser degree has been followed by most other countries. In the process, considerable administrative costs have been avoided.

There is, however, one important caveat to the foregoing case against command-and-control. Where transaction costs of defining levels, measuring, monitoring and policing are high, compared with the benefits available, markets may fail. This has certainly been accepted in policy arrangements for combating domestic pollution from a great many minor sources. It would not be cost-effective to attempt to police hundreds of thousands of chimneys. Nor, for the present, is it cost-effective to introduce taxes or tradable rights on vehicle emissions. These matters constitute the heart of the 'externalities' or spillover case against the use of markets.

*Operations of Taxes and Tradable Rights Regimes*
Pollution taxes involve setting a charge per unit of emissions sufficient to achieve the required level of reduction. The emitter has a financial incentive to reduce emissions to the point where the profit loss due to a unit reduction in emissions is equal to the damage costs involved.

In a system of marketable pollution permits, the regulatory authority allocates, on some basis, permits equal to a determined aggregate quantity of emissions. The permits are tenable for a defined period (or perhaps indefinitely) and tradable. Trading of permits among emitters will then establish a market-determined price of emissions. The market price of a permit then signals damage costs, and emitters have financial incentives to respond by reducing emissions, as is true of a tax.

Both taxes and marketable rights therefore put a price on scarce rights to emit pollutants. As a result, each instrument prompts emitters to reveal their true costs of reducing emissions. By creating incentives for firms to explore all options for minimising the costs of reducing pollution, both instruments strengthen firms' incentives to actively seek out and adopt effective emission-reducing technologies.

# Trade-offs in Pollution Control

In determining a tax or total number of marketable permits, the regulatory authority must balance the costs the community bears due to pollution against the costs it bears when emitters reduce the output of valued activities and/or increase production costs. Thus the authority requires information about how changes in aggregate emissions of the pollutant affect the value of pollution damages and the total benefits to emitters. As discussed, public decision makers will in fact have great difficulty in obtaining accurate information about these matters. The complexity of the implementation decisions stemming from these difficulties is reduced when an economic instrument approach is used, because the authorities need not be aware of the detailed solutions available on a firm by firm basis (household emissions of pollutants are ignored in the remainder of this paper, to concentrate on the implications of taxes and marketable permits for industry). People place different values on the absence of pollution and on the benefits they obtain from being permitted to pollute. Why then can the levels of pollution not simply be left to the people directly affected?

One reason is that pollutants can be expensive to measure; another is that it is often difficult to identify sources and recipients of particular emissions; a third is that it may be hard to get agreement on the values attached to emissions, given the lack of comparable market situations. So private negotiations between affected parties may be rejected or break down.

The most important reason for the absence of negotiations between emitters and recipients of pollution is that usually many people are harmed by the same emissions of a pollutant. As a result, action to reduce emissions of a pollutant commonly benefits many people — it is a collective or public good. In the case of public goods (unlike private goods), individuals cannot easily choose a different level of abatement, and a different level of compensation, from their neighbours. Partly because of this, individuals who will benefit from reductions in pollution may prefer to free-ride — to leave it to their fellows to act to have emissions reduced. Individual recipients reason that their contribution to collective action will make little or no difference, but that they will reap the benefits of reduced emissions regardless. Thus they may decide to make no contribution at all. If many or most recipients think likewise, there will be no private negotiation to reduce emissions. Thus it is left to public agencies to control emissions of pollutants that affect large numbers of people.

Can a government pollution control agency identify the optimum level of emissions? To get emission standards right, the agency has to know the costs of abatement and demand for each incremental unit of emission. It may obtain its information from the political process and/or direct from emitters and recipients. There is, however, no reason to expect that any of these sources will provide accurate information, since in the political arena, unlike the marketplace, individuals rarely have to back up their stated preferences with their own money. Thus emitters have incentives to exaggerate abatement costs or to persuade the agency to set lenient standards (provided they do not expect to be compensated for reducing emissions); conversely, recipients have incentives to exaggerate damage costs, so long as they do not have to pay for the resulting tight standards.

## Alternative Distributions of Rights

The disposition of property rights to release pollutants into the environment affects the distribution of income and welfare between emitters and recipients of pollution. If emitters have a legal right to emit, the community will have to pay them to reduce emissions, by paying subsidies or purchasing emission rights. If recipients have the legal right to be free of emissions, would-be emitters must pay recipients or the community for emissions, either by paying tax on emissions or by purchasing emission rights.

Both pollution taxes and marketable rights can, in principle, be structured to achieve a variety of distributional outcomes. In the case of taxes, different starting allocations of rights can be achieved by designating an emissions standard, together with a tax on emissions in excess of the standard and a subsidy on reductions below the standard. In the case of marketable permits, different allocations of rights can be achieved by combinations of free distribution and auctioning of permits.

The major problem in designing pollution control instruments is the difficulty for public decision makers in the identification of schedules of costs and damages. Without these calculations it is impossible to determine the optimum level of emissions. Thus a major criterion for choosing between instruments is their relative advantage in generating reliable information about the benefits and costs of abatement.

As a producer of emissions, a firm has a vast array of options for reducing its emissions. These may include the combination of alternatives already discussed, that is, to:

- reduce output or change the output mix;
- change the input mix used in production (the production process), so that the ratio of emissions to product is reduced;

- add emission controls at the end of the production process, relocate production to an alternative site or vary the timing of emissions.

In reacting to pollution, the recipient also has several options, some analogous to those available to the emitter. These include to:

- bear the costs;
- alter consumption and production activities to reduce damage;
- adopt measures to insulate activities from damage;
- relocate.

The true marginal damage cost curve will incorporate the least costly combinations of these options for each recipient at each level of emissions. This point would be very difficult to identify even in the absence of the previously outlined valuation problems. And like cost of abatement, costs of damage, particularly for recipients as a group, will be dynamic, varying with changes in prices, the technologies of consumption and production, and with recipients' attitudes to pollution.

## Comparing Taxes and Marketable Permits

*Information and efficiency*

Where the regulatory authority simply aims to achieve pre-determined aggregate emission standards in a least-cost manner, marketable permits have an advantage in that the target is built into the instrument being employed. To attain the target using taxes, and not knowing firms' costs of adjustment, the authority may have to alter the tax several times in a process of iteration towards the target level of emissions.

Marketable permits are often thought of as having a substantial advantage involving minimal intervention subsequent to the initial distribution of permits. But their countervailing disadvantage is that there is no feedback from the price at which permits trade (at the equivalent of the tax) to the aggregate level of permits. It may be that a fixed aggregrate level of permits would be traded at a lower price; this means that greater abatement could have been achieved for the expected cost. The reverse may also be true; the price of permits might skyrocket indicating that the abatement is being achieved at a far higher cost than was planned.

The level of permits could, of course, be adjusted to take such matters into account but such actions would undermine a major advantage of permits, which provides greater freedom from arbitrary change. Such freedom provides a more favourable environment for long-term planning and investment in emitter industries and for the recipients of pollution. The likelihood of continual adjustments either in taxes or permit levels by the regulatory authority makes industries more dependent on government decisions, thereby discouraging investments that involve long lead times and payback periods.

*Distributional Effects*

Some people favour taxes over tradable rights because the former allow meeting of goals while lowering other taxes. Such a lowering may be possible but this is only one side of the story.

Imposing a new tax on atmospheric pollution assumes that it is the recipient, rather than the polluter, who has the rights to clean air. In fact, ownership of those rights is rarely clear cut. The polluter seized them in the first instance when they had little value and usually with no opposition from recipients of the pollution. (Indeed, the recipients may see the presence of the polluter as advantageous in providing job opportunities or other economic advantages.) If, after becoming established, the producer is required to incur unanticipated expenditures, then the community is engaging in a form of expropriation. Expropriation creates adverse incentives to productive investment and would therefore markedly reduce living standards. So the case for taxes is not quite so clear cut as a superficial examination would imply. Opposition to tradable rights is misplaced when it is on the grounds that such action rewards 'anti-social' behaviour by incumbent polluters.

Although taxes or auctioning of quotas accords with notions of fairness in making the polluter pay for a 'good', the environment, that is usually considered to be owned by the whole community, demand for such payment is not necessarily the appropriate approach. Rights may more appropriately be assigned to those who have first claimed them, especially when, at the time of seizure, the rights were not considered to be especially valuable. Vesting rights to the present polluters and allowing these to be traded is a *de jure* recognition of a *de facto* situation. Of course, it may be argued that the *de facto* recognition did not extend to the transferability of the rights and some community compensation is warranted on these grounds.

As Hahn (this volume) has shown in his review of the implementation of taxes and charges in the United States, all the tax and marketable permit systems studied placed great importance on the distributional status quo. Most taxes actually imposed were too low to have much impact on the behaviour of emitters, and most tax revenues were used to subsidise investments in pollution control in the emitting industries. Marketable permits were given to the holders of current emission licences ('grandfathered'), implying government acceptance of emitters' rights to their initial legal emission levels.

*Transactions Costs and 'Thin Markets'*
With taxes, there are no transactions costs; each emitter simply responds directly to the incentive provided by the tax. In contrast, trades of permits involve the costs of identifying exchange partners and revelation of willingness to pay and to accept. If these transactions costs are large relative to anticipated gains from acquisition or sale of permits, there will be little exchange, and the desired least-cost configuration of emissions will not be achieved. Hahn has identified limited trading between firms in the case of air and water pollution permits, and extensive trading of permits for the use of lead in petrol.

Hahn's findings are partially explained by regulatory restrictions on permissible trades. Another explanation is the small numbers of potential traders in many permit markets, often leading to strategic behaviour towards firms that are major competitors in the final product market. For example, the most important potential traders of marketable permits for biological oxygen demand along the Fox River in Wisconsin are pulp and paper mills. There was only one trade in this market in its first six years of operation.

*Flexibility of Environmental Standards and Sovereign Risk*
The true costs of abatement and damage for a region will shift over time, due to changes in final product prices, input costs, production and abatement technology, industry and population location, and so on. Efficient use of resources over time involves a trade-off between (i) variability in taxes or the aggregate quantity of permits, to reflect these economic changes; and (ii) security of property rights and other 'rules of the environmental game', so that firms' and households' planning and investment will not be inhibited, to the detriment of economic growth and people's welfare.

Pollution taxes remain under direct government control, able to be readily changed in response to new scientific, technical or political information. Marketable permits are likely to be increasingly regarded as valuable private property, a basis for longer term decision making, and correspondingly difficult to change.

As knowledge of the environment, production technology and desired emission standards change, those with a benign view of government will see taxes as facilitating desirable flexibility in environmental policy.

On the other hand, once we admit the possibility of government error or objectives other than economic efficiency, marketable permits are more attractive because of the constraints they are likely to impose on precipitate or purely self-serving government action. Thus, for example, there may be few political and legal impediments preventing a regulatory authority or a minister setting taxes to maximise Treasury revenues, to the detriment of the environment and community welfare. Uncompensated variations in the numbers or terms and conditions of marketable permits are likely to be subject to greater political and legal constraints than changes in taxes, because permits are viewed as private property. Important in this respect is the High Court of Australia's interpretation of the requirements of 'just compensation' specified in section 51 (xxxi) of the Constitution as requiring 'full and adequate' compensation for the compulsory acquisition of property rights by the Commonwealth Government.

*Uncertainty and the Choice Between Taxes and Permits*
The choice between taxes and marketable permits does make a difference if the regulator is uncertain about the incremental costs of emission reductions, but has information about the relative slopes of the incremental pollution damage and abatement curves. The cost of the errors involved in misjudging the optimum quantity of emissions are in direct proportion to the errors themselves. Therefore taxes result in less costly errors than marketable permits when changes in emission levels cause a greater change in emitters' profits than in recipients' costs of pollution damage and vice versa (Baumol and Oates 1988, 67–70).

# Conclusion

Pollution and some other inevitable spillovers from production often have highly dispersed effects. While command-and-control regulations may be employed to counter unwanted side effects from production, market instruments such as taxes and tradable rights are preferable. With perfect knowledge of the different costs and benefits of pollution and a perfect political system to develop and administer specified regulatory approaches, command-and-control regulation would provide the optimum mix of additional cost and lower pollution. However, regulatory systems are less than perfect and market instruments allow some well documented deficiencies of command-and-control regulation to be diminished.

A tax on pollution or granting a tradable right to pollute enlists the self-interest of firms in seeking cost-effectiveness. The firms themselves, in order to reduce their taxes or to profit from sales of surplus rights, will implement the most efficient pollution control approaches. They will also have an incentive to seek out new, more cost-effective means of abating pollution. Market instruments, therefore, allow increased abatement, the desired level of abatement at a lower cost or a mixture of the two.

# References

Baumol, W.J. and Oates, W.E. (1988) *The Theory of Environmental Policy*, 2nd edn, Prentice-Hall, New Jersey.

Crandell, R.W. (1983) *Controlling Industrial Pollution*, Brookings, Washington DC.

Levin, M.H. (1985) 'Building a Better Bubble at EPA', *Regulation* March/April, 33–42.

# 4

# *Towards Ecologically Sustainable Development: The Role and Shortcomings of Markets*

## Peter Kinrade

### Introduction

The past fifteen years have seen neoclassical economics and its various 'free market' offshoots replace Keynesian economics as the dominant economic philosophy around the world. Often referred to as 'economic rationalism' in Australia, this philosophy promotes the free play of markets, 'unhindered' by government intervention and control, as the best means of achieving an efficient allocation of resources and thereby maximising the welfare of society. Neoclassical economics has also entered the environmental debate, with many of its exponents arguing that the appropriate balance between environmental protection and economic development can best be achieved through market mechanisms, whether by means of market-based incentives and/or the privatisation of environmental 'assets'.

This chapter seeks to highlight the shortcomings of this approach as a means of achieving ecologically sustainable development (ESD), which emphasises the integration, rather than simply the balancing, of economic, social and environmental considerations.[1]

In this chapter it is argued that if ESD is accepted as a desirable goal of Australian society, then a mixed or integrated policy approach, including regulatory intervention and institutional reform, will be necessary to achieve that goal. Improving the operation of markets does have a role to play in the transition to an ecologically sustainable society, but only as a complement to a range of other approaches. An approach to environmental and social concerns that is based solely or primarily on increasing the role of markets and improving the efficiency of resource allocation will not move society towards ESD, except by default. Indeed, a 'market transactions' approach to environmental protection could, in many cases, produce outcomes directly at odds with the principles of ESD.

It is also argued that markets should not have a role in determining environmental objectives. Determination of these objectives is ultimately up to society, through democratic processes. Given available public opinion, though, the principles of ESD would seem to be a good starting point.

## Ecologically Sustainable Development

The concept of sustainability was probably first promoted in a cohesive fashion in 1972 at the United Nations Conference on the Human Environment, but it was not until the release of 'Our Common Future' in 1987 by the World Commission on Environment and Development (WCED 1987) that the term 'sustainable development' was firmly established on the international agenda.

However, the oft quoted WCED report (also known as the 'Brundtland Report') contains a number of inconsistencies, not least of which is that economic growth, regardless of its pattern, is regarded as an objective in itself rather than as a means to particular ends. Nevertheless, at the time of its release, it represented a milestone in the environment and development debates in highlighting the links between global environmental, social and economic concerns.

Sustainable development served as a major organising principle at the United Nations Conference on Environment and Development (UNCED) in Rio de Janeiro, Brazil, in June 1992. The conference was attended by delegates from over 150 United Nations (UN) member countries, including many heads of government. It produced a set of common principles for sustainable development (the Rio Declaration) and a detailed agenda for action based on these principles (AGENDA 21). The conference also witnessed the signing of two significant conventions — the Framework Convention on Climate Change and the Convention on Biodiversity. As a consequence of UNCED, the UN General

Assembly has now also established a Commission on Sustainable Development.

Notwithstanding these developments, the outcomes from the conference are disappointing from the point of view of many community-based non-government environment and aid organisations (NGOs). In particular, the contents of the two conventions and of AGENDA 21 are considerably weaker than expectations of NGOs. Furthermore, at this stage it would appear that the comprehensive actions, value shifts and resources required to address North–South inequities and Third World debt, and to incorporate environmental considerations into the economic/development/ trade agenda, are unlikely to be forthcoming. The election of Democrat Bill Clinton to the US Presidency, with Al Gore as his environmentally credible Vice-President, may improve this situation, but it seems unrealistic to expect too much from one national political leader.

### The ESD Process in Australia

In Australia, a two-year long ESD process culminated with the release of the National Strategy for Ecologically Sustainable Development (NSESD) in December 1992 (Commonwealth of Australia 1992). The Australian Conservation Foundation (ACF), in conjunction with the World Wide Fund for Nature (WWF), actively participated in the first 15 months of the process through its representation on eight of the nine sectoral working groups.[2] Participation in the deliberations of the working groups was limited and the final reports, released in November 1991, represented a series of compromises (see Hare 1991, for a detailed assessment of the ESD Working Group process and the Final Working Groups' Reports). Nevertheless, the reports contain enough substance to provide the basis for the taking of concrete steps towards ESD in Australia, provided the Working Groups' recommendations are implemented vigorously and as an integrated package.

However, the Working Groups' recommendations were subjected to intergovernmental negotiations through 1992. These negotiations, which effectively excluded NGOs, unions and industry, saw a revisionist approach to the ESD Working Groups' recommendations, with many being significantly watered down and others being rejected altogether. The resulting National Strategy lacks direction and merely picks the easy issues and avoids acting on the difficult ones — an outcome that the ACF had forewarned against (see Hare 1991, 8). Futhermore, progress by governments on implementation of the NSESD has, to date, been totally inadequate.

The partial breakdown of the ESD process in Australia does not invalidate ESD as a long-term societal objective. The basic principles of ESD still hold and attainment of those principles can and should be sought through policy development and grass roots action independently of the formal inter-governmental ESD process. The breakdown of the process does mean, however, that pursuit of ESD has largely been removed from the mainstream political agenda. This will make the task of moving towards an ecologically sustainable society more difficult in the future.

Until now, much of the debate surrounding ESD in Australia — what it means and how it might be achieved — has occurred largely within bureaucratic and academic circles and has excluded the general public. This situation probably stems from a combination of inadequate public consultation and participation processes, the failure of mainstream media to pick up on the debate, and the nebulous nature of the term 'ecologically sustainable development'. Nonetheless, extensive public opinion research during the ESD process suggests that Australian society intuitively supports the concept of ESD. While the majority of Australians have little knowledge of the two-year ESD process and principles, most support the notion of 'development without harming the environment' (ANOP 1991, 53). This suggests that ESD, in a general sense, is indeed a goal of Australian society.

The principles of ESD are themselves problematic, being open to considerable interpretation. This leaves the concept of ESD — or sustainable development — open to the charge that it can and does mean all things to all people. The ambiguity of ESD has, to some extent, contributed to the breakdown of the official process, for there was never complete agreement over what it is participants in the process should be trying to achieve in detailed terms (let alone how they could achieve it). Despite this lack of consensus over detailed objectives, a general consensus did emerge from the ESD process in Australia about the broad principles of ESD, if not always their precise meanings. The broadly agreed principles of ESD are:

- the improvement of individual and community well-being and welfare by following a path of economic progress that does not impair the welfare of future generations;
- the provision of equity within and between generations;
- protection of biological diversity and the maintenance of ecological processes and systems;
- recognition of the global dimension; and
- an anticipatory and precautionary policy approach.[3]

*Achieving ESD in Australia*

Aside from debate over details of the principles of ESD, discussion during the ESD process centred around what is the desired level of environmental protection — consistent with the principles of ESD — and the means by which to achieve that protection.

During, and subsequent to, the ESD process considerable emphasis has been placed on the efficiency of market-based approaches to environmental protection and development. The assumption underlying this view is that the 'appropriate' level of environmental protection in Australia can substantially be achieved through market transactions, provided markets are adjusted to give value to environmental and other externalities. Furthermore, a strong emphasis has been placed on market-based instruments as the most 'efficient' means of achieving the desired outcome in Australia, with the proviso that any market adjustments should be globally harmonised. This approach has been favoured by neoclassical economists in government departments and agencies, notably the key finance and development departments such as Treasury and Primary Industries, as well as by sections of industry (see, for example, BCA 1991, 9–10; Industry Commission 1991, 1992).

Even more market-orientated in their approach are the 'free market environmentalists' from the Libertarian and Public Choice schools of economics. Essentially, they argue that the most appropriate way to deal with environmental problems is to assign property rights to environmental assets such as species, wilderness areas, aquatic systems and airsheds, thereby creating markets in environmental protection. The 'optimal' level of environmental protection will then be achieved by bidding between players in the market. This idea was first propounded in a paper by Coase (1960). In Australia it is now advocated most strongly by public policy 'think tanks' such as the Tasman Institute and the Institute of Public Affairs (see, for example, Bennett and Block 1991; Moran, Chisholm and Porter 1991).

Yet both the neoclassical and free market approaches to environmental protection often conflict with the societal goal of ESD.

The free market approach to environmental issues is of particular concern. This chapter argues that the notion of 'optimal' environmental protection favoured by free market economists, to be achieved through market bidding processes, is inconsistent with the principles of ESD. Furthermore, through the market bidding approach, the fundamental ESD principles of 'inter-' and 'intragenerational equity' and 'protection of biodiversity' are likely to be contravened, since low-income earners, future generations and other species have an unequal or no role in the market bidding process.

A strict neoclassical approach to environmental problems is also likely to be inconsistent with ESD principles, since it relies considerably on an ability to price non-market values, including option values and existence values, to arrive at an optimal level of environmental protection.

To illustrate these arguments, the principles of ESD have been applied to major environmental concerns in three examples.

In the first example it is argued that the notion of 'optimal environmental pollution', favoured by free market and some neoclassical economists, is in breach of the 'intergenerational equity' and 'precautionary' principles and is therefore inconsistent with both the outcomes and processes required for ecological sustainability.

In the second example it is argued that protection of bio-diversity and ecological integrity in Australia can only be achieved through a package of measures that includes extensive government intervention. Market instruments or the allocation of property rights are unlikely to achieve a level of protection commensurate with ecological sustainablity.

In the third example — an examination of the greenhouse issue — it is argued that even if policy directions are determined without reference to markets, market-based approaches to reducing emissions will not necessarily be the most efficient and effective means of achieving the desired outcome.

# Example 1: Pollution — 'Optimal' Does Not Equal 'Sustainable'

The issue of pollution, both aquatic and atmospheric, has come to the fore on the Australian politico-environmental agenda in the past couple of years. In December 1992, the cornerstone of the Prime Minister's Statement on the Environment was a commitment to restore the Murray–Darling river basin to 'ecological balance' by ensuring that 'no longer will effluent, rubbish and chemicals be pumped into the system' (Keating 1992, 3). The statement essentially received bipartisan support. Similarly, during the 1993 federal election campaign, the greatest area of policy convergence between the two major parties occurred in relation to pollution.[4]

This political focus may be attributed, in part, to major pollution concerns that have received increasing media attention, notably, sewage in Melbourne and Sydney waterways and beaches, toxic algal blooms (partially attributable to increased nutrient loadings) in major rivers, lead pollution and photo-chemical smog. The attention may also be due to an unstated perception within political circles that these so-called 'brown-green' issues (e.g. pollution) are more easily dealt with than 'green-green' ones (e.g. nature conservation).

Yet despite the development of new strategies such as the National Water Quality Management Strategy (see ANZECC 1992), the political focus on pollution issues has yet to be translated into clear long-term goals for air and water pollution.

*Problems With 'Optimal' Pollution*

The orthodox economist's approach to pollution is to aim for an 'optimal' or 'efficient' level of pollution by seeking to reduce pollution to the point at which the present value of the net benefit is maximised. That point is reached when the marginal costs of controlling the pollution equal the marginal benefits to society of the reduced environmental damage. Many relevant government departments and agencies in Australia appear to favour this approach including, for example, the Resource Assessment Commission (RAC 1992).

Jacobs (1991) argues that the orthodox approach is funda-mentally flawed because it rests on the notion that all environ-mental values can be priced. A significant proportion of the environment's value, such as its value to future generations and geographically removed people, cannot be known and therefore cannnot be included in the valuation process (quite apart from the 'intrinsic value' of the environment). Furthermore, as Pearce, Markandya and Barbier (1989) argue, if sustainable development is to be achieved, then not only should environmental values be priced and integrated into project appraisal, but development and associated environmental degradation should also be subject to a 'sustainability constraint' to ensure that natural capital is not reduced. It is on this basis that Pearce and Turner (1990) argue that if we are to ensure sustainable development then the notion of an 'optimal' level of pollution needs to be modified to one of a sustainable level of waste. This modification amounts to an implicit rejection of 'optimal pollution' when it leads to the deple-tion of natural capital.

An understanding of the concept of natural capital is crucial to this discussion. Natural capital refers to the diverse range of matter and processes including air and water quality, soil, species, ecosystems and natural cycles such as the hydrological cycle and the carbon cycle. Its maintenance is considered by the ACF to be essential to ensuring intergenerational equity and therefore essential to the attainment of ESD (see Hare et al. 1990). Natural *capital* is distinguished from natural *resources* by a number of characteristics including non-substitutability, uncertainty and irreversibility.[5] The characteristic of non-substitutability is particularly important. Unlike natural resources, natural capital cannot be replaced by human-made capital. A lost species or an irreversibly damaged waterway (within human time frames) and their attached values and amenities cannot be replaced by a new technology or manufactured product.

The traditional neoclassical approach to sustainability is based implicitly on the notion that human-made capital and natural capital are substitutable in the same way that human-made resources and natural resources are substitutable. Similarly, free market economists do not acknowledge fundamental ecological or thermodynamic constraints to economic activity. Instead, they place a great deal of faith in the ability of humankind to find substitutes for natural resources (see, for example, Baden and Stroup 1991; Chant et al. 1991). Yet this faith conflates the distinction between natural resources and natural capital: plastics may replace wood, but we have no means of remaking extinct species.

*Towards Pollution Prevention*
If an 'optimal' level of pollution is potentially inconsistent with ESD, then what level of pollution is definitely sustainable?

Pearce and Turner (1990) suggest that the sustainable level of waste should be based on the assimilative capacity of the receiving environment. Assimilative capacity is the natural environment's ability to receive waste that is harmless by volume and nature to human health, ecosystems and ecological processes. In practical terms, though, given lack of baseline information about ecosystems and ecological processes, determining the assimilative capacity of the environment is problematical. In many cases it may be impossible to determine, particularly over a short time frame. For these reasons, the use of 'assimilative capacity' has been rejected in many scientific circles (Campbell 1984; ANZECC 1992). Until and unless assimilative capacities can be defined over a long time frame, based on a comprehensive understanding of ecological processes and the impacts of pollution on those processes, no level of waste discharge can be deemed with certainty to be an assimilable level. Thus in practical terms, to be certain of achieving ecological sustainability, we need to adopt the long-term objective of 'pollution prevention' based on progressive reductions in pollution in order to increase confidence that pollution is being brought within ecologically sustainable levels.

Pollution prevention is increasingly being viewed as a realistic goal. Zero discharge is already a goal of the US *Clean Water Act* (see Blake et al. 1992). Furthermore, Swiss industrialist and representative of the Business Council for Sustainable Development, Stephen Schmidheiny, argues that:

> The commonsense, precautionary response to burgeoning pollution problems is to seek to prevent pollution before it happens. Where it is already occurring, the aim should be to eliminate the source of the problem rather than attack symptoms through often expensive 'end of pipe' methods such as filters, scrubbers, treatment plants, and incineration'
>
> (1992, 99).

He also quotes an executive of Volvo, who stressed that in the long run, 'we must use materials in our processes that do not give rise to hazardous emissions at all' (1992, 99).

It should be stressed, however, that pollution prevention is a long-term ESD objective. In many cases, the technology or processes are not currently available or are completely unviable economically. That is why pollution reduction is a practicable approach in the short to medium term. This approach relies on setting pollution targets that are reduced over time and are risk adjusted, according to the best available scientific knowledge of the effects on health and ecosystems of different substances. Discharges or emissions should be set at levels sufficiently low to ensure that their concentrations in receiving environments are well *below* levels considered safe for human health *and* for ecosystems. Sensitive ecosystems should receive a higher level of protection. Furthermore, the added risks associated with toxic and biocumulative discharges point to a need for such discharges to be eliminated over a much shorter time frame.

The pollution reduction/prevention approach is also consistent with the precautionary principle of ESD. The precautionary principle places the burden of proof in decision making on establishing that ecosystems will be protected in the face of uncertainty about the impacts of pollution. In other words, scientific uncertainty should not be taken as a reason for postponing preventative actions.

Many environment protection agencies have, in part, already adopted this principle when determining 'safe' levels of water quality. The Victorian Environment Protection Authority, for example, determines the permissible level of non-cumulative toxicants on the basis of the threshold level of measurable harmful effects for sensitive species (the threshold level being risk adjusted according to the level of protection sought). However, the toxicity tests on which the threshold levels are based are not sensitive enough to be adequate indicators of ecosystem health. Due to information gaps, the area of water quality risk assessment is controversial, highlighting the difficulty of assessing risk to ecosystems of discharges, about which there is, comparatively, little information.

In summary, an objective of pollution reduction leading towards pollution prevention is the most rational and prudent course to adopt in order to achieve consistency with the intergenerational and precautionary principles of ESD. Outcomes achieved through this objective, in terms of the volume and nature of pollutants discharged into receiving ecosystems, could well differ substantially from the 'optimal' pollution levels favoured by free market economists and many neoclassical economists.

*An Integrated Package to Achieve Pollution Reduction*
The instruments by which the pollution reduction targets are achieved are also at issue. As outlined by Jacobs in chapter 2 of this volume, neoclassical economists tend to favour market instruments as the most 'efficient' means of achieving a particular environmental objective. Yet even if neoclassical economists — as described in category 'C' of Jacobs' taxonomy — can agree that governments and the community, and not markets, should determine pollution objectives the taxes and charges that those economists favour as being less distortionary than regulations may not suffice for the task.

Of course, taxes can encourage polluters to reduce their pollution. The revenue raised from such charges can also be used to compensate for the environmental degradation or natural capital depletion caused by the pollution (or in economists' terms, 'correct for the market distortion'). They cannot, however, always ensure that particular pollution targets or objectives are necessarily achieved; often, markets may not be competitive or there may be other intervening variables that defy economic analysis.

This is why the most appropriate approach to pollution reduction, within an ESD framework, is to use a cost-effective combination of instruments to achieve specified pollution reduction targets that have been set by governments in consultation with the community. Taken on a case by case basis, this will generally mean that a proscriptive component (e.g. standard setting) is necessary, particularly in relation to air and water quality.[6] However, other instruments, including taxes and charges and information and education programs, will often prove valuable and effective complements to the legal regulations. Given present uncertainties about the impacts of pollution on bio-diversity and ecological processes, improved air and water quality monitoring programs will also be an important component of a pollution reduction package.

The integrated approach defended here is similar to that set out in category 'F' of Jacobs' taxonomy.

Finally, it is worth examining tradable emission permits (TEPs or simply tradable permits) in the context of the preceding discussion. Tradable permits are increasingly being viewed as an efficient means of achieving environmental objectives, since they can combine the purported flexibility of markets with the certainty of outcomes provided through regulations. Only in the USA have they been applied to pollution issues to any great extent, and the results, both from an environmental and economic viewpoint, are fairly encouraging (see Stavins 1990 and Hahn in this volume).

The small successes to date of tradable permits have been used by neoclassical and free market economists alike to proclaim the benefits of market-based approaches to environmental protection. In the case of the latter, tradable permits have even been pro-moted as an example of the successful application of private property rights to environmental protection (see, for example, Stroup 1991). However, tradable permits are clearly distinguish-able from privatisation measures, which involve the relinquishment of government control. That is, tradable permits, to be successful in achieving environmental objectives, will always entail a strictly enforceable regulatory component, based on predetermined objec-tives. Ideally, the total pollution quota permitted will diminish over time and there will also be restrictions on the concentration and distribution of the permits to avoid pollution 'hotspots' developing within particular areas. Thus a tradable permit should really be viewed more as a combination of regulatory and market instruments rather than a market instrument *per se*.

# Example 2: Conservation of Biodiversity and Ecological Integrity

The conservation of biodiversity and maintenance of ecological integrity is viewed by many in the environment movement as perhaps the key principle of ESD. According to Amos, Kirkpatrick and Giese:

> Biodiversity describes the full range of living things. It is the variety and number of species of organisms, the variation within a species

and the ways in which they interact with each other in communities and ecosystems. Ecological integrity concerns the health and condition of an ecosystem and the ability of its species to evolve

(1993, i).

Biodiversity and ecological systems are valued not only for their human use values in supplying food, clothing, fuel, pharmaceuticals, a wide range of other commodities, spiritual and recreational values, as well as a host of 'ecological services' such as soil formation and pollination. Ecological systems also help to maintain basic life support processes for humankind and all other species. In addition, environmentalists believe that other species have the right to exist and evolve naturally, simply because they exist. In other words, species are understood to possess intrinsic or existence value, over and above their use value to humans.

Of all the principles of ESD, the conservation of biodiversity and the maintenance of ecological integrity probably best encapsulate the view that humans are part of, not apart from and superior to, the natural world and that economic activity needs to take place within ecological constraints.

*Recognising Ecological Constraints*
Jacobs (1993) has neatly summarised the major divide that has arisen over the interpretation of the ESD principles. He refers to two sustainable development paradigms: a 'weak' one and a 'strong' one. Those who subscribe to the weak paradigm essentially argue that we can and should trade ecological sustainability off against short-term objectives such as the level of economic activity. On the other hand, the strong sustainable development paradigm focuses on the limits or constraints to economic activity that the pursuit of ecological sustainability will necessarily entail.

There is no doubt that most sections of the environment movement in Australia subscribe to the strong paradigm. Many environmentalists are prepared to countenance trade-offs between some environmental protection goals and other goals such as freedom of movement, at least in the medium term. For example, environmentalists may be prepared to accept the loss of human well-being arising from a certain level of pollution due to motor vehicle emissions, against the loss of well-being that would occur if all emissions were required to be eliminated immediately. However, most would probably agree that the conservation of biodiversity and ecological integrity should be a fundamental constraint on economic activity in both the medium and long term. Under no circumstances should there be a trade-off of species for 'dollars in the bank'.

*Species Trade-offs*

This viewpoint marks another major point of divergence between
free market and (at least) some neoclassical approaches to
environment protection and the *ecologically* sustainable development approach. Either through intent or outcome the market-
oriented approaches appear to countenance at least some trade-
off of biodiversity protection against other objectives.

Free market economists are sceptical of the notion that there
are or should be ecological constraints to economic activity. They
also fail to give full consideration to non-financial values, including ecological service values, option values and the existence
values of species, when assessing social welfare or well-being.[7] For
example, Moran, Chisholm and Porter are quite explicit in rank-
ing the relative values of wealth and natural assets in determining
social welfare: 'Placing obstacles in the way of wealth generation
which mining development brings is more likely to impede the
pursuit of overall community well-being than to prevent the
destruction of natural assets which would be valued greatly now
or in the future' (1991, 159). This is a direct assertion that
human wealth is more important than the natural environment —
an assertion that fails to explore the longer term interdependencies between human welfare and ecological welfare.

*Concerns With the Property Rights Approach*

Furthermore, a private property rights approach to environmental
protection without regulation, as favoured by free market economists, will almost certainly lead to a trade-off of species and
ecosystems for other objectives, although some free market economists resist this interpretion:

> With a robust regime of property rights over land, the owners of
> land have a strong incentive to take care of their asset not only for
> current but for future use. Similarly a complete property rights
> system over ecosystems or even individual species making up an
> ecosystem, can ensure their conservation
>
> (Bennett 1991, 273).[8]

This approach is all very well if the holder of property rights to
ecosystems or a species can envisage a direct economic benefit
from protecting or managing them, but when no such benefits are
immediately apparent, the environmental defence of private property rights breaks down. The notion that land holders will
protect their land for future generations is highly questionable. In
rural Australia, for example, decades of private property rights,
established through freehold and perpetual leasehold title, have

been accompanied by poor management practices, including wholesale clearing of native vegetation, leading to well documented problems of soil erosion, salinity and the degradation of waterways and contributing to the loss of species and ecosystems.

Property rights advocates will often try to explain away this situation as being the consequence of government failure, information failure or the absence of full freehold title (Dumsday and Chisholm 1991). While accepting that lack of information and poor government policies — including, until 1983, tax write-offs for vegetation clearance under section 51 of the *Income Tax Assessment Act* (Cwlth) — have been partly responsible for this situation in the past, removal of taxation and other subsidies and greatly improved information networks, through programs such as Landcare, have not prevented the continuation of large-scale clearing of remnant vegetation on both freehold and leasehold land.[9] In Queensland for example, hundreds of thousands of hectares of native vegetation are cleared annually, approximately half being on private land. And in Western Australia, in the south-west corner alone, an estimated 50 000 hectares are cleared annually, mostly on freehold land (Cameron and Elix 1991). Continuation of these practices will almost certainly hasten the demise of species and ecosystems regionally, and perhaps nationally, as well as contributing to continued land and waterways degradation, unless restrictions and reserves are introduced.

An inevitable conclusion to be drawn from this discussion is that the allocation of property rights among competing users will not work to ensure the protection of biodiversity unless there are sufficient bidders in the market who are prepared to bid for the interests of species and ecosystems. Free market economists argue that this is a feasible notion and point to the successes of bodies such as the Nature Conservancy in the United States in achieving private land conservation (Anderson 1991).

However, even if we were to assume that Australia's financial resources and philanthropic traditions were able to match those of the United States (which they presently do not), this approach would not go even close to securing and managing the extensive system of reserves and regulations required to protect biodiversity in Australia. In addition to a large network of areas owned privately or in trust in the United States for biodiversity protection, the United States has a system of publicly owned protected areas that is far more extensive than currently exists in Australia.[10] In addition to purchasing private land, the US Nature Conservancy spends a sizeable proportion of its time and resources lobbying the US Federal Government to protect and expand these protected areas. Thus, the free market economists' defence of the practices of the Nature Conservancy is highly selective and misleading.

### The Need for Government Intervention

This is not an argument against the appropriateness of organisations being set up to achieve private land conservation. Nor is it an argument for the abolition of private property rights. Rather, it is an argument for additional measures to ensure the protection of ecosystems and species. Government intervention, including restrictive regulation, cannot be overlooked as part of a package of measures designed to achieve this end. From an ACF perspective, the package must necessarily include measures such as vegetation clearance controls, legislation to protect endangered species and the creation of a comprehensive and representative system of reserves protected by law (Amos, Kirkpatrick and Giese 1993).

Although many such interventionist measures may be anathema to free market economists, as well as to those neoclassical economists who do not accept the need for ecological limits or constraints to economic activity, we must come back to the major point at issue concerning objectives. That is, this group of economists are concerned primarily with achieving an *optimal* level of environmental protection and with *economically* efficient outcomes. Unfortunately, these objectives do not necessarily give rise to ecologically sustainable outcomes. Although government intervention should not be seen as a cure-all in this matter, intervention is essential to ensure the protection of biodiversity and to put into effect constraints on economic activity that are necessary to achieve ecologically sustainable development.

## Example 3: Controlling Greenhouse Gas Emissions — Are Market Instruments the Most Efficient?

In this third and final case study claims by neoclassical and free market economists that market-based instruments are necessarily the most efficient means of limiting the emission of anthropogenic greenhouse gases are examined. The point at issue here is not whether the enhanced greenhouse effect is a real threat,[11] nor how Australia and the international community should respond to that threat.[12] Rather, given a specific objective for achieving emission reductions, are market mechanisms *necessarily* the most efficient means of achieving that objective?

*Recent Carbon Tax Studies*
Following the adoption of an interim planning target for greenhouse gas emissions by the Australian Government in 1991, numerous studies have been undertaken to determine the economic implications for Australia of meeting greenhouse gas emission targets. Some of the more publicised studies, including those by the Industry Commission and the Tasman Institute,[13] purport to demonstrate that stabilisation and/or reduction of carbon dioxide emissions in Australia is best achieved through a carbon tax, but only at considerable economic cost. A critical examination of the methodology, assumptions and conclusions of these studies, however, suggests that they are severely flawed and put into doubt the assertion by neoclassical and free market economists that market-based instruments are necessarily the most efficient means of achieving environmental protection.[14]

The studies in question have taken a broadly consistent approach to the issue of carbon dioxide emission reductions. They have adopted a 'top down' methodological approach, using neoclassical economic models to assess the implications for the Australian economy of meeting carbon dioxide emission targets. The studies are characterised by starting from the same basic, profit maximising behavioural assumption. This assumption suggests that the market for energy is essentially perfect and that there are no opportunities for cost-effective fuel switching or improvements in energy efficiency. Based on this assumption, the studies then further assume that the optimal instrument for achieving emission reductions in Australia is through a broadly based market mechanism, such as a carbon tax, since other forms of intervention, for example regulation, will inevitably distort the market.

*Questionable Assumptions and Market Failure*
The above assumptions are, at best, questionable though, and there has been little attempt to substantiate them in any of the studies. In theory, energy prices under perfect market conditions should optimise the allocation of resources, including the adoption of cost-effective efficiency and renewable technologies. In practice this does not happen. Numerous studies have documented how market failure provides barriers to the uptake of efficient and renewable energy technologies and practices (e.g. IEA 1989; Grubb 1990; Reddy 1991). Some of the major barriers include the following:

- 'Up-front' costs of renewable energy and energy efficiency technologies to consumers are proportionally high when compared with traditional energy technologies. Even though the total lifecycle costs of the renewable technologies may be lower than the traditional energy technologies, consumers are often deterred by the initial capital costs, which they generally must finance themselves. The capital costs of traditional energy sources, on the other hand, are generally financed by the energy utility.

- Associated with the first point, individuals and firms are usually only prepared to finance the 'up-front' capital costs of energy technologies if the payback period for their investment is relatively short. Utilities, on the other hand, are prepared to accept much longer payback periods for their investments in traditional energy sources.
- There is an absence of institutional support (e.g. maintenance and repair services, advisory services, marketing support and sales outlets) for energy efficient products, whereas there are large and powerful institutions supporting traditional energy supply.
- The price structures for fossil fuels and electricity contain hidden subsidies and cross-subsidies, and do not incorporate 'external' environmental and social costs of their use.
- The rate of replacement of the existing stock of inefficient energy-using products is slow.
- For many businesses, energy is only a small fraction of total cost and hence the pursuit of cost savings through greater energy efficiency is a low priority.
- There is a general lack of expertise and information with respect to energy efficiency and renewable energy.

The Industry Commission and the Tasman Institute accept only that information barriers exist, and make only passing reference to the possibility of other barriers. On that basis, and without undertaking further analysis of their own, both bodies reject the notion that cost-effective energy efficiency measures can be implemented. The Industry Commission concludes that 'On the evidence available to it, the Commission does not consider that most such changes could be implemented without net cost' (Industry Commission 1991, Vol. I, 239). Similarly, the Tasman Institute concludes that: 'Contrary to the findings of the DASETT commissioned Deni Greene studies, using less energy and different forms of energy will be costly. If as these studies maintain, there are private gains to be made, usages will reduce automatically' (Tasman Institute 1991, 5).

Yet this position is contradicted by results from a comprehensive range of Australian energy use studies (see for example

Deni Greene 1990; Wilkenfeld 1990; ABARE 1991). The studies provide substantial evidence of cost-effective energy savings that are not being achieved due to energy market failure. Opportunities for cost-effective emission reductions are particularly evident in the commercial and residential sectors. For example, a range of proposals for reduction of commercial sector lighting could, according to one analysis, reduce energy consumption by approximately 20 petajoules per annum, with simple payback periods of between minus 73 years and zero years (EMET Consultants 1991)!

However, the results of such studies appear to be ignored. The Industry Commission and Tasman Institute opt to overlook the complication of possible market failure and to choose instead a market-based instrument that fits comfortably within their own ideological framework, namely a carbon tax. A carbon tax is selected on the grounds that it 'has been effective in the past and there is no reason to suggest that it would not be as effective as needed in the future' (Industry Commission 1991, Vol. I, 121). Similarly, the Tasman Institute argues that such a market instrument 'allows the decentralised decision making of the market to bring about efficient solutions. Such solutions are certain to be more efficient than if governments impose technologies' (Tasman Institute 1991, 10).

These claims are not substantiated, however. The only evidence proffered in support of price-related instruments comes from the Industry Commission, which argues that oil price increases in the 1970s and 1980s were associated with subsequent major improvements in the efficiency of energy use in the United States and other industrialised countries (Industry Commission 1991, 121). Work by David Greene (1990), though, suggests that it was regulatory measures, such as the corporate average fuel economy (CAFE) standards in the USA, rather than price increases, which were largely responsible for efficiency improvements.[15] His work is supported by Schipper et al. (1992), who found that fuel economy improved far more in the USA than in any other country between 1973 and 1988, principally due to the CAFE standards. Little change to fuel economy occurred in Europe, where no binding standards were imposed.

*Disadvantages of Carbon Taxes*
There are also three significant disadvantages of carbon taxes that the Industry Commission and the Tasman Institute have failed to acknowledge.

Firstly, carbon taxes are broad, blunt and indiscriminate. They do not take account of different marginal abatement costs between different classes of energy users. A broadly based carbon tax will necessarily have to be large, therefore, to influence the behaviour of energy users who have high marginal abatement costs, either because they are efficient users of energy already, or because alternatives to their existing patterns of energy consumption are not readily available.

Secondly, a carbon tax is likely to have major equity implications. It is a regressive tax, since low income earners generally spend a larger proportion of their disposable income directly on energy consumption than do higher income earners.

Finally, because of uncertain and irregular energy demand elasticities (the degree to which the demand for energy changes in response to energy price changes), it is highly uncertain that a particular rate of carbon tax would achieve its intended emissions reduction objective anyway.

These concerns do not amount to a rejection of the carbon tax as a potential future policy instrument. The importance of energy prices to long-term trends in energy consumption cannot be denied. However, it seems clear that *while energy market distortions remain widespread*, the cost-effectiveness of market-based measures, such as carbon taxes, will be greatly diminished. Instead, the initial policy focus should be on removing the energy market distortions through a carefully targeted and integrated package of policy measures.

A similar approach is favoured in a recent report by the International Energy Agency (IEA 1993). The IEA, generally known for its neoclassical approach to energy and related policy issues, in this instance argues for what it terms a 'regulatory-incentive' approach to stabilising carbon dioxide emissions in the OECD countries in preference to a carbon tax being introduced in isolation (1993, 14).

The final Greenhouse Report of the ESD Working Group Chairs (1992) also recommends the implementation of a broad package of measures in Australia to tackle the issue, including institutional reforms of energy markets, national energy performance standards, codes and labelling, government infrastructure and procurement programs, research and development and incentives, as well as price reforms such as the removal of subsidies. The ACF believes that the package would be enhanced if it were at least partially funded through a small carbon levy on domestic fossil fuel consumption.[16] The primary purpose of such a levy would not be directly to reduce demand for carbon based fuels. Rather, by funding a transition package, it would help to compensate for the rundown in natural capital being caused by the combustion of fossil fuels.

# Conclusion

The three examples examined in this chapter — pollution control, the conservation of biodiversity and ecological integrity, and the control of greenhouse gas emissions — are sufficient to demonstrate that market-based approaches to environmental protection, both in terms of objectives and methods, may often be inconsistent with the goal of ecologically sustainable development. If we are to move society towards ESD, then an integrated policy approach is necessary to place constraints on the operation of markets.

In many circumstances, taxes and other market-based approaches will be useful components of an integrated policy approach. Market-based measures can be used to implement the 'polluter pays principle' and enable the transition to ESD to occur as efficiently as possible. However, the determination of environmental and social objectives should not be left to the market.

In arguing for government constraints on the operation of markets to achieve ESD, it is important to recognise the distinction between general community interests and the private interests of market players. Such interests are not coterminous, although they do overlap. ESD is very much about making community choices. There are many ways in which the private interests of market players may be enlisted to serve the community interest, but in those cases where they do not coincide, the community interest must prevail.

However, government intervention through regulations, financial incentives and publicly funded programs is not sufficient by itself to achieve ESD. Community participation in the formulation and implementation of policy will be vital to the attainment of ESD. No policy approach, regardless of how well conceived and how carefully implemented, will achieve ESD in the long run without widespread community support and value shifts. Neither governments nor markets can induce those value shifts. At best, they can merely help to facilitate them.

# Endnotes

1. In Australia and increasingly elsewhere, the phrase 'sustainable development' is generally now prefixed with 'ecologically' to circumvent inappropriate derivations that have arisen, such as 'sustained development' and 'sustainable growth' and to highlight the need for development to be underpinned by ecological sustainability.
2. However, these two groups did not participate in the Forestry Working Group on the grounds that this working group would

duplicate work already being undertaken by the Resource Assessment Commission in its Forest and Timber Industry Inquiry.

3. These principles are included in the National Strategy for ESD (see Commonwealth of Australia 1992a, 8–9). A detailed discussion of the principles from the perspective of major Australian environmental groups can be found in Hare et al. (1990).

4. A questionaire containing 50 questions was sent by the Australian Conservation Foundation to all major parties during the election campaign. Both major parties provided detailed responses.

5. Natural capital is subject to a degree of uncertainty not generally associated with natural resources. For example, there is a great deal of uncertainty about the capacity of species to withstand modifications to ecosystems. Under these circumstances a precautionary policy approach is advisable. Similarly, changes to natural capital are often irreversible. The loss of a forest ecosystem, for example, or of a species within that ecosystem is irreversible. A natural resource, such as a forest plantation, however, is essentially replaceable.

6. Even economists from the OECD, noted for their advocacy of 'freeing up' markets, agree that tax-based measues will not always be suitable substitutes for a framework of pollution control regulations (OECD 1993).

7. Option values represent an expression of preference to protect an environment so that an individual, group or society has a wider range of options for its future use.

8. The example often cited to bolster this argument is the improved conservation status of African elephants in Zimbabwe achieved as a consequence of property rights for the elephants being vested in the hands of local people. Local Zimbabweans have an incentive to protect and manage elephant herds because they receive a share of the money paid for tusks taken from elephants that have been culled.

9. The notable exception to this situation is South Australia, which has introduced legislation to restrict clearing on private and public land.

10. The proportion of land set aside as protected areas in the United States is 8.6 per cent, compared with only 4.7 per cent in Australia (ABS 1992).

11. The ACF accepts mainstream science on the enhanced greenhouse effect, as set out by the Intergovernmental Panel on Climate Change. On that basis, and in accordance with the precautionary principle of ESD, action is considered necessary to reduce the emission of greenhouse gases.

12. The ACF supports the interim planning target adopted by Federal Cabinet in October 1991, which is to reduce emissions of greenhouse gases not controlled by the Montreal Protocol to 20 per cent below their 1988 levels by 2005, but not the attached provisos relating to international competitiveness. Measures set out in the National Greenhouse Response Strategy (December 1992) are not sufficient to meet that target. The ACF further believes that the United Nations Framework Convention on Climate Change should be strengthened at the first session of the Conference of Parties — possibly with protocols — to include *binding commitments* from

developed countries to reduce emissions.
13. The studies examined include Industry Commission (1991); Tasman Institute (1991, 1992) and London Economics (1992).
14. For a detailed review of these studies refer to Kinrade (1992) and Eckersley (1993).
15. The Corporate Average Fuel Economy (CAFE) standards were legislated in the US in 1975. The legislation set fuel efficiency standards on all new vehicles (imported and locally manufactured), based on a corporate average, with the standards to improve steadily over time. New fleet average fuel consumption dropped from 16.5 litres/100 kilometres in 1973 to 8.2 litres/100 kilometres in 1988. A proposal to tighten the CAFE standard further to 5.9 litres/100 kilometres by 2010 was defeated in Congress in 1990. Average new fleet fuel consumption in Australia is estimated to be approximately 9–10 litres/100 kilometres.
16. Most recently, ACF has proposed a levy of $A8.00 per tonne of carbon ($A2.20 per tonne of carbon dioxide) (ACF 1994).

# References

Amos, N., Kirkpatrick, J.B. and Giese, M. (1993) *Conservation of Biodiversity, Ecological Integrity and Ecologically Sustainable Development: A Discussion Paper*, Australian Conservation Foundation, Melbourne.

Anderson, T.L. (1991) 'The Market Process and Environmental Amenities' in J. Bennett and W. Block (eds), *Reconciling Economics and the Environment*, Australian Institute for Public Policy, Perth.

ANOP Research Services (1991) *The Environment and the ESD Process: An Attitude Research Analysis, Vol. 1*, Report prepared for the Department of Arts, Sport, the Environment, Tourism and Territories (DASETT) and the ESD Secretariat.

ANZECC. (1922) *Australian Water Quality Guidelines for Fresh and Marine Waters*, Australian and New Zealand Environment and Conservation Council, Canberra.

Australian Bureau of Agricultural and Resource Economics (ABARE). (1991) *Projections of Energy Demand and Supply: Australia 1990–91 to 2004–05*, Australian Government Publishing Service (AGPS), Canberra.

Australian Bureau of Statistics (ABS). (1992) *Striking a Balance: Australia's Development and Conservation*, AGPS, Canberra.

Australian Conservation Foundation (ACF). 1994 *Investing in the Future: Federal Budget 1995–96*, Submission to the Federal Government, December, Australian Conservation Foundation, Melbourne.

Baden, J. and Stroup, R.L. (1991) 'Natural Resource Scarcity, Entrepreneurship and the Political Economy of Hope' in J. Bennett and W. Block (eds), *Reconciling Economics and the Environment*, Australian Institute for Public Policy, Perth.

Bennett, J. (1991) 'Conclusion' in J. Bennett and W. Block (eds), *Reconciling Economics and the Environment*, Australian Institute for Public Policy, Perth.

Bennett, J. and Block, W. (1991) *Reconciling Economics and the Environment*, Australian Institute for Public Policy, Perth.

Blake, D., Ford, L., Freedman, P., Marti, J. and Melton, L. (1992) 'Zero Discharge: A Goal Whose Time Has Come?' *Water Environment and Technology* October 1992.

Business Council of Australia (BCA). (1991) *Achieving Sustainable Development*, BCA, Melbourne.

Cameron, J. and Elix, J. (1991) *Recovering Ground*, ACF, Melbourne.

Campbell, I.C. (1984) 'Assimilative Capacity Challenged', *Search* 17, 154–55.

Chant, J., McFetridge, D., Smith, D. and Nurick, J. (1991) 'The Economics of the Green Society' in J. Bennett and W. Block (eds), *Reconciling Economics and the Environment*, Australian Institute for Public Policy, Perth.

Coase, R. (1960) 'The Problem of Social Cost', *Journal of Law and Economics* 3 (October 1960), 1–44.

Commonwealth of Australia. (1992) *National Strategy for Ecologically Sustainable Developmentt*, AGPS, Canberra.

Dumsday, R.G. and Chisholm, A.H. (1991) 'Land Degradation: Economic Causes and Cures' in J. Bennett and W. Block (eds), *Reconciling Economics and the Environment*, Australian Institute for Public Policy, Perth.

Eckersley, R. (1993) 'Re-interpreting "No Regrets": A Green Critique of the Greenhouse Response Strategy' in S.L. Pfueller, M.A. Hooper and D.H.P. Harvey (eds), *Greenhouse and the Energy Regions: Proceedings*, Monash Distance Education Centre, Churchill, Victoria, 1993.

Ecologically Sustainable Development Working Group Chairs. (1992) *Greenhouse Report*, AGPS, Canberra.

EMET Consultants Pty Ltd. (1991) *Evaluation of Costs of Options for Greenhouse Gas Reductions in Energy Use, Commercial Sector Lighting*, Department of Primary Industries and Energy, Canberra.

Greene, David. (1990) 'CAFE or Price: An Analysis of Federal Fuel Economy Regulations and Gasoline Prices on New Car MPG, 1878–89', *The Energy Journal* 11(3), 37–57.

Greene, Deni. (1990) *A Greenhouse Energy Strategy: Sustainable Energy Development for Australia*, A Report prepared for the Department of Arts, Sport, the Environment, Tourism and Territories (DASETT).

Grubb, M. (1990) *Energy Policies and The Greenhouse Effect*, Volume One: Policy Appraisal, The Royal Institute of International Affairs, Dartmouth, UK.

Hare, W.L. (ed.). (1991) *Ecologically Sustainable Development: Assessment of the Working Group Reports*, ACF, Melbourne.

Hare, W.L., Marlow, J.P., Rae, M.L., Gray, F., Humphries, R. and Ledgar, R. (1990) *Ecologically Sustainable Development: A Submission*, ACF, Melbourne.

Industry Commission. (1991) *Costs and Benefits of Reducing Greenhouse Gas Emissions*, Report No. 15, Volumes I & II, AGPS, Canberra.

Industry Commission. (1992) *Water Resources and Waste Water Disposal*, Report No. 26, AGPS, Canberra.

International Energy Agency (IEA). (1989) *Energy Conservation in IEA Countries*, OECD, Paris.

International Energy Agency (IEA). (1993) *World Energy Outlook to the Year 2010*, IEA/OECD, Paris.

Jacobs, M. (1991) *The Green Economy*, Pluto Press, London.

Jacobs, M. (1993) *Environmental Economics, Sustainable Development and Successful Economies*, RAC Occasional Paper No. 4, AGPS, Canberra.

Keating, P. (1992) 'Australia's Natural Environment: A Natural Asset', Statement on the Environment, 21 December, Adelaide.

Kinrade, P. (1992) *Implications for the Australian Economy of Meeting Carbon Dioxide Emissions Targets: A Review of Recent Carbon Tax Studies*, ACF, Melbourne.

London Economics. (1992) *The Impact of Global Warming Control Policies on Australian Industry*, Volumes I & II, London Economics, London.

Moran, A., Chisholm, A. and Porter, M. (eds). (1991) *Markets, Resources and the Environment*, Allen and Unwin, Sydney.

OECD. (1993) *OECD Letter* 2(3), 3–6.

Pearce, D., Markandya, A. and Barbier, E.B. (1989) *Blueprint for a Green Economy*, Earthscan Publications, London.

Pearce, D.W. and Turner, R.K. (1990) *Economics of Natural Resources and the Environment*, Harvester Wheatsheaf, London.

Resource Assessment Commission (RAC). (1992) *Coastal Zone Inquiry Draft Report*, AGPS, Canberra.

Reddy, A.K.N. (1991) 'Barriers to Improvements in Energy Efficiency', *Energy Policy* 19(3), April.

Schipper, L., Steiner, R., Figueroa, M.J. and Dolan, K. (1992) 'Fuel Prices, Automobile Fuel Economy, and Fuel Use for Land Travel: Preliminary Findings from an International Comparison', International Energy Studies, Energy Analysis Program (Draft).

Schmidheiny, S. (1992) *Changing Course: A Global Business Perspective on Sustainable Development*, MIT Press, Cambridge, Massachusetts.

Stavins, R.N. (1990) 'Innovative Policies for Sustainable Development in the 1990s: Economic Incentives for Environmental Protection', paper prepared for the United Nations Economic Commission for Europe and The United States Environmental Protection Agency Workshop on *The Economics of Sustainable Development*, Washington DC, January 23–26.

Stroup, R.L. (1991) 'Chemophobia and Activist Environmental Antidotes: Is the Cure More Deadly than the Disease?' in J. Bennett and W. Block (eds), *Reconciling Economics and the Environment*, Australian Institute for Public Policy, Perth.

Tasman Institute. (1991) *Global Warming — Its Economics and Politics*, Tasman Institute, Melbourne.

Tasman Institute. (1992) *Carbon Taxes: Effects on Prices and Incomes*, Tasman Institute, Melbourne.

Wilkenfeld, G. (1990) *Greenhouse Gas Emissions from the Australian Energy System: The Impact of Energy Efficiency and Substitution*, NERDDP Grant Report No. 1379.

World Commission on Environment and Development (WCED). (1987) *Our Common Future*, Oxford University Press, Melbourne.

# Part III

## *New Environmental Policy Instruments in Practice*

# 5

# Financial Incentives: The British Experience

## Michael Jacobs

## Introduction

Until 1988–89 environmental control in the United Kingdom, and the associated policy debate, was almost entirely regulatory. The basic assumption was that *if* controls were necessary, a legislative framework should be provided, and within this framework government departments or agencies would be empowered to set specific product standards, issue pollution consents or otherwise regulate polluters and resource users. Environmental behaviour was binary in form: it was either legal or illegal, with some negotiation allowed to determine the boundary. The use of financial incentives or 'market-based mechanisms' to control behaviour was almost unknown.

There were a few exceptions. Airline companies have for some time had to pay fees related to noise at airports, and producers of effluent have faced sewerage charges. Charging was also used as a back-up to regulatory systems of pollution control and resource use through administrative charges and 'non-compliance fees', although as these are not strictly related to environmental damage they do not really count as financial incentives. In the countryside, subsidies have been available to landowners for habitat management.

1988–89 was the year in which public — and therefore political — concern about the environment exploded. Although national media interest in the environment has declined since then, public concern has barely diminished, and the policy fall-out within the machinery of government remains high. In particular, the influence of the so-called Pearce Report (Pearce, Markandya and Barbier 1989), which was commissioned by the Department of the Environment and published in 1989, continues to be felt. As yet, little has actually changed on the ground, but the terms of the policy debate have been considerably altered.

## Financial Incentives: The New Agenda

In one or two areas a new approach is already evident, though there is little to suggest that the new measures were introduced as part of any wider conceptual change in policy making. Differential taxation on unleaded petrol was indeed introduced before the Pearce Report appeared. Given the existing taxation of petrol it did not require much environmental economics to realise that making unleaded cheaper than leaded would encourage its use. Rather more sophisticated has been the introduction of 'recycling credits', which allow waste disposal authorities to reimburse waste collection bodies who divert part of the waste stream into recycling. Such credits, which in many cases have been passed on to voluntary salvage groups, have provided a useful incentive to recycling, although many other obstacles, notably the lack of markets for recycled products, have constrained this activity. Apart from these cases, however, the use of financial incentives has been developed in policy research rather than in practice.

Following the Pearce Report, the government's much-heralded White Paper on the Environment, *This Common Inheritance* (Her Majesty's Government 1990), was expected to contain a number of proposals for financial incentives. Much to the chagrin of the environmental economists, both within and outside government, it did not. An appendix provided a nice little summary of Pearce's arguments but the text said only that further research on such measures would be done. This was interesting evidence of the resistance of the environmental policy community to the proposed new approach, a resistance to which I shall return.

By the end of 1992 things had changed, however. In its annual review of progress on the White Paper, the government made the following declaration (using the term 'economic instruments' for financial incentives): 'In future, there will be a general presumption in favour of economic instruments. The intention is that new regulations should be limited to cases where economic instruments ... are either not available or require regulatory underpinning' (Her Majesty's Government 1992).

I doubt very strongly whether the government will or can live up to this commitment — in particular, the requirement that economic instruments have to be *unavailable* rather than merely less effective practically rules out regulation altogether. It is also not clear whether implementation of European directives, which are almost entirely regulatory, is excluded from this commitment. But whether or not the claim can be fulfilled, the shift in thinking is evident.

This shift has come from a combination of four sources. The first is a general dislike of regulation. 'Deregulation', with its accompanying rhetoric about reducing the size of government, cutting bureaucracy and liberating markets, has been a theme of the Conservative Government since 1979. Financial incentives are often presented as alternatives to regulation, even though they are really just another form of it (see chapter 2 in this volume). This allows necessary environmental control to be exercised without loss of ideological face. Second, the orthodox environmental economists' arguments about the greater efficiency and incentive to environmental improvement of 'market mechanisms' naturally appeals to Tories with a predisposition to favour market-based policies. Taxes and charges are seen as giving firms greater choice over their response to environmental control, and therefore as more libertarian than regulatory instruments. (Some of these arguments, of course, carry environmental weight as well.)

Third, the past few years have seen major proposals for changes in the institutional structure of regulation. The government's proposal for a new, all-embracing environment agency has placed the currently separated agencies dealing with water, air and solid waste onto the defensive. These agencies have traditionally had very strong regulatory cultures, which in the 1970s and 1980s provided the strongest source of resistance to environmental economists' prescriptions. Faced with abolition or merger, however, resistance has declined. The general shift in the culture of government bodies towards the market (including internal cost centre management, competitive tendering and performance-related pay) has also probably had an effect. Certainly there is much more interest in financial incentives within the agencies than there used to be. Fourth, the Treasury has finally realised the revenue-raising potential of green taxes and charges. Since nothing happens in British government without Treasury approval, this has probably been the most important change of all.

The new commitment has emerged so far in a number of research projects and consultative documents on particular types of financial incentive. The most important are:

- water pollution charges;
- tradable water extraction permits;
- tradable permits for sulfur dioxide emissions;
- landfill levies for solid waste;
- road pricing (motorway tolls and urban congestion charging);
- tradable credits for motor manufacturers to encourage the development of more fuel efficient cars.

In addition, the European Community has stimulated a major debate with its proposals for a Europe-wide carbon tax. Elsewhere, the Countryside Commission has conducted research into the use of various kinds of charges, principally aimed at revenue raising, for leisure activities in the countryside.

In none of the above areas have definite policy changes been set out in legislation, but they will not be long in coming. Interestingly, there are as yet no proposals for product charges (for example, on pesticides, artificial fertilisers or heavy metal batteries) or for deposit-refund schemes on bottles and other containers, even though many such measures have been used in other European countries. (The latter measures have been researched but are regarded as being very expensive.) There are also no current proposals, outside the water field, for tradable resource extraction permits, despite their obvious relevance to current issues, like overfishing in the North Sea.

It should also be said that there are no proposals for the privatisation of environmental assets to generate property rights. Indeed, there has been no debate in the UK about this kind of 'free market environmentalism' at all. This is rather surprising, as many other *laissez-faire* ideas have found their way into the mainstream of British Conservative politics in the past 15 years, and the environment would have been a good new arena for privatising zeal. But it has not happened, and does not seem likely to.

## The Environmentalists' Response

Naturally enough, this shift in government policy has brought forth responses from the business community, from the environmental lobby and from opposition parties. The reaction of the environmental movement has clearly changed in the period since the Pearce Report first brought the idea of financial incentives into the open. At that time, almost all the environmental organisations were opposed. A general feeling that market-based instruments were a form of deregulation — when regulation of one sort or other has been the universal goal of the environmental movement — was combined with a moral outrage that such instruments constituted 'licences to pollute'. Whereas regulations broadcast a clear message that pollution was wrong — illegal — taxes and tradable permits allowed it, so long as the polluter was rich enough to pay for it. The economists' arguments about efficiency cut little ice, since any savings would accrue to the companies themselves and were invisible to the general public.

This attitude, however, has changed markedly in the past three years. The blanket opposition to financial incentives has been replaced by a more discriminating response to different types of measure. This change is partly due to the recognition that financial instruments are not just an academic idea but have become a central part of the government's policy thinking: a more considered and issue-based response is therefore required. More positively, it has generally been acknowledged that financial incentives can be effective, and may offer solutions to environmental problems (such as in the waste field) where regulation cannot.

*Decision Rights*
It is interesting to observe the way in which the environmental movement has responded to the different proposals now on offer. I believe that it reveals an important issue in environmental economics, one that environmental economists are wont to ignore. In general, environmental organisations oppose financial incentives when they are put forward as a change to an existing regulatory regime. This is the case, for example, in the air and water pollution fields. But they give them a more favourable hearing when applied to issues not currently subject to much regulation, as in landfill levies and product charges.

At first sight this does not appear particularly logical. Why should whatever happens to be the current situation — of which environmentalists, after all, are highly critical — determine the groups' response? It is not completely consistent either. Most environmental organisations have been lukewarm (at best) towards the carbon tax, and opposed to water metering, while attitudes towards road pricing have been notably ambivalent. (These are also areas where there is little current environmental regulation.)

There is an explanation, I believe, for these attitudes. What the environmentalists are responding to is not primarily the efficacy of the proposed measure in comparison with the current situation. Rather, it is the implicit change that incentives propose to the *distribution of decision rights* between the different actors involved.

By decision rights I mean the rights people or firms have to use or 'consume' environmental goods; effectively, that is, their rights to decide what happens to such goods. Decision rights over any particular good can be shared between different actors (hence the preference for this term over the more common 'property rights'). Different environmental control measures effectively allocate decision rights in different ways. In general, the continuum in Table 5.1 may be drawn up. The example of a polluter is used, but it could equally be an extractor or user of resources.

**Table 5.1** A continuum of decision rights in relation to pollution

| Decision rights with polluter (resource user) | |
| --- | --- |
| | 1. Pollution is allowed and the community must pay to clean it up or assimilate it |
| | 2. The polluter must pay to pollute but is subsidised for improving the environment |
| | 3. It is illegal for the polluter to pollute the environment, but he/she is subsidised for improving it |
| | 4. The polluter is charged for polluting per unit of pollution. |
| | 5. It is illegal for the polluter to pollute beyond a certain amount |
| | 6. It is illegal for the polluter to pollute at all |
| | 7. The polluter is legally obliged to improve the environment |
| Decision rights with community | |

Attitudes towards environmental issues are often based on implicit beliefs about the 'proper' allocation of decision rights, because these in turn reflect notions of *fairness*. But they also reflect different notions of what might be *legitimate public regulation of externalities*, and these are subject to change. For example, in the 19th century it would have been unthinkable for the state to tell a private householder what he or she could do on his or her land. But in the 20th century the externalities of land use were recognised, and the town and country planning system now enshrines the principle that the 'community' (through the local authority) can exercise veto powers over land use proposals — up to a point. (The idea that the 'presumption in favour of development' should be reversed would further shift effective decision rights from landowner to community.)

The concept of decision rights illuminates what is going on in attitudes towards financial incentives. In air and water pollution, where regulatory regimes (emissions and technology standards) are used, the allocation of decision rights is located quite near to the 'community' end of the polluter–community continuum: pollution is illegal above a certain amount (position 5). The introduction of a charge or permit system would then shift the allocation towards the polluter, since pollution would be allowed, subject to payment (position 4). By contrast, in the case of landfill, waste producers have almost unlimited rights to landfill space; local planning authorities are obliged by law to find holes in the ground sufficient to meet demand (position 1). In this case, therefore, introducing a landfill charge would shift the allocation of decision rights towards the community (position 4).

Thus in general, the attitude of environmentalists (and quite possibly the general public) towards financial incentives reflects the movement in the allocation of decision rights they represent. Whatever the current situation, they want a shift in favour of the community.

The exceptions are for domestic energy and water taxes and various charges for use of the countryside. Why? Because it is widely felt that people have *right*s to use at least an 'allowance' of these environmental goods in a way that they don't have rights to use up landfill space or consume petrol, batteries, pesticides or other candidates for (relatively non-controversial) product charges. The ambivalence in attitudes towards road pricing is a reflection of a genuine uncertainty about whether personal mobility and the use of public roads should be a 'right' or — nowadays — a luxury.

What is interesting about these attitudes on the part of the environmental movement is that they are political and symbolic in nature rather than economic. To orthodox environmental economists, decision rights are (almost) irrelevant. What matters is the efficiency by which a particular environmental standard is reached, that is, the total cost of achieving it. The instrument by which this is done is seen as value-neutral. The economist's concern is the end-result, expressed in terms of financial cost, not the political implication of the means employed. By contrast, to the environmentalist — untrained, generally, in economics — cost is a marginal criterion of judgment. Since (in general) the savings that result from financial incentives accrue to firms, that is, to those responsible for the problem in the first place, their benefits are not particularly prized.

More importantly, the environmental organisations' position reflects the fact that their primary function, unlike that of the economists, is not the making of more efficient environmental policy. At root, environmental organisations are concerned to articulate a political position. This is grounded in the belief that the degradation of the environment by private interests is *wrong*, not that it is inefficient. The natural world is a common inheritance that belongs to all. Wherever possible, therefore, its use should be decided by the community as a whole, and private use only allowed so long as the condition of the environment is maintained for the next generation. Agreed environmental standards should take the form of legal prohibitions, as with any other kind of wrongdoing. Free private use is only sanctioned where the environment provides for basic needs required by all — such as in the case of water and domestic energy — or where its use by individual citizens is precisely an expression of common ownership (as in the use of the countryside).

The ideal policy position for the environmentalist, therefore, is at the bottom of the continuum, where all decision rights are held with the community. Actual policies are judged on the political criterion of whether or not they move towards this position, rather than on economic grounds of efficiency. This argument can be described as *symbolic* in nature because, as we have seen, the same policy can be opposed in one case and advocated in another, not on the basis of its intrinsic characteristics but because of the *change in the fundamental 'nature' of public policy that it represents* in the different circumstances.

This fundamental difference in the discourses of economists and environmentalists, and consequently in their perception of environmental policy instruments, may throw some light on why they have found it difficult to talk to one another. It is interesting to observe how, as the environmental movement becomes more economically 'literate' (i.e. as the economic discourse gains a foothold), the economists' arguments begin to carry more weight. For example, the argument that (unlike regulatory methods) financial incentives often encourage continuous improvement in environmental performance has had a noticeable effect on old positions. Yet there is no guarantee that such 'rational' arguments, grounded in the discourse of economics, will prevail at large. This is because politicians — who ultimately make the policy decisions — frequently find the symbolic discourse of politics more comfortable. Like the environmentalists they see the (implicit) concept of decision rights more clearly than that of efficiency. For conservative politicians the prescription lies in the opposite direction — they wish to see the allocation of decision rights move in the direction of environmental privatisation rather than community control. But the basic understanding, interestingly, is the same.

## The Business Response

The response of the business sector to the new proposals for financial incentives has also been mixed. On the one hand, most businesses are instinctively in favour of policies based on 'the market' and against regulation; they have therefore found it difficult to argue against the introduction of financial incentives. Moreover, public concern for the environment (and business rhetoric in support of it) is such that few large businesses can now argue that environmental improvement is unnecessary. (This would have been the standard argument 10 years ago.) This has led to the remarkable outcome that some of Britain's largest companies, including oil producers like BP and Shell, and the Society of Motor Manufacturers and Traders, are now publicly on the record as supporting a carbon tax.[1]

On the other hand, the introduction of financial incentives will almost certainly cause additional costs to the firms affected. This is obviously true in those areas where financial incentives are proposed as new measures altogether, rather than as replacements for regulatory instruments. These include road pricing and landfill levies. But it is also the case in the fields of water and air pollution control, where the proposal is to change the nature of the regime rather than to impose new standards. The industries affected have realised that whereas regulations only require them to pay for environmental improvements up to the level of the standard, pollution charges are levied on *the whole* of a company's dis-charges, not just on the part that exceeds the desired pollution level. The company therefore pays, in addition to the cost of the required pollution control, an effective 'rent' on its use of the environment (Pezzey 1988). Since under existing regulatory regimes property rights to use of the environment have effectively been vested in the company, this is regarded as a retrograde step, as well as a more costly one.

*Hypothecation and the Charge/Tax Distinction*
This ambivalence on the part of the business community appears to be resolving itself in an interesting compromise. The emerging view is that if financial incentives are introduced, the revenues should not go into the general coffers of the Treasury, but should be recycled back into the industry. Ideally they should be spent on subsidies to help the firms affected invest in better equipment; alternatively (or in addition) they could go towards more general research into environmentally improved technologies. Such a 'hypothecation' of revenues is common in other European countries, notably Germany and the Netherlands, where it has been practised with water pollution charges for some years. The revenues from Sweden's pesticide and fertiliser product charges are similarly devoted to research on alternatives. But hypo-

thecation is anathema in Britain. Or rather, it is anathema to the Treasury, which has long held the belief that all revenues accruing to the government should go to consolidated revenues, and none should be earmarked for specific purposes. This, it is believed, would fatally compromise the ability of government to decide each year how its income is to be spent, and therefore its flexibility of response to changing circumstances.

This debate about hypothecation is an important one, for it draws attention to the distinction between 'taxes', 'charges' and 'fees'. Public debate about financial incentives has tended not to separate these terms — it has been helpful to use the shorthand phrase 'green taxes' — but there are important differences. These differences, it should be noted, are not necessarily those that have traditionally been highlighted in the field of public finance, where the terms are generally defined in other ways; but they are important in the context of environmental policy making. There are three principal criteria by which the three kinds of instrument can be distinguished: their purpose, their degree of universality, and the department of government that administers them.

The principal purpose of a *tax* is to raise revenue. A tax is a universal measure: it is paid in exactly the same way by a very large number of economic actors across the economy. The revenues raised are consequently substantial. Tax rates are set in the annual government Budget, and the revenues are collected by the Treasury.

By contrast, a *charge* — in the sense being used here[2] — is an administrative measure whose primary purpose is to change behaviour, not to raise revenue. Charges are levied on a relatively small number of actors in very specific circumstances, possibly at different rates. Charge rates are set by an individual environment department or agency, which is then able to use the revenues as it decides. They do not go to the Treasury. The revenues are generally used for further environmental improvement, either by direct hypothecation as subsidy to the firms on whom the charge is levied, or for some other associated expenditure.

The third kind of instrument is here called a *fee*. This is a payment made in return for the provision of a specific government service. Its purpose is to cover the costs of providing that service. In the environmental context, fees are often paid to environment departments or agencies to cover the context of licensing and regulation. They are not intended to raise additional revenue over and above this,[3] and like charges they tend to be paid by a relatively small number of actors in specific regulated fields.

Given these definitions, the question then is: what kind of instruments are being proposed by the advocates of financial incentives? In the first place, very few of them are fees; environmental licensing fees *have* been widely proposed and introduced, but — precisely because they are simply payments to cover the cost of government services — they are relatively uncontroversial.

Some financial incentives are clearly charges. Thus air and water pollution levies are designed to change firms' environmental behaviour. They are imposed on a very specific and rather small number of discharging companies. Moreover they vary according to the particular circumstances of the pollution — firms located on different estuaries or in areas of different air quality will pay different rates. In nearly all cases they are therefore set and the revenues collected by an environment department or agency, not by the Treasury. In most cases, the revenues are then hypothecated, that is, used by that department or agency for further environmental improvement.

By contrast, some proposed incentives clearly fall into the 'tax' category. Levies on domestic and commercial energy and on petrol would be paid by practically everyone, at universal rates. Because of the volume of consumption, the revenues would be very large, and the macro-economic effects pervasive. They could therefore not avoid being fiscal measures, administered by the Treasury. (Indeed, revenues from an energy/carbon tax would be so large that it is almost always assumed that other taxes would be reduced in compensation.)

But other proposed measures could be either charges or taxes. For example, a landfill levy is normally discussed as if it were an administrative charge, its primary purpose to reduce the volume of waste produced and to increase the rate of recycling, and its rate therefore set by the environment department. But solid waste is a pervasive environmental effect caused by all economic actors, both domestic and commercial. Moreover the large amount of waste produced means that the revenues accruing from a levy could be very large. So it could just as easily be regarded as a tax, its rate set and its revenues received by the Treasury. Road use has similar characteristics, so motorway tolls could also fall into either category. They could either be a charge levied by the transport department, the revenues hypothecated for expenditure on (say) public transport; or a tax levied by the Treasury to add to general government revenues.

And herein lies the rub. For there is potentially a major conflict emerging between the possible purposes of financial incentives. Orthodox environmental economists, most environmentalists and virtually all of the business lobby are interested in environmental *charges*. They want incentives to change behaviour: to reduce environmental damage. They therefore wish to see such measures

LIVERPOOL JOHN MOORES UNIVERSITY
LEARNING SERVICES

introduced (if at all) as part of the wider package of environmental control, integrated coherently with other regulatory and public spending instruments. It naturally makes sense therefore for financial incentives to be in the control of those government departments (environment, transport, industry, etc.) that are responsible for the wider policy framework in each field. Thus a landfill levy would be handled as part of a coherent policy towards waste, including measures to encourage minimisation and recycling, etc; road pricing would be part of an integrated transport strategy that included land use planning and investment in public transport; and so on. Perhaps most importantly, the rates at which the charges were set would reflect their purpose: either to change behaviour directly, or to raise revenues that would be hypothecated for spending on environmental improvement.

But this is not how the Treasury sees it at all. Their interest in financial incentives is purely as *taxes* — as sources of revenue that would go straight to the Treasury. There would be no question of charge rates being set by other departments — they would be part of the Budget. This, of course, frightens both industry and environmentalists, though for different reasons. The former foresee their environmental activities being regarded as cash cows for the Treasury, with ever higher rates of tax. The latter fear that once the Treasury was dependent on environmental revenues it would have a vested interest in ensuring that environmental damage continued. (They cite the alleged reluctance of governments to act against smoking, because the revenues from tobacco tax are so large.)

The upshot is that the next few years may see an interesting and unexpected alliance of business leaders and environmental organisations. Both groups will support (if new controls are needed) the introduction of environmental charges, controlled by environmental departments and hypothecated for environmental improvement. But they will oppose proposals for Treasury-controlled environmental taxes (particularly energy taxes), which do little to change environmental behaviour and whose purpose is simply to raise general revenue.

## The Opposition Parties

This potential alliance may lead to some discomfort for the British opposition parties, who will find themselves on the side of the Treasury. This is because both Labour and the Liberal Democrats (1993) are also now flirting with the idea of environmental taxes — *not* directly as a means of environmental control, but specifically as a means of raising government revenue.

The thinking behind this is simple enough. Both the opposition parties, but especially Labour, are widely perceived (and perceive themselves) as having a problem. They wish to raise government spending on employment measures, education, the health service and the welfare state. But this requires higher taxation, and the Tories have been so successful in instilling a culture of low taxation that the British people will not vote for any increase in income tax. The opposition parties must therefore either abandon their spending plans in order to get elected, or stick to them and be defeated again. Or — and this is why they are interested in the environmental debate — they must find some other way of raising taxes.

What both parties are now looking at — the Liberal Democrats in public, Labour as yet only behind the scenes — is a shift in the burden of taxation away from labour, savings and income, towards energy, resources, waste and pollution. Such a shift could only be gradual at first, but the intended purpose is unmistakable. Taxation should be raised on environmentally damaging activities that society does not like rather than on those — employment, savings, income earning — that it does. It may even be possible, the policy analysts suggest, for income tax to be *reduced* if environmental taxes can be raised sufficiently to compensate. An energy tax is the obvious candidate as the major revenue raiser. The possibility of over-compensation, so that the total tax take can be increased, has not been overlooked.

The rationale here is not just electoral. There is both some impeccable neoclassical economics and some radical green theory in there too. The economics is based on the recognition that environmental damage is a negative externality, and taxing it is therefore a correction of a market distortion. By contrast employment, savings and income are positive goods whose taxation, though perhaps necessary, is economically inefficient. Any shift in the burden of taxation will therefore generate overall efficiency gains.

The green argument is that such a shift in the burden of taxation, if taken far enough, will change the structure of the economy. Energy and resource use, pollution and waste would become more expensive, and labour would become cheaper. It would therefore become more profitable to employ people than to use energy and resource-intensive and polluting technologies. The structure of the economy would change, leading to higher employment, an increase in labour-intensive sectors, and a reduction in environment-intensive ones.[4]

The Labour Party is still some way off agreeing to such proposals and making them public, though the Liberal Democrats have already done so. But already the obstacles have appeared. One was already evident: an energy tax would impose significant costs on certain heavy manufacturing industries, which might damage their competitive position. The European Community's proposals for a carbon-based energy tax — now shelved — exempted such industries for this reason. But the other obstacle has been created by the Conservative Government.

In April 1993 the government announced in its Budget that from 1994 VAT (sales tax) would be levied on domestic fuel. It needed to raise money to reduce its Budget deficit; playing the green card, it also argued that an energy tax would help to cut carbon dioxide emissions. The uproar was instantaneous and by the end of 1993 had not declined. In Britain nearly 6 million households, many of them pensioners, suffer from what is known as 'fuel poverty', that is, they are too poor, and their homes are too badly insulated, to keep warm. Every winter thousands of elderly people die from hypothermia and other cold-related diseases, and many households are plagued by respiratory and other illnesses caused by damp. Taxing domestic fuel, by 8 per cent in the first year, and then 17.5 per cent from the second, was certain to make this already intolerable situation much worse.

For the opposition parties there was only one possible response. They condemned the measure. Environment spokespeople for both Labour and the Liberal Democrats did try to argue that they were not opposed to taxing energy in principle, it was just this particular form. If a program of investment in insulation and more efficient heating systems were introduced, energy prices could rise and people would still pay less — and be warmer. Such a program would even pay for itself. But such subtleties were crowded out by the simple soundbites of opposition. It will be very difficult now for either of the opposition parties to come out in favour of any kind of energy taxation.

How these conflicts will be resolved promises to be one of the more interesting questions in British politics over the next decade. Some financial incentives will be relatively uncontroversial — both Labour and the Liberal Democrats will have no trouble supporting various kinds of pollution charges. But others will cause the same problems as VAT on domestic fuel, raising bitter potential conflicts between environmental and social objectives.

In many parts of Britain there are already water shortages, and these seem likely to spread over the coming years. Should Labour and the Liberal Democrats support a shift from flat-rate water charges to water metering and charging according to use? This would create incentives to save water, but might well lead to higher water costs for poorer family households. Urban and motorway traffic congestion is now reaching crisis proportions, with growth forecasts that clearly cannot be accommodated by the existing road system and increasing damage to health from air pollution. Should the opposition parties support road pricing? This would force the polluter to pay, but it would also restrict mobility for the poorest households while allowing the rich to carry on driving and polluting.

These potential conflicts are not insoluble. There are ways of improving the environment that are paid for primarily by better off households rather than poorer ones. Energy and water tariffs can be adjusted, for example, so that the first units — those to which people have a 'right' — are cheap, with excessive consumption very expensive. Transport policy can be based on providing local services that reduce the need to travel and public transport that *improves* the mobility of the poor (who do not have cars). But solutions such as these are complex, detailed, and prone to be misrepresented in the simple slogans that pass for politics. To the orthodox economist, financial incentives tend to look like straightforward, rational solutions to basic externality problems. The real world is rather different.

# Endnotes

1. *The Guardian*, 8.5.93. The business lobby's view was put in its response to the government's proposals for carbon dioxide reduction.
2. In some other contexts and jurisdictions, a 'charge' is sometimes treated as being synonymous with a 'fee' for service; in this discussion, I draw a distinction between a charge and a fee. I reserve the term 'fee' as a payment in return for particular government services.
3. In Australia, the imposition of excise duties (i.e. sales taxes on goods) is an exclusive power of the Federal Government under the Constitution. If any state imposes fees that are disproportionate to the service provided, such 'fees' can be in danger of being characterised as a sales tax in disguise and therefore will be declared unconstitutional by the High Court of Australia.
4. A shift in the structure of taxation on these lines has been explored in von Weizsacker and Jesinghaus (1992) and Repetto et al. (1992).

# References

*The Guardian*. (1993) 8 May.

Her Majesty's Government. (1990) *This Common Inheritance*, HMSO, London.

Her Majesty's Government. (1992) *Second Annual Review of the Environment White Paper*, HMSO, London.

Liberal Democrats. (1993) *Taxing Pollution Not People*, London.

Pearce, D. Markandya, A. and Barbier, E. (1989) *Blueprint for a Green Economy*, Earthscan, London.

Pezzey, J. (1988) 'Market Mechanisms of Pollution Control: "Polluter Pays", Economic and Practical Aspects' in R.K. Turner (ed.), *Sustainable Environmental Management: Principles and Practice*, Belhaven Press, London.

Repetto, R., Dower, R.C., Jenkins, R. and Goeghagen, J. (1992) *Green Fees: How A Tax Shift Can Work for the Environment and the Economy*, World Resources Institute, Washington DC.

von Weizsacker, E.U. and Jesinghaus, J. (1992) *Ecological Tax Reform*, Zed Books, London.

# 6

# *Economic Prescriptions for Environmental Problems: Lessons from the United States and Continental Europe*

## Robert W. Hahn

It is not easy to sit in an ivory tower and think of ways to help solve the world's environmental problems. As one who frequently engages in this exercise, I can attest to this fact. One of the dangers with ivory tower theorising is that it is easy to lose sight of the actual set of problems that need to be solved, and the range of potential solutions. In my view, this loss of sight has become increasingly evident in the theoretical structure underlying environmental economics, which often emphasises elegance at the expense of realism.

In this chapter, I will argue that both normative and positive theorising could greatly benefit from a careful examination of the results of recent innovative approaches to environmental management. The particular set of policies examined here involve two tools that have received widespread support from the economics community: marketable permits and emission charges (Pigou 1932; Dales 1968; Kneese and Schultze 1975). Both of these tools represent ways to induce businesses to search for lower cost methods of achieving environmental standards. They stand in stark contrast to the predominant command-and-control approach in which a regulator specifies the technology a firm must use to comply with regulations. Under highly restrictive conditions, it can be shown that both of the economic approaches share the desirable feature that any gains in environmental quality will be obtained at the lowest possible cost (Baumol and Oates 1975).

Until the 1960s, these tools only existed on blackboards and in academic journals, as products of the fertile imagination of academics. However, some countries have recently begun to explore the use of these tools as part of a broader strategy for managing environmental problems. This chapter chronicles the experience with both marketable permits and emission charges. It also provides a selective analysis of a variety of applications in the United States and Continental Europe and shows how the actual use of these tools tends to depart from the role that economists have conceived for them.

# The Selection of Environmental Instruments

In thinking about the design and implementation of policies, it is generally assumed that policy makers can choose from a variety of 'instruments' for achieving specified environmental quality objectives. The selection of instruments for addressing environmental quality can be divided into two broad categories: quantity mechanisms and pricing mechanisms. Table 6.1 provides a broad overview of these mechanisms.

**Table 6.1**  Mechanisms for environmental control

| |
|---|
| **I. Quantity mechanisms** |
|     A. Standards |
|         1. Technology-based standards |
|         2. Performance standards |
|     B. Market approaches |
|         1. Marketable permits |
|         2. Reducing market barriers |
| |
| **II. Pricing mechanisms** |
|     A. Taxes and charges |
|     B. Subsidies or subsidy elimination |
|     C. Marginal cost pricing in regulated industries |

*Source*: Hahn (1993, 115)

Standards are the dominant instrument for environmental control in the United States and throughout most of the developed world. Technology-based standards, which involve the specification of particular technologies (e.g scrubbers to control sulfur dioxide emissions), are sometimes referred to as 'command-and-control' regulation because they leave firms with little flexibility in meeting environmental targets. Performance-based standards are more flexible than technology-based standards insofar as they define a particular performance measure (e.g. car exhaust emission specifications) and allow firms to choose the best means of meeting the standard.

Market approaches allow firms considerably more flexibility than technology-based standards while also providing, in theory at least, continuing incentives for innovation. The implementation of marketable permits involves several steps. First, a target level of environmental quality is established. Next, this level of environmental quality is defined in terms of total allowable emissions. Permits are then allocated to firms, with each permit enabling the owner to emit a specified amount of pollution. Firms are allowed to trade these permits among themselves. Assuming firms minimise their total production costs, and the market for these permits is competitive, it can be shown that the overall cost of achieving the environmental standard will be minimised (Montgomery 1972). Marketable permits are generally thought of as a 'quantity' instrument because they ration a fixed supply of a commodity, in this case, pollution.

The reduction of market barriers can also promote conservation and more efficient resource use. For example, electricity markets could be improved by lowering the entry barriers for firms wishing to supply electricity and by introducing competitive bidding on new capacity. US state and federal policy appears to be moving towards allowing a more competitive generation sector.

The polar opposite of quantity instruments are pricing instruments, such as taxes, charges and subsidies. Instead of limiting the quantity of output of pollutants, pricing instruments charge polluters a fixed amount for each unit of pollution, or in the case of subsidies, encourage environmental improvements (e.g. tax credits for developing more environmentally benign technologies). A third mechanism would have regulators set prices on the basis of marginal cost as distinct from average cost. In many regulated industries, particularly energy markets (e.g. gas and electricity), prices tend to reflect average costs.

In each case, pricing instruments provide firms with an incentive to economise on the amount of pollution they produce (or resources they consume). If all firms are charged the same price for pollution, then marginal costs of abatement are equated across firms, and this result implies that the resulting level of pollution is reached in a cost-minimising way.

The environmental economics literature generally focuses on the selection of instruments that minimise the overall cost of achieving prescribed environmental objectives, particularly marketable permits and emissions charges. Economists have attempted to estimate the effectiveness of these approaches. Work by Plott (1983) and Hahn (1983) reveals that implementation of these ideas in a laboratory setting leads to marked increases in efficiency levels over traditional forms of regulation, such as setting standards for each individual source of pollution. The work based on simulations using actual costs and environmental data reveals a similar story. For example, in a review of several studies examining the potential for marketable permits, Tietenberg (1985, 43–44) found that potential control costs could be reduced by more than 90 per cent in some cases. Naturally, these results are subject to the usual cautions that a competitive market actually must exist for them to hold true. Perhaps, more importantly, the results assume that it is possible to easily monitor and enforce a system of permits or taxes. The subsequent analysis will suggest that the capacity to monitor and enforce can dramatically affect the choice of instruments.

Following the development of a normative theory of instrument choice, a handful of scholars began to explore reasons why environmental instruments are actually selected. This positive environmental literature tends to emphasise the potential winners and losers from environmental policies as a way of explaining the conditions under which we will observe such policies. For example, Buchanan and Tullock (1975) argue that the widespread use of source-specific standards rather than a fee can be explained by looking at the potential profitability of the affected industry under the two regimes. After presenting the various case studies, I will review some of the insights from positive theory and see how they square with the facts.

The formal results in the positive and normative theory of environmental economics are elegant. Unfortunately, they are not immediately applicable, since virtually none of the systems examined below exhibits the purity of the instruments that are the subject of theoretical inquiry. The presentation here highlights those instruments that show a marked resemblance to marketable permits or emission fees. Together, the two approaches to pollution control span a wide array of environmental problems, including toxic substances, air pollution, water pollution and land disposal.

## Marketable Permits

Marketable permits are now receiving increased attention as a policy tool in both developed and developing countries. This section reviews five applications in the United States: the control of water pollution on a river in Wisconsin; the trading of emissions rights of various pollutants regulated under the *Clean Air Act*; the trading of lead used in gasoline; the control of non-point sources of pollution in Colorado; and the 1990 amendments to the *Clean Air Act* dealing with acid rain. The performance of these programs exhibits dramatic differences, which can be traced back to the rules used to implement the different mechanisms.

### Wisconsin Fox River Water Permits

In 1981, the state of Wisconsin implemented an innovative program aimed at controlling biological oxygen demand (BOD) on a part of the Fox River (Novotny 1986, 11).[1] The program was designed to allow for the limited trading of marketable discharge permits. The primary objective was to allow firms greater flexibility in abatement options while still maintaining environmental quality. The program is administered by the state of Wisconsin in accord with the federal *Water Pollution Control Act*. Firms are issued five-year permits, which define their wasteload allocation. This allocation defines the initial distribution of permits for each firm.

Early studies estimated that substantial savings, to the order of US$7 million per year, could result after implementing this trading system (O'Neil 1983, 225). However, actual cost savings have been minimal. Since the start of the program, there has only been one trade. Given the initial fanfare about this system, its performance to date has been disappointing.

A closer look at the nature of the market and the rules for trading reveals that the result should not have been totally unexpected. The regulations are aimed at two types of dischargers: pulp and paper plants and municipal waste treatment plants. David and Joeres (1983) note that the pulp and paper plants have an oligopolistic structure, and thus may not behave as competitive firms in the permit market. Moreover, it is difficult to know how the municipal utilities will perform under this set of rules, since they are subject to public utility regulation (Hahn and Noll 1983). Trading is also limited by location. There are two points on the river where pollution tends to peak, and firms are divided into 'clusters' so that trading will not increase BOD at either of these points. There are only about six or seven firms in each cluster (Patterson 1987). Consequently, markets for wasteload allocations may be quite thin.

In addition, Novotny (1986) has argued that several restrictions on transfers may have had a negative impact on potential trading. Any transaction between firms requires modifying or reissuing permits. Transfers must be for at least a year; however, the life of the permit is only five years. Moreover, parties must waive any rights to the permit after it expires, and it is unclear how the new allocation will be affected by trading. These conditions create great uncertainty over the future value of the property right. Added to the problems created by these rules are the restrictions on eligibility for trades. Firms are required to justify the 'need' for permits. This effectively limits transfers to new dischargers, plants that are expanding, and treatment plants that cannot meet the requirements, despite their best efforts. Trades that only reduce operating costs are not allowed. With all the uncertainty and high transactions costs, it is not surprising that trading has got off to a very slow start.

While the marketable permit system for the Fox River was being hailed as a success by economists, the paper mills did not enthusiastically support the idea (Novotny 1986, 15). Nor have the mills chosen to explore this option once it has been implemented. Indeed, by almost any measure, this limited permit trading represents a minor part of the regulatory structure. The mechanism builds on a large regulatory infrastructure where permits specifying treatment and operating rules lie at the centre. The new marketable permits approach retains many features of the existing standards-based approach. The initial allocations are based on the status quo, calling for equal percentage reductions from specified limits. This 'grandfathering' approach has a great deal of political appeal for existing firms. New firms must continue to meet more stringent requirements than old firms, and firms must meet specified technological standards before trading is allowed.

*Emissions Trading*
By far, the most significant and far-reaching program in the United States is the emissions trading policy. Started in the 1970s, the policy attempts to provide greater flexibility to firms charged with controlling air pollutant emissions.[2] Because the program represents a radical departure in the approach to pollution regulation, it has come under close scrutiny by a variety of interest groups. Environmentalists have been particularly critical. These criticisms notwithstanding, the EPA Administrator Lee Thomas (1986) characterised the program as 'one of EPA's most impressive accomplishments'.

Emissions trading has four distinct elements. Netting, the first program element, was introduced in 1974. Netting allows a firm that creates a new source of emissions in a plant to avoid the stringent emission limits that would normally apply by reducing emissions from another source in the plant. Thus, net emissions from the plant do not increase significantly. A firm using netting is only allowed to obtain the necessary emission credits from its own sources. This is called *internal trading* because the transaction involves only one firm. Netting is subject to approval at the state level, not the federal.

Offsets, the second element of emissions trading, are used by new emission sources in 'non-attainment areas'.[3] The *Clean Air Act* specified that no new emission sources would be allowed in non-attainment areas after the original 1975 deadlines for meeting air quality standards passed. Concern that this prohibition would stifle economic growth in these areas prompted the EPA to institute the offset rule. This rule specified that new sources would be allowed to locate in non-attainment areas, but only if they 'offset' their new emissions by reducing emissions from existing sources by even larger amounts. The offsets could be obtained through internal trading, just as with netting. However, they could also be obtained from other firms directly, which is called *external trading*.

'Bubbles', though apparently considered by the EPA to be the centerpiece of emissions trading, were not allowed until 1979. The name derives from the placing of an imaginary bubble over a plant, with all emissions exiting at a single point from the bubble. A bubble allows a firm to sum the emission limits from individual sources of a pollutant in a plant, and to adjust the levels of control applied to different sources so long as this aggregate limit is not exceeded. Bubbles apply to existing sources. Initially, every bubble had to be approved at the federal level as an amendment to a state's implementation plan. In 1981, the EPA approved a 'generic rule' for bubbles in New Jersey, which allowed the state to give final approval for bubbles. Since then, several other states have followed suit.

Banking, the fourth element of emissions trading, was developed in conjunction with the bubble policy. Banking allows firms to save emission reductions above and beyond permit requirements for future use in emissions trading. While EPA action was initially required to allow banking, the development of banking rules and the administration of banking programs has been left to the states.

The performance of emissions trading can be measured in several ways. A summary evaluation that assesses the impact of the program on abatement costs and environmental quality is provided in Table 6.2.

For each emissions trading activity, an estimate of cost savings, environmental quality effect, and the number of trades is given. In

**Table 6.2**  Summary of emission trading activity during
1974–1986

| Activity | Estimated number of internal transactions | Estimated number of external transactions | Estimated cost savings (US$ millions) | Environmental quality impact |
|---|---|---|---|---|
| Netting | 5 000 to 12 000 | None | $26 to $300 in permitting costs: $500 to $12 000 in emission control costs | Insignificant in individual cases Probably insignificant in aggregate |
| Offsets | 1 800 | 200 | See text | Probably insignificant |
| Bubbles: • federally approved | 40 | 2 | $300 | Insignificant |
| • state approved | 89 | 0 | $135 | Insignificant |
| Banking | Less than 100 | Less than 20 | Small | Insignificant |

*Source*: Hahn and Hester (1989b)

each case, the estimates are for the entire life of the program. As
can be seen from the table, the level of activity under various
programs varies dramatically. More netting transactions have
taken place than any other type, but all of these have necessarily
been internal. The wide range placed on this estimate, 5000 to
12 000, reflects the uncertainty about the precise level of this
activity. An estimated 2000 offset transactions have taken place,
of which only 10 per cent have been external. Fewer than 150
bubbles have been approved. Of these, almost twice as many have
been approved by states under generic rules than have been
approved at the federal level, and only two are known to have
involved external trades. For banking, the figures listed are for the
number of times firms have withdrawn banked emission credits
for sale or use. While no estimates of the exact numbers of such
transactions can be made, upper bound estimates of 100 for
internal trades and twenty for external trades indicate the fact that
there has been relatively little activity in this area.

Cost savings for both netting and bubbles are substantial.
Netting is estimated to have resulted in the most cost savings,

with a total of between US$525 million and over US$12 billion from both permitting and emissions control cost savings.[4] By allowing new or modified sources to locate in areas that are highly polluted, offsets confer a major economic benefit on firms that use them. While the size of this economic benefit is not easily estimated, it is probably in the hundreds of millions. Federally approved bubbles have resulted in savings estimated at US$300 million, while state bubbles have resulted in an estimated US$135 million in cost savings. Average savings from federally approved bubbles are higher than those for state approved bubbles. Average savings from bubbles are higher than those from netting, which reflects the fact that bubble savings may be derived from several emissions sources in a single transaction, while netting usually involves cost savings at a single source. Finally, the cost savings from the use of banking cannot be estimated, but is necessarily small given the small number of banking transactions that have occurred.

The performance evaluation of emissions trading activities reveals a mixed bag of accomplishments and disappointments. The program has clearly afforded many firms flexibility in meeting emission limits, and this flexibility has resulted in significant aggregate cost savings — in the billions of dollars. However, these cost savings have been realised almost entirely from internal trading. They fall far short of the potential savings that could be realised if there were more external trading. While cost savings have been substantial, the program has led to little or no net change in the level of emissions relative to the emissions that would have resulted with less flexible regulation.

The evolution of the emissions trading can best be understood in terms of a struggle over the nature and distribution of property rights. Emissions trading can be seen as a strategy by regulators to provide industry with increased flexibility while offering environmentalists continuing progress toward environmental quality goals. Meeting these two objectives requires a careful balancing act. To provide industry with greater flexibility, the EPA has attempted to define a set of property rights that places few restrictions on their use. However, at the same time, the EPA had to be sensitive to the concerns of environmentalists and avoid giving businesses too clear a property right to their existing level of pollution. The conflicting interests of these two groups have led regulators to create a set of policies that are specifically designed to de-emphasise the explicit nature of the property right. The high transactions costs associated with external trading have induced firms to eschew this option in favor of internal trading or no trading at all.

Like the preceding example of the Fox River, emissions trading is best viewed as an incremental departure from the existing approach. Property rights were grandfathered. Most trading has been internal, and the structure of the *Clean Air Act*, including its requirement that new sources be controlled more stringently, was largely left intact.

*Lead Trading*

Lead trading stands in stark contrast to the preceding two marketable permit approaches. It comes by far the closest to an economist's ideal of a freely functioning market. The purpose of the lead trading program was to allow gasoline refiners greater flexibility during a period when the amount of lead in gasoline was being significantly reduced. (For a more detailed analysis of the performance of the lead trading program, see Hahn and Hester 1989a.)

Unlike many other programs, the lead trading program was scheduled to have a fixed life from the outset. Inter-refinery trading of lead credits was permitted in 1982. Banking of lead credits was initiated in 1985. The trading program was terminated at the end of 1987. Initially, the period for trading was defined in terms of quarters. No banking of credits was allowed. Three years after initiating the program, limited banking was permitted, which allowed firms to carry over rights to subsequent quarters. Banking has been used extensively by firms since its inception.

The program is notable for its lack of discrimination among different sources, such as new and old sources. It is also notable for its rules regarding the creation of credits. Lead credits are created on the basis of existing standards. A firm does not gain any extra credits for having been a large producer of leaded gasoline in the past. Nor is it penalised for being a small producer. The creation of lead credits is based solely on current production levels and average lead content. For example, if the standard were 1.1 grams per gallon, and a firm produced a 100 gallons of gasoline, it would receive rights entitling it to produce or sell up to 110 (100 × 1.1) grams of lead. To the extent that current production levels are correlated with past production levels, the system acknowledges the existing distribution of property rights. However, this linkage is less explicit than those made in other trading programs.[5]

The success of the program is difficult to measure directly. It appears to have had little impact on environmental quality. This is because the amount of lead in gasoline is routinely reported by refiners and is easily monitored. The effect the program has had on refinery costs is not readily available. In proposing the rule for banking of lead rights, the EPA estimated that resulting savings to refiners would be approximately US$228 million (US EPA 1985a). Since banking activity has been somewhat higher than anticipated by the EPA, it is likely that actual cost savings will exceed this amount. No specific estimate of the actual cost savings resulting from lead trading have been made by the EPA.

The level of trading activity has been high, far surpassing levels observed in other environmental markets. In 1985, over half of the refineries participated in trading. Approximately 15 per cent of the total lead rights used were traded. Approximately 35 per cent of available lead rights were banked for future use or trading (US EPA 1985b, 1986). In comparison, volumes of emissions trading have averaged well below 1 per cent of the potential emissions that could be traded.

From the standpoint of creating a workable regulatory mechanism that induces cost savings, the lead market has to be viewed as a success. Refiners, though initially lukewarm about this alternative, have made good use of this program. It stands out amidst a stream of incentive-based programs as the 'noble' exception in that it conforms most closely to the economists' notion of a smoothly functioning market.

Given the success of this market in promoting cost savings over a period in which lead was being reduced, it is important to understand why the market was successful. The lead market had two important features that distinguished it from other markets in environmental credits. The first was that the amount of lead in gasoline could be easily monitored with the existing regulatory apparatus. The second was that the program was implemented after agreement had been reached about basic environmental goals. In particular, there was already widespread agreement that lead was to be phased out of gasoline. This suggests that the success in lead trading may not be easily transferred to other applications in which monitoring is a problem, or environmental goals are poorly defined. Nonetheless, the fact that this market worked well provides ammunition for proponents of market-based incentives for environmental regulation.

### Non-point Sources of Pollution
An interesting potential application for marketable permits has arisen in the area of non-point source pollution.[6] In 1984, Colorado implemented a program that would allow limited trading between point and non-point sources for controlling phosphorus loadings in Dillon Reservoir (Elmore et al. 1984). Firms receive an allocation based on their past production and the holding

capacity of the lake. At this point in time, no trading between point and non-point sources has occurred.

As in the case of emissions trading, point sources are required to make use of the latest technology before they are allowed to trade. The conventional permitting system is used as a basis for trading. Moreover, trades between point and non-point sources are required to take place on a two for one basis. This means for each gram of phosphorus emitted from a point source under a trade, 2 grams must be reduced from a non-point source. Annual cost savings are projected to be about US$800 000 (Kashmanian et al. 1986, 14); however, projected savings are not always a good indicator of actual savings, as was illustrated in the case of the Fox River.

EPA is also considering using marketable permits as a way of promoting efficiency in the control of chlorofluorocarbons and halons, which lead to the depletion of stratospheric ozone.[7] In its notice of proposed rulemaking, the EPA suggested grandfathering permits to producers based on their 1986 production levels, and allowing them to be freely traded. This approach is similar to earlier approaches the EPA adopted for emissions trading and lead trading.

*The 1990 Amendments to the* Clean Air Act
The growth in public concern over environmental problems during the late 1980s prompted President Bush to introduce significant amendments to the *Clean Air Act* in 1990 to deal with acid rain, smog and air toxics.[8] The most innovative feature of the amendments has been the heavy reliance placed on market-based incentives to reduce emissions from electric utilities (mainly coal-fired plants) that contribute to acid rain. The acid rain amendments in Title IV of the Act seek to reduce annual sulfur dioxide emissions by ten million tons by the year 2000 (from a 1980 baseline) and to reduce nitrogen oxide emissions to two million tons (from their projected levels in the year 2000).

By giving utilities considerable flexibility in choosing how to achieve the specified emission reductions (i.e. they may buy, sell, trade or bank their allowances) considerable cost savings are expected. The Act established a two-phase program. Phase I — 1 January 1995 until 1 January 2000 — affects 110 of the highest emitting electric utilities in the United States (other plants and industrial sources not affected by the program are given the option of participating) (Hahn and May 1994, 3). Phase II begins in 2000, when the program will be expanded to include most existing fossil-fired electric generating units (Hahn and May 1994, 3). The affected utilities are allocated tradable allowances based on their past fuel usage and statutory emission limits. Allowances are dated by years and may be used in the relevant year or 'banked' for use in subsequent years. In addition to allowing private trades, the Act enables the EPA to hold annual auctions — intended partly as a mechanism for helping to provide a price signal in the private market and partly to provide a supply of allowances to new entrants in the market.

Economic theory would predict that, in a competitive market, the price of an allowance in any given period would equal or exceed the discounted price of an allowance for a subsequent period (a relationship that follows directly from the ability of firms to bank allowances). The prices would also reflect the marginal costs of control in their respective periods, appropriately discounted (Hahn and May 1994, 6). However, this theory assumes settled rules, the absence of political biases and low transaction costs.

To date, the level of trading has been lower than predicted. Nonetheless, the behaviour of the allowance market suggests that prices are likely to be linked between Phases I and II in a predictable manner that is broadly consistent with economic theory. However, market performance is crucially affected by the trading rules that are adopted by the EPA and 48 state regulatory agencies subject to different political pressures. It is therefore hardly surprising that some potential cost savings have not been realised given that utilities already operate in highly regulated environments and there are differences in regulations across states. Although all of the potential cost savings that are theoretically available have not been achieved, the greater flexibility provided by allowance trading has produced greater cost savings than would otherwise be the case under alternative command-and-control regulation (for a more detailed discussion, see Hahn and May 1994).

One of the concerns raised by environmentalists is that allowance trading may produce 'hotspots' in ecologically sensitive areas or that it may otherwise generate an unfair distribution of environmental quality across different regions (Hahn and May 1994, 10). However, if the pre-1990 *Clean Air Act* is taken as the relevant baseline, then the regional shifts in emissions due to trading are likely to be relatively trivial compared with the overall reductions that are achieved by the Act (1994, 11). Moreover, the experience to date indicates that the total volume of Phase I trades, and hence the distributional impact, has been relatively small when compared with the total stock of allowances, although this might change in the future (1994, 11–12).

Estimating the size of the cost savings remains an important exercise for a proper appreciation of the future success of the program. However, such estimates may prove to be less important for the implementation of other market-based initiatives involved with the acid rain program than the political *perceptions* of the major interest groups. For example, if environmentalists believe that environmental goals are not being met, or if governments frequently change the rules for trading, then the program is unlikely to pass the 'rigours of the political market' (Hahn and May 1994, 14). While it is too early to predict how this market approach will be judged, it appears that leading members of the business community and environmental community are satisfied with the results.

The behaviour of the allowance market to date is broadly consistent with the predictions of economic theory. The data show that prices have declined over time and that predicted and actual prices are converging. In addition, there appears to be an economic link between the price of Phase I and Phase II allowances. Clearly, economic theory has much to offer in demonstrating that there are real efficiency gains to be had by the introduction of greater flexibility in the allowance market.

The applications covered in this section illustrate that there is a rich array of mechanisms that come under the heading marketable permits. The common element seems to be that the primary motivation behind marketable permits is to provide increased flexibility in meeting prescribed environmental objectives. This flexibility, in turn, allows firms to take advantage of opportunities to reduce their expenditures on pollution control without sacrificing environmental quality. However, the rules of the marketable permits can sometimes be so restrictive that the flexibility they offer is more imaginary than real. The increased interest in market-based approaches can be expected to continue into the future. President Clinton has voiced his support for using flexible approaches for environmental problem solving. Recently, the Clinton administration held a high-level conference aimed at identifying 'win-win' situations for the environment and the economy. Market-based approaches were central to this discussion.

## Charges in Practice

Charge systems in four countries are examined in this section. Examples are drawn from France, Germany, the Netherlands, and the United States. Particular systems were selected because they were thought to be significant either in their scope, their effect on revenues, or their impact on the cost-effectiveness of environmental regulation. While the focus is on water effluent charges, a variety of systems that cover other applications are briefly mentioned at the end of the section.

*Charges in France*
The French have had a system of effluent charges on water pollutants in place since 1969 (Bower et al. 1981). The system is primarily designed to raise revenues, which are then used to help to maintain or improve water quality. Though the application of charges is widespread, they are generally set at low levels.[9] Moreover, charges are rarely based on actual performance. Rather, they are based on the expected level of discharge by various industries. There is no explicit connection between the charge paid by a given discharger and the subsidy received (Bower et al. 1981, 126). However, charges are generally earmarked for use in promoting environmental quality in areas related to the specific charge. The basic mechanism by which these charges improve environmental quality is through judicious earmarking of the revenues for pollution abatement activities.

In evaluating the French charge system, it is important to understand that it is a major, but by no means dominant, part of the French system for managing water quality. Indeed, in terms of total revenues, a sewage tax levied on households and commercial enterprises is larger in magnitude (Bower et al. 1981, 142). Moreover, the sewage tax is assessed on the basis of actual volumes of water used. Like most other charge systems, the charge system in France is based on a system of water quality permits, which places constraints on the type and quantity of effluent a firm may discharge. These permits are required for sources discharging more than some specified quantity (Bower et al. 1981, 130).

Charges appear to be accepted as a way of doing business in France now. They provide a significant source of revenues for water quality control. One of the keys to their initial success appears to have been the gradual introduction and raising of charges. Charges started at a very low level and were gradually raised to current levels (Bower et al. 1981, 22). Moreover, the range of pollutants on which charges are levied has expanded considerably since the initial inception of the charge program.[10]

*Charges in Germany*
The German system of effluent charges is very similar to the French system. Effluent charges cover a wide range of pollutants (Brown and Johnson 1984, 934, 939). The charges are used to cover administrative expenses for water quality management and to subsidise projects that improve water quality (1984, 945). The bills that industry and municipalities pay are generally based on

expected volume and concentration (1984, 934). Charges vary by industry type as well as across municipalities. Charges to municipalities depend on several variables, including size of the municipality, desired level of treatment, and the age of equipment (1984, 938).

Charges have existed in selected areas of Germany for decades (Bower et al. 1981, 299). Management of water quality is delegated to local areas. In 1981, a system of nationwide effluent charges was introduced (Bower et al. 1981, 226). The Federal Government provided the basic framework in its 1976 *Federal Water Act and Effluent Charge Law* (Brown and Johnson 1984, 930). Initially, widespread use of charges was opposed by industry. After losing the initial battle, industry focused on how charges would be determined and their effective date of implementation (Brown and Johnson 1984, 932). While hard data are lacking, there is a general perception that the current system is helping to improve water quality.

*Charges in the Netherlands*
The Netherlands has had a system of effluent charges in place since 1969 (Brown and Bressers 1986, 4). It is one of the oldest and best administered charge systems, and the charges placed on effluent streams are among the highest. In 1983, the effluent charge per person was US$17 in the Netherlands; US$6 in Germany and about US$2 in France (1986, 5). Because of the comparatively high level of charges in the Netherlands, this is a logical place to examine whether charges are having a discernible effect on the level of pollution. Bressers (1983), using a multiple regression approach, argues that charges have made a significant difference in several pollutants. This evidence is also buttressed by surveys of industrial polluters and water board officials, which indicate that charges had a significant impact on firm behaviour (Brown and Bressers 1986, 12–13). This analysis is one of the few existing empirical investigations of the effect of effluent charges on resulting pollution.

The purpose of the charge system in the Netherlands is to raise revenue that is used to finance projects that will improve water quality (Brown and Bressers 1986, 4). Like its counterparts in France and Germany, the approach to managing water quality uses both permits and effluent charges for meeting ambient standards (1986, 2).[11] Permits tend to be uniform across similar dischargers. The system is designed to ensure that water quality will remain the same or get better (1986, 2). Charges are administered both on volume and concentration. Actual levels of discharge are monitored for larger polluters, while small polluters often pay fixed fees unrelated to actual discharge (Bressers 1983, 10).

Charges have exhibited a slow, but steady increase since their inception (Brown and Bressers 1986, 5). This increase in charges is correlated with declining levels of pollutants. Effluent discharge declined from 40 population equivalents in 1969 to 15.3 population equivalents in 1980, and it was projected to decline to 4.4 population equivalents in 1985 (1986, 10). Thus, over 15 years, this measure of pollution declined to the order of 90 per cent.

As in Germany, there was initial opposition from industry to the use of charges. Brown and Bressers (1986, 4) also note opposition from environmentalists, who tend to distrust market-like mechanisms. Nonetheless, charges have enjoyed widespread acceptance in a variety of arenas in the Netherlands.

One interesting feature of the charge system in the Netherlands relates to the differential treatment of new and old plants. In general, newer plants face more stringent regulation than older plants (Brown and Bressers 1986, 10). As we shall see, this is also a dominant theme in American regulation.

## Charges in the United States

The United States has a modest system of user charges levied by utilities that process waste water, encouraged by federal environmental regulations issued by the Environmental Protection Agency (EPA). They are based on both volume and strength, and vary across utilities. In some cases, charges are based on actual discharges, and in others, a rule of thumb, related to average behaviour. In all cases, charges are added on to the existing regulatory system, which relies heavily on permits and standards.

Both industry and consumers are required to pay the charges. The primary purpose for the charges is to raise revenues to help meet the revenue requirements of the treatment plants, which are heavily subsidised by the Federal Government. The direct environmental and economic impact of these charges is apparently small (Boland 1986, 12). They primarily serve as a mechanism to help to defray the costs of the treatment plants. Thus, the charges used in the United States are similar in spirit to the German and French systems already described. However, their size appears to be smaller, and the application of the revenues is more limited.

## Other Fee-based Systems

Several other fee-based systems have not been included in this discussion. Brown (1984) did an analysis of incentive-based systems to control hazardous wastes in Europe and found that a number of countries had adopted systems, some of which had a marked economic effect. The general trend was to use either a tax on waste outputs or a tax on feedstocks that are usually correlated with the level of waste produced. Companies and government officials were interviewed to ascertain the effects of these approaches. In line with economic theory, charges were found to induce firms to increase expenditures on achieving waste reduction through a variety of techniques including reprocessing of materials, treatment, and input and output substitution. Firms also devoted greater attention to separating waste streams because prices for disposal often varied by the type of waste stream.

The United States has a diverse range of taxes imposed on hazardous waste streams. Several states have land disposal taxes in place. Charges exhibit a wide degree of variation across states. For example, in 1984, charges were US$.14/tonne in Wisconsin and US$70.40/tonne in Minnesota (US CBO 1985, 82). Charges for disposal at landfills also vary widely. The effect of these different charges is very difficult to estimate because of the difficulty in obtaining the necessary data on the quantity and quality of waste streams, as well as the economic variables.

*Lessons about the Implementation of Charges*
The preceding analysis reveals that there is a wide array of fee-based systems in place designed to promote environmental quality. In a few cases, the fees were shown to have had a marked effect on firm behaviour; however, in the overwhelming majority of cases studied, the direct economic effect of fees appears to have been small. Several patterns repeat themselves through these examples.

First, the major motivation for implementing emission fees is to raise revenues, which are then usually earmarked for activities that promote environmental quality.[12] Second, most charges are not large enough to have a dramatic impact on the behaviour of polluters. In fact, they are not designed to have such an effect. They are relatively low and not directly related to the behaviour of individual firms and consumers. Third, there is a tendency for charges to increase faster than inflation over time. Presumably, starting out with a relatively low charge is a way of testing the political waters as well as determining whether the instrument will have the desired effects.

# Implementing Market-based Environmental Programs

An examination of the charge and marketable permits schemes reveals that they are rarely, if ever, introduced in their textbook form. Virtually all environmental regulatory systems using charges and marketable permits rely on the existing permitting system. This result should not be very surprising. Most of these approaches were not implemented from scratch. Rather, they were grafted onto regulatory systems in which permits and standards play a dominant role.

Perhaps, as a result of these transaction costs, the level of cost savings resulting from implementing charges and marketable permits is generally far below their theoretical potential. Cost savings can be defined in terms of the savings that would result from meeting a prescribed environmental objective in a less costly manner. As noted earlier, most of the charges to date have not had a major incentive effect. We can infer from this that polluters have not been induced to search for a lower cost mix of meeting environmental objectives as a result of the implementation of charge schemes. Thus, it seems unlikely that charges have performed terribly well on narrow efficiency grounds. The experience on marketable permits is similar. Hahn and Hester (1989b) argue that cost savings for emissions trading fall far short of their theoretical potential. The only apparent exception to this observation is the lead trading program, which has enjoyed very high levels of trading activity.

The example of lead trading leads to another important observation: in general, different charge and marketable permit systems exhibit wide variation in their effect on economic efficiency. On the whole, there is more evidence for cost savings with marketable permits than with charges.

While the charge systems and marketable permit systems rarely perform well in terms of efficiency, it is important to recognise that their performance is broadly consistent with economic theory. This observation may appear to contradict what was said earlier about the departure of these systems from the economic ideal. However, it is really an altogether different observation. It suggests that the performance of the markets and charge systems can be understood in terms of basic economic theory. For example, where barriers to trading are low, more trading is likely to occur. Where charges are high and more directly related to individual actions, they are more likely to affect the behaviour of firms or consumers.

If these instruments are to be measured by their effect on environmental quality, the results are not very impressive. In general, the direct effect of both charges and marketable permits on environmental quality appears to be neutral or slightly positive. The effect of lead trading has been neutral in the aggregate. The effect of emissions trading on environmental quality has probably been neutral or slightly positive. The direct effect of charges on polluter incentives has been modest, although the indirect environmental effect of spending the revenue raised by charges has been significant.

The evidence on charges and marketable permits points to an intriguing conclusion about the nature of these instruments. Charges and marketable permits have played fundamentally different roles in meeting environmental objectives. Charges are used primarily to improve environmental quality by redistributing revenues. Marketable permits are used primarily to promote cost savings.

## Towards a More Complete Theory of Instrument Choice

The positive theory of instrument choice as it relates to pollution control has been greatly influenced by the work of Buchanan and Tullock (1975). They argue that firms will prefer emission standards to emission taxes because standards result in higher profits. Emission standards serve as a barrier to entry to new firms, thus raising existing firms' profits. Charges, on the other hand, do not preclude entry by new firms, and also represent an additional cost to existing firms. Their argument is based on the view that industry is able to exert its preference for a particular instrument because it is more likely to be well-organised than consumers.

While this argument is elegant, it misses two important points. The first is that within particular classes of instruments, there is a great deal of variation in the performance of instruments. The second is that most solutions to problems involve the application of multiple instruments. Thus, while the Buchanan and Tullock theory explains why standards are chosen over an idealised form of taxes, it does little to help to explain the rich array of instruments that are observed in the real world. In particular, under which situations would we be likely to observe different mixes of instruments? Several authors have explored these different issues for instrument choice within this basic framework (Coelho 1976; Yohe 1976; Dewees 1983). The basic insight of this work is that the argument that standards will be preferred to taxes depends on the precise nature of the instruments being compared.

Another weakness in the existing theory is that the instruments are not generally used in the way that is suggested by the theory. Most emissions charges, for example, are used as a revenue-raising device for subsidising abatement activity, but a few also have pronounced direct effects on polluters. Most marketable permit approaches are designed to promote cost savings while maintaining environmental quality. However, the different types of trading schemes perform with widely varying success.

The data from the examples given earlier can be used to begin to piece together some of the elements of a more coherent theory of instrument choice. For example, it is clear that distributional concerns play an important role in the acceptability of user charges. The revenue from such charges is usually earmarked for environmental activities related to those contributions. Thus, charges from a noise surcharge will be used to address noise pollution. Charges for water discharges will be used to construct treatment plants and subsidise industry in building equipment to abate water pollution. This pattern suggests that different industries want to make sure that their contributions are used to address pollution problems for which they are likely to be held accountable. Thus, industry sees it as only fair that, as a whole, they get some benefit from making these contributions.

The 'recycling' of revenues from charges points up the importance of the existing distribution of property rights. This is also true in the case of marketable permits. The 'grandfathering' of rights to existing firms based on the current distribution of rights is an important focal point in many applications of limited markets in pollution rights (Rolph 1983; Welch 1983). All the marketable permit programs in the United States place great importance on the existing distribution of rights.

In short, all of the charge and marketable permit systems described earlier place great importance on the status quo. Charges, when introduced, tend to be phased in. Marketable permits, when introduced, usually are optional in the sense that existing firms can meet standards through trading of permits or by conventional means. In contrast, new or expanding firms are not always afforded the same options. For example, new firms must still purchase emission credits if they choose to locate in a non-attainment area, even if they have purchased state-of-the-art pollution control equipment and will pollute less than existing companies. This is an example of a 'bias' against new sources. While not efficient from an economic viewpoint, this pattern is consistent with the political insight that new sources do not 'vote' while existing sources do.

Though the status quo is important in all applications studied here, it does not, by itself explain the rich variety of instruments that are observed. For example, there has been heated controversy over emissions trading since its inception, but comparatively little controversy over the implementation of lead trading. How can economists begin to understand the difference in attitudes towards these two programs?

There are several important differences between emissions trading and lead trading. In the case of lead standards, there appears to be agreement about the distribution of property rights, and the standard that defined them. Refiners had the right to put lead in gasoline at specified levels during specified time periods. Lead in gasoline was reduced to a very low level at the end of 1987. In contrast to lead, there is great disagreement about the underlying distribution of property rights regarding emissions trading. Environmentalists continue to adhere to the symbolic goal of zero pollution. Industry believes and acts as if its current claims on the environment, without any emission reductions, represent a property right.

In the case of lead trading, output could be relatively easily monitored using the existing regulatory apparatus. This was not so for the case of emissions trading. A new system was set up for evaluating proposed trades. This was, in part, due to existing weaknesses in the current system of monitoring and enforcement. It was also a result of concerns that environmentalists had expressed about the validity of such trades.

The effect that emissions trading was likely to have on environmental quality was much less certain than that of the lead trading program. Some environmentalists viewed emissions trading as a loophole by which industry could forestall compliance, and Hahn and Hester (1989b) found some evidence that bubbles were occasionally used for that purpose. The effects of lead trading were much more predictable. Until 1985, there was no banking, so the overall temporal pattern of lead emissions remained unchanged under the program. With the addition of banking in 1985, this pattern was changed slightly, but within well-defined limits.

To accommodate these differing concerns, different rules were developed for the two cases. In the case of lead trading, rights are traded on a one-for-one basis. In contrast, under emissions trading, rights are not generally traded on a one-for-one basis. Rather, each trade must show a net improvement in environmental quality. In the case of lead, all firms are treated equally from the standpoint of trading. In the case of emissions trading, new firms must meet stringent standards before being allowed to engage in trading.

This comparison suggests that it is possible to gain important insights into the likely performance and choice of instruments by understanding the forces that led to their creation. Analysing the underlying beliefs about property rights to pollution may be vital both for the political success of the measure and for how well it works in terms of pure economic efficiency.

This view of efficiency is similar to, but should not be confused with, the notion of efficiency advanced by Becker (1983). Becker argues that government will tend to choose mechanisms that are more efficient over those that are less efficient in redistributing revenues from less powerful to more powerful groups. To the extent that his argument is testable, I believe it is not consistent with the facts. For example, the United States currently has a policy that directs toxic waste dumps to be cleaned up in priority order. The policy makes no attempt to examine whether a greater risk reduction could be attained with a different allocation of expenditures. Given a finite budget constraint, this policy does not make sense from a purely economic viewpoint. However, it might make sense if environmentalists hoped that more stringent policies would emerge in the future. Or it might make sense if Congress wanted to be perceived as doing the job 'right', even if only a small part of the job got done.

A second example can be drawn from emissions trading. It is possible to design marketable permit systems that are more efficient and ensure better environmental quality over time (Hahn and Noll 1982; Hahn 1990), yet these systems have not been implemented. Environmentalists may be reluctant to embrace market alternatives because they fear it may give a certain legitimacy to the act of polluting. Moreover, they may not believe in the expected results. Thus, for Becker's theory to hold in an absolute sense, it would be necessary to construct fairly complicated utility functions. The problem is that the theory does not explicitly address how choices are made by lobbyists, legislators and bureaucrats (Campos 1987).

These choices may be made in different ways in different countries. How can it be explained, for example, that a large array of countries use fees, while few countries currently use marketable permits for environmental protection? Noll (1983) has argued that the political institutions of different countries can provide important clues about regulatory strategy. In addition, the comparison of lead trading and emissions trading revealed that the very nature of the environmental problem can have an important effect on interest group attitudes.

Interest group attitudes can be expected to vary across countries. In the Netherlands, Opschoor (1986, 15) notes that environmental groups tend to prefer charges while employer groups prefer regulatory instruments. Barde (1986, 10–11) notes that the political 'acceptability' of charges is high in both France and the Netherlands. Nonetheless, some French airlines have refused to pay noise charges because the funds are not being used (1986, 12). In Italy, there has been widespread opposition from industry and interest groups (Panella 1986, 6, 22). While German industry has accepted the notion of charges, some industries have criticised the differential charge rates across jurisdictions. In the United States, environmentalists have shown a marked preference for regulatory instruments, eschewing both charges and marketable permits. These preferences may help to explain the choice of instruments in various countries as well as the relative utilisation of different instruments. In addition, interest groups in different countries will share different clusters of relevant experiences, which will help to determine the feasible space for alternatives.

In short, existing theories could benefit from more careful analysis of the status quo, of underlying beliefs about property rights, and about how political choices are actually made in different countries.

## Implications for System Design and Performance

This review of marketable permits and charge systems in the United States and Europe has demonstrated that regulatory systems involving multiple instruments are the rule rather than the exception. The fundamental problem is to determine the most appropriate mix, with an eye to both economic and political realities.

In addition to selecting an appropriate mix of instruments, attention needs to be given to the effects of having different levels of government implement selected policies. It might seem, for example, that if the problem is local, then the logical choice for addressing the problem is the local regulatory body. However, this is not always true. Perhaps the problem may require a level of technical expertise that does not reside at the local level, in which case some higher level of government involvement may be required. What is clear from a review of implementing environmental policies is that the level of oversight can affect the implementation of policies. For example, Hahn and Hester (1989b) note that a marked increase in bubble activity is associated with a decrease in federal oversight.

Because marketable permit approaches have been shown to have a demonstrable effect on cost savings without sacrificing environmental quality, this instrument can be expected to receive more widespread use. One factor that will stimulate the application of this mechanism is the higher marginal costs of abatement that will be faced as environmental standards are tightened.

A second factor that will tend to stimulate the use of both charges and marketable permits is a 'demonstration effect'. Several countries have already implemented these mechanisms with some encouraging results. The experience gained in implementing these tools will stimulate their use in future applications. A third factor that will affect the use of both of these approaches is the technology of monitoring and enforcement. As monitoring costs go down, the use of mechanisms such as direct charges and marketable permits can be expected to increase. The combination of these factors leads to the prediction that greater use of these market-based environmental systems will be made in the future.

## Acknowledgment

This research was funded in part by the National Science Foundation. I would like to thank Gordon Hester and the editor for helpful comments. The views expressed herein are those of the author and do not necessarily reflect the views of the institutions with which he is affiliated.

## Endnotes

1. BOD is a meaure of the demand for dissolved oxygen imposed on a water body by organic effluents.
2. Pollutants covered under the policy include volatile organic compounds, carbon monoxide, sulfur dioxide, particulates, and nitrogen oxides (Hahn and Hester 1989b).
3. A non-attainment area is a region that has not met a specified ambient standard.
4. The wide range of this estimate reflects the uncertainty that results from the fact that little information has been collected on netting.
5. One of the reasons the EPA set up the allocation rule in this way was to try to transfer some of the permit rents among producers. This will not always occur, however, and depends on the structure of the permits market as well as the underlying production functions.
6. Point sources represent sources that are well-defined, such as a factory smoke stack. Non-point sources refer to sources whose emission points are not readily identified, such as fertiliser run-off from farms.
7. Ozone depletion leads to increased ultraviolet radiation, which has been linked to increases in the incidence of skin cancer and cataracts.
8. Air toxics refer to carcinogenic pollutants such as benzene and asbestos.
9. Charges cover a wide variety of pollutants, including suspended solids, biological oxygen demand, chemical oxygen demand, and selected toxic chemicals.

10. For example, Brown (1984, 114) notes that charges for nitrogen and phosphorus were added in 1982.
11. Emission and effluent standards apply to individual sources of pollution whereas ambient standards apply to regions such as a lake or an air basin.
12. The actual application of fees is similar in spirit to the more familiar deposit-refund approaches that are used for collecting bottles and cans.

# References

Barde, J. (1986) 'Use of Economic Instruments for Environmental Protection: Discussion Paper', *ENV/ECO/86*.164, OECD, September 9, 27 pp.

Baumol, W. and Oates, W. (1975) *The Theory of Environmental Policy*, Prentice-Hall, Englewood Cliffs, NJ.

Becker, G. (1983) 'A Theory of Competition Among Pressure Groups for Political Influence', *Quarterly Journal of Economics* XCVII, 371–400.

Boland, J. (1986) 'Economic Instruments for Environmental Protection in the United States', *ENV/ECO/86*.14, OECD, September 11, 83 pp.

Bower, B. et al. (1981) *Incentives in Water Quality Management: France and the Ruhr Area*, Resources for the Future, Washington, DC.

Bressers, J. (1983) 'The Effectiveness of Dutch Water Quality Policy', Twente University of Technology, Netherlands, mimeo, 31 pp.

Brown, G., Jr. (1984) 'Economic Instruments: Alternatives or Supplements to Regulations?' *Environment and Economics*, Issue Paper, Environment Directorate OECD, June, 103–20.

Brown, G., Jr and Bressers, J. (1986) 'Evidence Supporting Effluent Charges', mimeo, September, 28 pp.

Brown, G., Jr and Johnson, R. (1984) 'Pollution Control by Effluent Charges: It Works in the Federal Republic of Germany, Why Not in the U.S.', *Natural Resources Journal* 24, 929–66.

Buchanan, J. and Tullock, G. (1975) 'Polluters' Profits and Political Response: Direct Controls Versus Taxes', *American Economic Review* 65, 139–47.

Campos, J. (1987) 'Toward a Theory of Instrument Choice in the Regulation of Markets', California Institute of Technology, Pasadena, California, mimeo, January 26, 30 pp.

Coelho, P. (1976) 'Polluters' Profits and Political Response: Direct Control Versus Taxes: Comment', *American Economic Review* 66, 976–78.

Dales, J. (1968) *Pollution, Property and Prices*, University Press, Toronto, Canada.

David, M. and Joeres, E. (1983) 'Is a Viable Implementation of TDPs Transferable?' in E. Joeres and M. David (eds), *Buying a Better Environment: Cost-Effective Regulation Through Permit Trading*, University of Wisconsin Press, Madison, Wisconsin.

Dewees, D. (1983) 'Instrument Choice in Environment Policy', *Economic Inquiry* XXI, 53–71.

Elmore, T. et al. (1984) 'Trading Between Point and Nonpoint Sources: A Cost Effective Method for Improving Water Quality', paper presented at the 57th annual Conference/Exposition of the Water Pollution Control Federation, New Orleans, Louisiana, 20 pp.

Hahn, R. (1983) 'Designing Markets in Transferable Property Rights: A Practitioner's Guide' in E. Joeres and M. David (eds), *Buying a Better Environment: Cost Effective Regulation Through Permit Trading*, University of Wisconsin Press, Madison, Wisconsin.

Hahn, R. (1990) 'Regulating Constraints on Environmental Markets', *Journal of Public Economics* 42, 149–75.

Hahn, R. (1993) 'Getting More Environmental Protection for Less Money: A Practitioner's Guide', *Oxford Review of Economic Policy* 9(4), 112–23.

Hahn, R. and Hester, G. (1989a) 'Marketable Permits: Lessons for Theory and Practice', *Ecology Law Quarterly* 16, 361–406.

Hahn, R. and Hester, G. (1989b) 'Where Did All the Markets Go?: An Analysis of EPA's Emission Trading Program', *Yale Journal on Regulation* 6, 109–53.

Hahn, R. and May, C. (1994) 'The Behaviour of the Allowance Market: Theory and Evidence', Working Paper, Center for Science and International Affairs, John F. Kennedy School of Government, Harvard University, March. 16 pp.

Hahn, R. and Noll, R. (1982) 'Designing a Market for Tradable Emissions Permits' in W. Magat (ed.), *Reform of Environmental Regulation*, Ballinger, Cambridge, Massachusetts.

Hahn, R. and Noll, R. (1983) 'Barriers to Implementing Tradable Air Pollution Permits: Problems of Regulatory Interaction', *Yale Journal on Regulation* 1, 63–91.

Kneese, A. and Schultze, C. (1975) *Pollution, Prices, and Public Policy*, The Brookings Institution, Washington, DC.

Kashmanian, R. et al. (1986) 'Beyond Categorical Limits: The Case for Pollution Reduction Through Trading', paper presented to the 59th Annual Water Pollution Control Federation Conference, October 6–9, 35 pp.

Montgomery, W.D. (1972) 'Markets in Licenses and Efficient Pollution Control Programs', *Journal of Economic Theory* 5, 395–418.

Noll, R. (1983) 'The Political Foundations of Regulatory Policy', *Zeitschrift fur die gesamte Staatswissenschaft* 139, 377–404.

Novotny, G. (1986) 'Transferable Discharge Permits for Water Pollution Control in Wisconsin', mimeo, December 1, 19 pp.

O'Neil, W. (1983) 'The Regulation of Water Pollution Permit Trading under Conditions of Varying Streamflow and Temperature' in E. Joeres and M. David (eds), *Buying a Better Environment: Cost-Effective Regulation Through Permit Trading*, University of Wisconsin Press, Madison, Wisconsin.

Opschoor, J. (1986) 'Economic Instruments for Environmental Protection in the Netherlands', *ENV/ECO/86*.15, OECD, August 1, 66 pp.

Panella, G. (1986) 'Economic Instruments for Environmental Protection in Italy', *ENV/ECO/86*.11, OECD, September 2, 42 pp.

Patterson, D. (1987) Telephone Interview, Bureau of Water Resources Management, Wisconsin Department of Natural Resources, Madison, Wisconsin, April 2.

Pigou, A. (1932) *The Economics of Welfare*, 4th edn, Macmillan and Co., London.

Plott, C. (1983) 'Externalities and Corrective Policies in Experimental Markets', *Economic Journal* 93, 106–27.

Rolph, E. (1983) 'Government Allocation of Property Rights: Who Gets What?', *Journal of Policy Analysis and Management*, 3, 45–61.

Thomas, L. (1986) Memorandum Attached to Draft Emissions Trading Policy Statement, Environmental Protection Agency, Washington, DC, May 19.

Tietenberg, T. (1985) *Emissions Trading: An Exercise in Reforming Pollution Policy*, Resources for the Future, Washington, DC.

US Congressional Budget Office. (1985) *Hazardous Waste Management: Recent Changes and Policy Alternatives*, May, US Government Printing Office, Washington, DC.

US Environmental Protection Agency. (1985a) 'Costs and Benefits of Reducing Lead in Gasoline, Final Regulatory Impact Analysis', Office of Policy Analysis, February.

US Environmental Protection Agency. (1985b) 'Quarterly Reports on Lead in Gasoline', Field Operations and Support Division, Office of Air and Radiation, July 16.

US Environmental Protection Agency. (1986) 'Quarterly Reports on Lead in Gasoline', Field Operations and Support Division, Office of Air and Radiation, March 21, May 23, July 15.

Welch, W. (1983) 'The Political Feasibility of Full Ownership Property Rights: The Cases of Pollution and Fisheries', *Policy Sciences* 16, 165–80.

Yohe, G. (1976) 'Polluters' Profits and Political Response: Direct Control versus Taxes: Comment', *American Economic Review* 66, 981–82.

# 7

# *Market-based Instruments: The Australian Experience*

## Peter Christoff

## Introduction

In Australia, there is an emerging perception that established methods and institutions for environmental management are failing to meet new challenges or to resolve persistent problems. Whereas the 1970s and 1980s delivered improvements in urban air quality, the 1990s threaten to deliver a slow reversal of such trends in major urban centres like Sydney and Melbourne. In rural regions, the trend towards environmental degradation continues. Toxic algal blooms, fed by agricultural nutrients, have spread for hundreds of kilometres along the Murray and Darling Rivers, causing chaos in Australia's agricultural heartland during the past few summers. A new wave of extinctions is predicted, in part because of ongoing clearing of remnant vegetation on private land, in a continent internationally renowned for the diversity of its endemic species. And, despite the establishment of targets for the stabilisation of carbon dioxide emissions, Australia's total contribution to global warming continues apace. Yet political action on new instruments for environmental protection, including tougher regulations and market-based measures, has generally been lacking.

When, in 1984, the OECD's Conference on Environment and Economics (OECD 1985) considered the environmental role of economic instruments, it set an agenda that has taken over a decade to be recognised by some of its member nations. The conference promoted market-based instruments as policy tools that could be potentially superior to direct regulation in provoking preventative environmental management by industry and for realising the Polluter Pays Principle. The conference examined a range of specific instruments (many of which were already in widespread use alongside, rather than as replacements for, environmental regulatory regimes) with regard to their revenue implications, distributive effects, environmental effectiveness and administrative requirements. These criteria, which would determine the political and social acceptability of individual instruments, subsequently became subjects for systematic consideration and review as the instruments were developed and implemented by OECD member countries (OECD 1986, 1989, 1994a,b).

After the conference, some nations — in particular, the Scandinavian countries, Germany and the Netherlands — continued to develop and implement a wide range of environmental economic instruments throughout the 1980s. Other nations, however, did little even to test and adopt those economic instruments already successfully deployed elsewhere. This has generally been the case for Australia. Despite a burst of interest in economic environmental policy instruments in the early 1980s, which coincided with a political climate that was increasingly dismissive of state intervention and enthusiastic for market-based solutions to a spectrum of social, economic and environmental problems, there had been little serious interest in the use of market-based instruments in Australia until the 1990s. Australia's use of these measures still lags behind most comparable OECD nations.

This chapter examines the use of market-based instruments for environmental management in Australia during the decade from 1984 to 1994, together with the impediments to their adoption and the prospects for change. It shows that, when it comes to integrated environmental decision making, Australia is still — as the former director of the Australian Conservation Foundation, Phillip Toyne, has dubbed it — a 'reluctant' nation (Toyne 1994). This reluctance may be attributed not only to political decisions (Toyne's focus) but also to deeply embedded features of Australia's political institutions and economy.

The significant shift towards the centralisation and national integration of Australian economic policy was largely achieved in 1942, when the Commonwealth Government assumed exclusive power to raise income taxes at the expense of the states. However, it was not until the 1970s that a similar process began for environmental policy when the Commonwealth Government chose to enter the field through an adventurous use of its constitutional powers.[1] Even so, the Commonwealth Government remains reluctant to override individual states with decisions reflecting national obligations to an expanding number of international environmental treaties. Incomplete, or perhaps failed, national integration with regard to environmental management is reflected in the fragmentary development and use of market-based instruments under Australia's federal system. Other related political, economic and institutional factors that contribute to the slow uptake of market-based instruments include:

- Australia's economic dependency on primary resource exploitation;
- the push towards micro-economic reform by minimising imposts on the private sector, which has predominated at all levels of government during the past decade;
- the degree of fragmentation and competition between states; and
- bureaucratic compartmentalisation between departments.

Paradoxically, while these factors initially served to delay serious consideration and implementation of market-based instruments, they have also generated a dynamic that is increasingly swinging the pendulum towards greater interest in such measures.

## Resisting Change — the 1980s

In 1987, the OECD surveyed the use of economic instruments for environmental protection among its member countries (OECD 1989). This report portrays Australia as a middle-ranking performer, set well behind the leading nations – Finland, Sweden, (West) Germany and the Netherlands – but comparable to Norway and the United States both in the number and mix of instruments applied. As in other OECD countries, environmental measures in Australia during the 1980s remained almost exclusively regulatory. Nonetheless, as in other OECD countries during the early and mid-1980s, academics and policy makers in Australia displayed both considerable interest in the application of economic instruments for environmental ends (DHAE 1983; DHAE 1984; HRSCEC 1987) and some awareness of measures already in use overseas (AEC 1982; OECD 1985; Ware 1985).

In Australia, isolated examples could be found of charges and levies with potential, if incidental, beneficial environmental outcomes. Measures in use at state level included container deposit schemes, fuel charges, entrance charges for certain popular state and national parks, licences for commercial timber harvesting and recreational hunting and fishing, and minor charges for the extraction or supply of water for agricultural purposes. At the national level, a small number of taxes offered incidental incentives or disincentives for actions affecting the environment.

Most existing measures were aimed at aspects of primary resource use. None reflected an explicit interest in resource conservation or management or a predominant intention to improve environmental outcomes. Almost without exception, they were solely intended as general revenue-raising measures and, as such, were usually designed not to alter or encumber the practices to which they were attached. For example, charges were generally too small to generate any positive environmental incentive. Indeed, timber and irrigation water resource rents were nominal and under-priced, leading to a loss to the state on investment and expenditure on related infrastructure. Where charges or fees obstructed industry development, they were reduced or discarded: for instance, deposits on recyclable glass bottles and jars, in common use during the 1960s and 1970s, lapsed in most states during the 1980s as disposable glass, plastic and aluminium containers came to dominate the market.

Moreover, the application of market-based instruments varied widely between states and lacked coordination across the country, with relatively little national intervention. Historically, the states adopted different institutional approaches to environmental management. For example, at the start of the 1980s, only three states had established EPA-like agencies[2] (the remaining states relied on a range of other administrative agencies and departments). States also adopted their own mix of regulatory and market-based measures, and different rates of incidence for identical instruments. In all, these arrangements reflected interstate competition to attract investment and, during the 1980s, the fragmentary and divergent (rather than convergent) nature of state environmental policies under Australia's federal system.

Perhaps the most widely quoted example, from this period, of an innovative economic instrument providing an identifiable positive environmental outcome is the pay-for-use water pricing scheme established in the Hunter District of New South Wales (NSW). By the end of 1982, the Hunter District Water Board was confronted by a massive and growing backlog in its maintenance works, water demand that would soon over-reach the limits of its three existing supply sources, and rising operation costs. In response, in 1982–83 the Board imposed a demand management strategy that included a two-tier water tariff (a fixed charge for the initial volume of water, and variable charges for amounts above the initial allocation). The new strategy led to a considerable increase in revenue and a 25 per cent decline in total consumption, thereby deferring the need for construction of a new dam for three decades at minimum (DAHE 1985; Paterson 1992). The success of the Hunter District scheme provided an icon for advocates of market-based systems of resource management and a spur for the introduction of similar water pricing systems elsewhere in Australia (EPAC 1992a). Nevertheless, during the 1980s this case stood alone during a time when the emphasis remained focused on the use of regulatory instruments to manage the volume and rate of exploitation of natural resources.

The role of the Commonwealth Department of Environment in promoting market-based instruments is notable during this period. At the start of the 1980s, it was still widely believed that the Commonwealth Government had very limited regulatory powers with regard to managing the environment outside its own territories. So it is not surprising that interest in new nonregulatory measures was spurred on by the federal Department of Environment.[3] Significant departmental initiatives included a national Conference on Conservation and the Economy, held in 1984 (DHAE 1984), the same year as the OECD Conference on Economic Instruments; the House of Representatives Standing Committee on Environment and Conservation Inquiry into *Fiscal Measures and the Achievement of Environmental Objectives* (HRSCEC 1987) — established following a request by the Minister for Home Affairs and Environment in 1983 — and a series of departmental papers and reports.

The 1984 conference provides a milepost for environmental (resource) policy development, in reflecting contemporary Australian problems and articulating a domestic policy agenda for finding new instruments for sustainable resource management in the agricultural, fishing, waste, forestry and water sectors. This agenda included key questions, such as how to:

- cost and treat land degradation, tree loss and the expansion of agriculture into remnant habitat on private land;
- assist in the allocation of fishing rights, increase the efficiency of the industry and limit the depletion of fish stocks;
- ensure that market prices reflected the full cost of waste management (which they did not do) and increase recycling and resource recovery opportunities;
- discover techniques and analyses that could 'promote the protection and efficient management of flora, fauna and natural areas, ... reflecting their value to the community in terms of scientific, cultural, tourism, existence values and their contribution to sustainable development' (DHAE 1984).

The 1986 House of Representatives Standing Committee Report also provides a good litmus for gauging Australian thinking and action on market-based instruments during this time. The committee observed how the Commonwealth was extending its influence over environmental policy through the use of its external affairs powers,[4] increasing its dominance over economic policy and, accordingly, increasing its power over the states (through the provision of general and special purpose grants). Consequently, the committee concentrated its attention on reviewing the environmental impact of Commonwealth taxes in the areas of forestry and conservation of native vegetation, land degradation and heritage conservation.

The report discussed the relative advantages and disadvantages of fiscal measures and direct regulatory controls in terms that were to be repeated during the next decade in the international literature on these measures. In doing so, the committee reflected untested assumptions about the likely real world performance of market-based instruments. Market-based measures were seen to provide flexibility of choice for producers seeking efficient means for reducing pollution, ongoing incentives towards abatement, overall cost-efficiency in implementation, and revenue for environmental restoration. Their perceived disadvantages included the methodological and political problems associated with determining an appropriate level for charges, and costs relating to administrative arrangements for monitoring and supervision. Overall, the committee considered that there may be merit in an environment program using a mixture of regulatory and other economic approaches (HRSCEC 1987, 15).

In its review, the committee found that most existing measures tended to *discourage* positive environmental outcomes, particularly in the areas of forestry and native vegetation clearing. Such positive measures as did exist were often cancelled out or overwhelmed by other measures. For instance, in Tasmania the government was providing financial incentives for private forestry in the form of cost subsidies to private landholders (HRSCEC 1987, 31). On the other hand, Commonwealth loans assisted the states in clearing native forests for softwood plantations, tax provisions gave industry an incentive to clear native vegetation on public and private land (perhaps the most significant single threat to biological diversity and the survival of native species in Australia), and the income tax regime worked as a disincentive to the establishment of plantations on private land (which over time would ease the pressure to harvest timber from native forests) (1987, 39). Similarly, the *Income Tax Assessment Act*, while providing deductibility for expenditure on tree planting, soil conservation and pest eradication under section 75D, did not specifically provide for expenditure on the retention of existing stands of native vegetation on farms.

The committee also heard evidence about the value of combining regulations with incentives to better achieve conservation objectives. For example, the South Australian Government gave evidence that, in addition to its controversial *Native Vegetation Management Act*, it provided a broader range of incentives and inducements to land holders to retain native vegetation and financial assistance where a drop in property value occurred as a result of new controls or restrictions imposed as a result of the new legislation (HRSCEC 1987, 55).[5] Other submissions supported the use of economic measures to influence farmers to reduce 'excessive degradation pressures', and provide low interest loans and subsidies to enable farmers to invest in conservation tillage technologies (1987, 69–70).

Consequently, the committee recommended that disincentives to long-term investment in private forestry be removed, that grants and loan schemes only be used where environmental benefits such as a reduction in logging of native forests could be identified, and that other sources of revenue, such as a levy on woodchip exports, be considered (HRSCEC 1987, 49). The committee also proposed an urgent review of taxation provisions applied to tree planting and for retention of native vegetation on private land, and for the development of cross-compliance measures to tie assistance to farmers (such as drought relief funding) to the implementation of conservation farming and soil conservation practices. Many of these proposals are still being urged almost a decade later (ACF 1994a,b).

At best, the 1980s saw national and state governments engaging in defensive measures, namely the *removal* of the most blatant environmentally detrimental economic incentives, such as accelerated depreciation for the initial clearing of native vegetation on private land and for the draining of wetlands.[6] As the Prime Minister's 1989 Environment Statement noted, 'It is vital also that governments ensure that they are not inadvertently encouraging environmental damage through tax concessions, subsidies and other special assistance' (DPMC 1989, 6).

Yet, despite the creation in 1989 of two major well-funded national programs to encourage revegetation and soil conservation,[7] few significant positive market-based incentives (or regulatory measures) were set in place during the 1980s. An even more pronounced lack of innovation may be observed in relation to urban and industrial pollution.

Why is this so? Observations in the 1987 House of Representatives Report provide some answers that are still relevant today. The most revealing comments in the report focus on the lack of integration between economic and environmental policy making — an ongoing problem for the widespread adoption of both market-based and regulatory environmental measures. This stems as much from a territorial protection of departmental turf and traditional 'client relations' as from a genuine lack of understanding of how and where integration must occur. For instance, Treasury suggested that

> there is no need for general macro-economic policies such as the determination of budgetary objectives, the structure and level of taxation, the conduct of monetary policy or the pursuit of prices and incomes policy to be assessed against specific environmental criteria, and that the effects on the environment of changes in such policies are likely to be so indirect and diffuse as to be incapable of precise measurement.
>
> (HRSCEC 1987, 9).

Other federal departments also displayed a high degree of resistance to suggestions for change that might disrupt well-established institutional arrangements with their 'client groups'. For instance, the Commonwealth Department of Resources and Energy

> ... advised the Committee that the regulatory approach has been in place for some time. The controls and the underlying policies are now seen as being well accepted and well understood by all parties involved in resource development. The Department considered that the information costs and other costs associated with making a large scale move to fiscal measures would outweigh the benefits that would be achieved.
>
> (HRSCEC 1987, 15)

In all, the committee found that both the Commonwealth and the states responded to environmental and economic problems without considering their interaction and reciprocal impacts. Observing that it was 'somewhat surprising that governments have not used fiscal measures to control the environmental impact of economic activities in the same way as they have used fiscal measures to control economic impacts', the committee singled out three broad reasons for the lack of integration between economic and environmental policy at this time. Most important was the different attitudes of decision makers in industry, government and the conservation movement. Industry leaders were concerned to maximise profits and, not surprisingly, opposed to measures designed to increase environmental benefits and industry costs. The conservation movement was suspicious of economic measures that 'attempt to define acceptable pollution measures in terms of economic efficiency'. Meanwhile, decision making by government seemed to be characterised by compartmentalisation between different departments with different approaches.

The second explanation was the lack of knowledge about the economic costs and benefits of environmental protection, compounded by a lack of research and communication between environmentalists and economists. Finally, there were the practical obstacles to implementation of statements of principle about the integration of 'conservation and development' that resulted from 'the division of constitutional power within the Australian federal system, the failure to develop suitable mechanisms and a resistance from those who perceive a conflict between environmental problems and economic development' (HRSCEC 1987, 2–5).

Beyond these general observations, the delayed use of economic instruments may also be attributed to the structural bias of the Australian state (at all levels) towards the facilitation of natural resource exploitation and the protection of related commercial and union interests. Australia is still a frontier state and economy, although one now increasingly straining under the political pressure to meet newly articulated and increasingly urgent national and international environmental demands. This structural bias is highlighted during environmental conflicts or when major environmental reforms are considered. In addition, problems of conflict resolution in the Australian federal system are exacerbated where differences over conservation or resource management are concerned: moves towards integration between different levels of government repeatedly collapse into policy gridlock as soon as the different levels begin pulling in opposing directions.

## The Response of State Environment Agencies

Resistance to market-based measures was not just confined to the national level of government nor was it necessarily conservative. Australian state-based pollution control and environment protection agencies have been modelled on the US Environmental Protection Agency (EPA) and its enabling legislation. During the 1980s, these agencies were still consolidating their first decade's work, establishing standards for air, water and waste emissions, and licensing significant individual industrial polluters. Direct regulation delivered considerable improvements in the management of point-source pollution and related environmental conditions. However, treatment of a range of more diffuse or less immediately obvious pollution sources (such as run-off from urban and rural land) were put to one side.

Moreover, the larger, 'ungovernable' issues and problems (such as climate change and ozone depletion, and control of diffuse greenhouse emissions), which mobilised public opinion in 1988–89, had not yet surfaced. Grabosky and Braithwaite, in their study of the compliance strategies of a wide range of government agencies, reported that 'while Australian environmental agencies have given greater or lesser consideration to regulation by market incentives, every one of them rejected it as impracticable' (1986, 37). Interestingly, the reason most commonly given for this rejection was 'the logistic impossibility of auditing honest measurement of emissions on which charges would be based' (1986, 37).

## Dilemmas of Reform

Following the flurry of interest in the early to mid-1980s, serious consideration of market-based instruments died away for the remainder of the decade. This may seem paradoxical, given the political and economic fascination with the market that prevailed in Australia during the decade. The 1980s were dominated by the 'economic rationalists',[8] who had largely 'captured' the national economic agenda through their influence and positions in Treasury and other industry and economic development portfolios (Pusey 1991; Carroll and Manne 1992). Throughout the 1980s and into the 1990s, under their influence, the federal Labor Government implemented a succession of decisions aimed at increasing national competitiveness by fostering greater international market exposure and global economic integration. These decisions included floating the Australian dollar, deregulating the finance sector, substantially reducing tariffs, proposing full or partial privatisation of a variety of public sector utilities and corporations, and reducing personal income and company tax rates. The reduction in direct taxes and the increased freedom to borrow directly from overseas sources were intended to foster investment in the Australian manufacturing sector. Instead, the combined effect of the economic reforms was a significant growth in speculative investment and — when overseas interest rates rose — ballooning national debt and unemployment. This new economic climate had unintended consequences for national and state environmental policy.

First, the national Labor Government's enthusiasm for deregulation during the 1980s did not extend to environmental matters, where the emphasis was on diffusing political conflict by creating administrative institutions and processes for the co-operative development of national environmental standards and policies by Commonwealth and state governments. In the late 1980s, 'the environment' rose to prominence in the Australian political agenda through the conjuncture of soaring international concern, a series of spectacular battles between conservationists and industry, the resultant conflict between state and federal governments over the fate of proposed or listed World Heritage sites, and the electoral vulnerability of the federal Labor Government to the 'green' vote (Christoff 1994). In combination, these phenomena forced the Federal Government to search for institutions, processes and agreements that might avert or manage and resolve environmental conflict. Between 1989 and 1992, the national government established the Commonwealth EPA, the Resource Assessment Commission, the InterGovernmental Agreement on the Environment (IGAE), and a process for developing a National Ecologically Sustainable Development (ESD) Strategy.[9] Nevertheless, environmental policy was never made integral to the dominant processes of economic policy development or implementation, and was again side-lined during the recessionary early 1990s. For instance, while recent recommendations for micro-economic reform in the electricity, gas and water sectors (Hilmer, Rayner and Taperell 1993) have direct repercussions for environmental outcomes,[10] environmental impacts have not loomed large in the associated policy deliberations.

Second, during the 1980s, economic deregulation strengthened the political standing of states, industries and companies heavily dependent on primary resource production. The significant reduction in tariffs, instead of shocking the manufacturing sector into international competitiveness, was almost terminal for manufacturing-based industries, regions and states. As a result, Australia became increasingly reliant on mineral, fuel and agricultural exports (in 1993, these provided some 61 per cent of export earnings) as the overall balance of payments situation deteriorated dramatically due an increase in foreign interest rate rises, an increase in processed imports, and a decline in the volume and value of manufactured exports (later reversed, albeit from a very low base, in the early 1990s). If full-cost recovery through resource rents was difficult to achieve before then, it became politically unattainable as the decade wore on. Instead, resource industries were wooed vigorously by states competing with each other, using pricing concessions, subsidies and infrastructural assistance to attract investment. Conflicts between conservationists and developers sharpened as resource exploitation was promoted as the necessary, indeed only, panacea for present economic woes. The industry lobby still plays on this theme relentlessly in the media, as do ministers with 'economic portfolios' in Cabinet.

Third, and paradoxically, by creating longer term fiscal problems for the Australian state, the economic reforms of the 1980s eventually increased interest in new revenue sources (including environmental taxes) but also made them politically difficult to establish. Significant reductions in Australian personal and company tax rates during the 1980s eroded the public sector revenue base. Thus the Commonwealth Government has had to fund elevated (recessionary) social welfare expenditure by increasing the public sector deficit and selling public sector assets. Neither of these strategies is viable over the longer term. Now the national Labor Government is being forced to look for additional revenue and sources of finance. However, Labor's direct tax cuts and promises of further tax reductions leave any attempt to reverse this trend politically vulnerable to attack by opposition parties and industry claiming that such moves threaten hard-won gains for market efficiency and improved investor confidence (despite the fact that Australia now has one of the lowest income tax rates among OECD countries). Meanwhile, socially regressive taxes are especially politically unpopular, particularly among Labor supporters who have experienced the harsh effects of Labor's deregulatory policies during the 1980s in the form of increased unemployment and a growing gap between poor and rich. (Labor was able to win the 1993 election largely through its vigorous opposition to new indirect taxes when the Liberal Opposition campaigned around the introduction of a broad-based goods and services tax [the GST].) In such a climate, environmental taxes and levies are vulnerable to challenge from both ends of the political spectrum. Two examples indicate the depth of these dilemmas for environmental–economic integration.

*Sinking the Leaded Petrol Excise*
When unleaded petrol was introduced in Australia in 1985–86, it was expected to supplant leaded fuel by 1990. By 1993 it had gained only 42 per cent of the market, a reflection of the age and the slow turnover of the nation's car fleet (partly a consequence of the recession). Also in 1993, several prominent reports focused public attention on the relationship between leaded petrol and the health impacts of lead pollution. In response, the then Minister for Environment, Ros Kelly, introduced an education program

encouraging drivers of the 30 per cent of cars manufactured before 1986 to transfer to unleaded petrol. She sought new regulations to cut lead levels in petrol, a move strongly resisted by the petroleum companies. She also examined the possibility of introducing a differential excise on leaded petrol to further encourage drivers to switch to cheaper lead-free petrol and/or buy new cars using this fuel. Other incentives, such as increased registration charges for older cars, were rejected.

Prior to the 1993–94 Budget, the Federal Government had canvassed the idea of a 5 cents per litre excise differential on leaded petrol as part of a general increase in petrol prices for revenue purposes. With headlines like 'ALP's petrol tax hits the true believers' and 'How super fuel tax hits the battlers' (complete with a socioeconomic map of Melbourne) (Munro 1993; Stapleton 1993), a fierce public debate ensued over the socially regressive impact of the ($200-a-year average) charge. The extra tax on leaded petrol was attacked by key social welfare organisations, the union movement and, predictably, the road transport lobby. When the petrol excise increase, with the differential excise between leaded and unleaded petrol rising to 5 cents per litre by 1995, was introduced in the Budget, no compensatory measures for low income earners were included with the proposal. Nor was the revenue raised hypothecated to fund public transport improvements, as had been suggested by environment organisations. The differential measure was rejected by the Greens and Australian Democrats in the Senate (Upper House), where they held the balance of power. The measure was portrayed as a revenue garnering exercise wrapped in 'green rhetoric,' but subsequently passed at a reduced rate of 2 cents per litre. Even so, the Commonwealth EPA's figures suggest that about 250 000 cars switched to unleaded petrol in the month following the introduction of this reduced measure. While, in 1995, the larger excise is still supported by conservationists — conditional on compensation being available for its regressive impacts (ACF 1994a,b) — it appears to be politically dead for the foreseeable future.

## Emitting a Carbon Tax

Australia is the third highest *per capita* producer of carbon dioxide emissions and is responsible for 1.1 per cent of total global emissions. Despite the federal government's commitment, under the Climate Change Convention, to stabilise total national carbon dioxide emissions at 1988 levels by the year 2000 and then reduce them by 20 per cent by 2005 (ESDWG 1991, 29), the total volume of emissions has continued to rise. Meanwhile, both the

Commonwealth and state governments have failed to implement even the 'no-regrets' regulatory and voluntary measures agreed under the National Greenhouse Response Strategy (NGRS) (AG 1993).

The use of tradable permits and carbon taxes as greenhouse response measures have been discussed by Australian policy makers for the past five years, without government action being taken (ESDWG 1991; Owen 1991; Price Waterhouse 1991). However, with worsening emission outcomes and an increasing implementation deficit for the NGRS, pressure to implement a carbon tax or levy is growing. Simultaneously, political interest has been aroused by the need for new revenue sources (including for environmental expenditure). A 'politically feasible' levy is believed to be around $A1.25 (US$1.00) per tonne of emitted carbon dioxide, as suggested by the federal Department of Environment. This is less than the $A2.20 (US$1.70) per tonne of carbon dioxide proposed by the Australian Conservation Foundation (ACF 1994a,b) but enough, if fully hypothecated, to fund measures sufficient to meet Australia's current emission reduction targets. (By comparison, five smaller or comparably sized economies of OECD nations have introduced carbon or energy taxes. They have applied rates of $A18.85 for general fuel consumption and $A9.90 for industry in Denmark; $A5.25 in Finland; $A3.25 in the Netherlands; $A62.60 and $A20 for coal, in Norway; and in Sweden, $A53.75 for general fuel consumption and $A13.85 for industry.)

As noted earlier, the primary industry lobby wields considerable political influence over policies affecting energy prices. Coal, crude oil and gas exports comprise over 18 per cent of Australia's total export earnings. Consequently, with Australia's current account deficit ballooning towards 6 per cent of GDP, taxing fuel exports is economically and politically unacceptable. A carbon tax has been strongly opposed by the Australian Coal Association, the Australian Mining Council, major mining corporations such as BHP, Alcoa and CRA, the Business Council of Australia, state electricity utilities and the national Electricity Supply Association, and mining unions. The 'economics ministers' (Industry; Primary Industry; Resources; Treasury; and Finance) are therefore not especially enthusiastic about such a tax, which they believe would also affect micro-economic reform and increase inflation and unemployment. Hypothecation is supported by the Minister for Environment (but not by Treasury) and by the minor parties in the Senate — the Greens and Australian Democrats — whose support is necessary to pass such a measure. The welfare lobby may support the socially regressive levy, but only if adequate compensatory measures are included. At the time of writing, the view of the key trade union body, the ACTU, is undecided.[11]

In all, there exists a formidable array of impediments to the national implementation of significant economic instruments. The Federal Government is riven along resource development and conservation factional lines. It is politically reluctant to over-ride or force the states' hand, and it is politically vulnerable to the interest groups arraigned in opposition to specific measures.

## A New Realism, a New Agenda? — the 1990s

Despite signs of policy paralysis, in the 1990s one can see both renewed Australian interest in market-based instruments and a new realism about the scope and limits of such mechanisms. As noted earlier, the explosion of environmental concern during 1988–89 increased political pressure for more efficient and ecologically sensitive forms of natural resource management. The revival of institutional interest in the use of market-based instruments is evidenced in the reports of the National Ecologically Sustainable Development Strategy Working Groups in 1991, in work by the Office of the Economic Policy Advisory Committee (EPAC) and the Departments of Environment; Finance; and Primary Industries and Energy (EPAC 1992a,b,c; ABARE 1993; Dept Fin. 1994) and a national 'roundtable' on such measures, recently convened by the NSW EPA. However, such thinking still remains marginal to much government activity around resource management. There is still no Australian counterpart to the highly influential report, *Blueprint for a Green Economy* (Pearce, Markayanda and Barbier 1989), commissioned by the UK Government.

The new realism perhaps derives from a growing appreciation of the complexities of 'state failure' and 'market failure' in the Australian context. The direct regulatory stratagem has not been seen to 'fail' or to have hit some mythical 'effectiveness frontier'. It has not conformed to the free marketeers' caricature of environmental regulations and regulatory agencies as inevitably 'static, inflexible and suboptimal' in their performance.[12] Such outcomes, where they exist, refer to a variable *political* phenomenon rather than to a permanent *structural* incapacity of regulatory agencies. Nevertheless, EPAs have had to confront the reality of chronic political resistance to environmental control and the ways in which deliberate under-resourcing of monitoring and enforcement capacities has generated environmental 'implementation deficits' in all Australian states. Such realities have, however, encouraged the EPAs to seek additional means to support or enhance existing regulatory approaches. Meanwhile, the critique of 'market failure' (the inability of markets to reflect and manage the full range of social and ecological values) in the environmental realm has, if anything, strengthened.

If, beyond these considerations, there has been a sea-change towards market-based instruments, this may be attributed to changes in the political composition of mainland state governments. Whereas during much of the 1980s all mainland governments (national and state) were Labor, by 1992 almost all state governments had fallen to the Liberals (conservatives). The new Liberal state governments came to power uninterested in national policy coordination under the guidance of a Labor national government, and even more powerfully ideologically driven by a belief in the disciplining force of the market and the greater efficiency of the private sector. They have set about vigorously implementing programs to reduce the size of the public sector overall and, specifically, to complete the program of corporatisation of public sector utilities initiated by their Labor predecessors. Corporate management structures and commercial accounting procedures have been established in most state water, fisheries, forestry and energy departments and utilities, as a prelude to full privatisation in many of these areas. The search for economic efficiency and a positive rate of return has led to job-shedding and the loss of skills and knowledge in the public sector. It is likely that environmentally detrimental outcomes will result from competition between rival corporations (as in the energy sector) if cost-cutting for market advantage ensues.

Nevertheless, commercialisation of heavily subsidised forestry and water services may lead — if accompanied by near or full-cost recovery, and rigorous environmental monitoring and enforcement — to long-sought greater efficiencies of resource use and the possible elimination of environmentally and economically marginal agriculture on marginal salt-prone land and logging in marginally productive state forests. Several major urban water supply authorities (in Sydney and Melbourne) are now implementing two-tier tariffs in order to introduce demand management through use-based pricing. Ironically, then, political changes at state government level appear to have loosened some of the knots that had hitherto constrained policy experimentation in this area and established, at best, a creative tension between federal and state levels (although at some cost to democratic rights and public controls over these resources and agencies).

First elected in 1988, the NSW Government exemplifies the willingness among the new Liberal state governments to push the free-market environmentalists' agenda for an extension of property rights to the environment and for greater use of market-based environmental instruments. In his opening address to the New Environmentalism conference in Sydney in 1991, the then Premier Nick Greiner announced that New South Wales was seeking an environment policy that 'was at the leading edge of environmental reform around the world'. The New Environmentalism was 'explicitly concerned with the institutional framework within which environmental decisions are being made'. Governments would be facilitators, wherever possible making 'the members of society themselves trade-off the costs and the benefits of particular decisions through the use of economic incentives and the allocation of true costs'. And they would be information providers, 'making sure that the community is made fully aware of the true costs and benefits of political decisions, including the costs imposed on private land holders, social costs and benefits and the costs and benefits being imposed on future generations'. The underlying vision was of a minimal state tending an open market and a pluralist society from 'outside' — a vision considerably at odds with the real-world material engagement of the state in economic, social and political life.

Greiner's vision assumes that the state can insulate itself politically by allowing the market to resolve conflict. Or as he put it, 'the market provides us with a mechanism for allocating scarce resources in a way which maximises community welfare while avoiding the pressures from purely sectional and sometimes selfish demands. Markets are able to make decisions that politicians lack the will or the information base to make' (Greiner 1991). This view simply denies the historical role of, and increasing pressure on, the state as a participant and mediator in environmental conflicts that *result* from competing and unequal power between property developers (including state agencies), chemical industries or timber companies, and environmentalists and local residents. It also assumes perfect knowledge. Establishing a system of limited property rights (as with the creation of markets for tradable permits) may work if the ecological knowledge on which the system is based is accurate. Given the state of ecological science, however, this is rarely possible. The state is constantly required to discipline and direct the market as ecological failures are revealed or new scientific understandings emerge.

Nevertheless, enlisting the arguments of overseas and local proponents of property rights, such as US consultant Robert Hahn and the Australian Tasman Institute, and drawing on American and New Zealand examples of permit trading and resource privatisation, the 'New Environmentalism' conference defined an agenda that the new NSW EPA (established later in 1991) would explore. Since then, the NSW EPA has employed advisers such as Hahn to examine a range of pollution charge systems and the potential and actual use of economic instruments for controlling emissions from point and non-point sources. The EPA's studies and related pilot projects place NSW in the forefront of work on economic instruments in Australia, including a tradable permit scheme to control salinity inputs to the Hunter River, measures to control phosphorus inputs to the Hawkesbury–Nepean River, and instruments to limit motor vehicle emissions (Bernauer and O'Shea 1994; Groenhout 1994; James 1994; Moore 1994a,b).

# Current use of Market-based Instruments[13]

A comprehensive review of Australian use of market-based instruments is beyond the scope of this chapter. Nevertheless, some general lessons may be drawn from a selection of major developments. The range of instruments currently used in Australia is given in Table 7.1 (which lists economic tools specifically introduced for their environmental impacts) and Table 7.2 (which lists those introduced for other purposes but with secondary or unintended environmental outcomes).[14] Some of these measures are discussed below.

There are few Australian examples of emission charges applied to discharges by load, level or concentration in Australia, despite the presence of the broad range of environmental pollutants — emissions to air, water and soil, aircraft and motor vehicle noise, and domestic and industrial waste — for which these charges have been successfully used overseas. James (1993) cites the South Australian *Marine Protection Act* (1990) as providing a rare example of a charge designed to have an incentive effect on effluent disposal. Charges for aircraft noise are now being considered for Sydney Airport, and, as noted earlier, a tax or levy for carbon dioxide emissions is also under discussion.

*User Charges*
User charges are widely employed throughout Australia by state and local governments in relation to domestic and industrial electricity and water supply, and waste water and solid waste disposal. However, water supply and domestic waste disposal charges generally only fund service provision, are levied through property rates, and have little incentive effect. Domestic water

**Table 7.1** Economic instruments with intended environmental impacts, Australia (1994)

| Instruments | National | State | Local |
|---|---|---|---|
| 1.   CHARGES AND LEVIES | | | |
| *Emission and effluent charges* | | | |
| Air | | x | |
| Water | | x | |
| Aircraft noise | (x)★ | | |
| *User charges* | | | |
| Industrial waste | | x | x |
| Municipal waste | | | x |
| Sewerage and sewage treatment | | x | x |
| *Product charges* | | | |
| *(including tax differentiation)* | | | |
| Leaded petrol | x | | |
| Recycled/ordinary paper | x | | |
| Beverage containers | | x | |
| Ozone depleting substances | x | | |
| *General environmental levies* | | x | x |
| 2.   DEPOSIT REFUND | | | |
| Beverage containers | | x | |
| 3.   TAX INCENTIVES | | | |
| *Tax subsidies, deductions or credits* | | | |
| Clean technologies | x | | |
| Capital expenditure on | | | |
|   soil conservation | x | | |
|   water conservation | x | | |
|   tree planting | x | | |
|   regeneration, native vegetation | x | | |
| Donations to environment groups | x | | |
| 4.   TRADABLE RESOURCE ENTITLEMENTS AND EMISSION RIGHTS | | | |
| Fishing | x | x | |
| Timber harvesting | | x | |
| Rural water use | | x | |
| Salt to rivers | | x | |
| Emissions to air | x | (x)★ | |
| 5.   OTHER | | | |
| Recycling incentives | | x | |
| Performance bonds | | x | |

★(x) means 'under consideration'
*Sources*: Bernauer and O'Shea 1994; Dept Fin. 1994; EPAC 1992a,b; James 1993, 1994; Jubb et al. 1992; Moore 1994a,b; OECD 1994a; SSCERA 1994

**Table 7.2**  Economic instruments with incidental environmental
impacts, Australia (1994)

| Sector or activity and instrument | National | State | Local |
|---|---|---|---|
| **Agriculture** | | | |
| Low sales tax rate for pesticides/fertilisers | − | | |
| Drought assistance | − | | |
| Diesel fuel rebate | − | | |
| Agricultural water use and supply charges | | + | |
| **Forestry** | | | |
| Diesel fuel rebate | − | | |
| **Hunting and fishing** | | | |
| Licences | | + | |
| **Mining** | | | |
| Diesel fuel rebate | − | | |
| **Manufacturing** | | | |
| Licence fees for waste disposal | | + | |
| Industrial water use | | | + |
| Industrial electricity use and supply charges | | + | |
| **Nature conservation** | | | |
| Entry fees to parks and conservation reserves | | + | |
| Tax deduction for gifts and legacies to environment protection organisations | + | | |
| **Transport** | | | |
| Fuel taxes, levies and excises | + | | |
| Fringe benefits tax on business car | + | | |
| Fringe benefits tax on work-related car parking | + | | |
| Limit to deductability of business trip costs | + | | |
| Tariff on imported used cars | − | | |
| Vehicle registration and compulsory insurance costs | | + | |
| Motor vehicle sales tax | + | | |
| Road toll charges | | + | |
| **Other** | | | |
| Domestic water use and supply charges | | + | |
| Domestic power and gas use and supply charges | | + | |
| Domestic waste disposal charges | | | + |

*Note*: + = positive impact;   − = negative impact (i.e. encourages degradation)
*Sources*: As for Table 7.1

charges are still mostly based on property values rather than imposed as a means of demand management, although there is a trend to user-pays charging. However, examples where charges are seen to have a clear incentive effect are still uncommon.

Charges for industrial and commercial solid waste, usually levied by volume and increasingly by weight, have a slight incentive effect. James (1993) notes that in NSW, the Sydney Water Board's Trade Waste Program uses charges that have resulted in a decrease in the volume of materials discharged to sewers, and a Waste Disposal Levy has been applied to household and industrial waste resulting in an increase in recycling. In South Australia, revenue from a solid waste charge is paid into a recycling development fund, and a recycle rebate scheme has been introduced in New South Wales to encourage and assist local councils to run domestic recycling programs.

*Product Charges*
In contrast to Europe, very few product charges are used in Australia. Differential taxes have been used to promote use of unleaded petrol and recycled paper. Fees designed to raise revenue to cover administrative costs associated with the regulation of phase-out (rather than as a disincentive to use) have been imposed on the import and manufacture of ozone-depleting substances (Dept Fin. 1994, 30). In relation to ozone management, James (1993, 20) points to the familiar problem of policy coordination among the Commonwealth and the states: 'Not all states have introduced specific controls, and where legislation has been passed, it differs between states. Some states have banned the use of ozone-depleting substances even though their use is permitted in others.'

*Deposit-refund Systems*
Despite overseas evidence proving the effectiveness of this instrument for encouraging waste minimisation and reducing littering, and widespread local recognition of the incentive value of deposit-refund systems (e.g. CEPA 1992; SSCERA 1994), only one Australian state has introduced such a scheme under legislation.[15] The South Australian *Container Deposit Act* (1975) has caused some direct substitution from cans to bottles (Jubb, Mastoris and van Vliet 1992, 19). Data indicate a decline in recyclable bottles going to waste in South Australia and suggest that the Act is having a beneficial effect on litter levels (CEPDG 1993, 153). Elsewhere in Australia, existing deposit recovery schemes have been dismantled under industry pressure and proposals for new legislation blocked.

*Tradable Emission and Resource Permits*

Only in the application of tradable permits has there been any real innovation with economic instruments in Australia over the past decade. Schemes have been established for trading resource rights for water, timber and fish, and for pollution rights for emissions to water (salt) and air (ozone-depleting substances). The experience has reflected both the limited circumstances in which such instruments may be successfully applied and specific features of the Australian environment and the nation's manufacturing sector.

Proponents of tradable permit schemes argue that they enhance traditional regulatory mechanisms by allowing polluters to meet predetermined environmental goals with greater flexibility and reduced costs (Hahn and Hester 1989). They also provide an ongoing incentive for industries to innovate, again to reduce costs and to profit from trade in excess credits (OECD 1989). However, such schemes are only feasible where potential savings are high enough to encourage industry innovation, where administrative and other costs are not prohibitive, and where there are sufficient sources to establish a viable market. Overall, it seems that tradable permits are most useful when applied to easily monitored resources such as water or 'gross' pollutants — such as sulfur oxides or salt — which predominantly are emitted from a confined number of point sources. However, the potential to establish schemes is limited where there are only a small to medium number of trading partners.

In Australia, successful establishment of tradable permit systems has predominantly occurred in the area of water resource management. Traditionally, water entitlements were fixed and 'attached' to land acquisition. Legislative systems for limited transferable water entitlements (TWE) have been introduced in New South Wales, Victoria and Queensland (with trial schemes also in Tasmania and Western Australia) in an attempt to increase efficiencies in irrigation water use. Generally, these schemes have been successful in helping to rationalise irrigation water use by reallocating water to more productive and economically valuable activities and regions (Millington 1991; Musgrave 1991; Pigram et al. 1992; James 1993). Restrictions on trading have included controls on volume, to prevent monopolisation of the resource, and to provide for environmental allocations (i.e. to protect flow requirements necessary to maintain instream ecological values). None of the systems are based on secure property rights, which remain with the state (Dept Fin. 1994, 28). In some areas, TWEs have provided environmental benefits as excess water has been traded away from currently salt-affected regions to more productive regions and enterprises.[16]

Australian attempts to establish tradable permit systems for emissions to air from stationary sources have reflected implementation problems experienced overseas. In both Sydney and Melbourne — Australia's major manufacturing centres — generally only a few enterprises are responsible for a substantial proportion of $SO_x$ and $NO_x$ emitted by stationary sources. These few enterprises also contribute only a relatively minor percentage of total emissions for certain chemicals (e.g. $NO_x$ and hydrocarbons). The bulk of such emissions are produced by vehicles. Generally, there are too few major industrial sources for feasible application of other aspects of tradable permit systems (bubbles, offsetting and netting), while establishing trading between smaller producers would produce greater administrative problems than under current licensing procedures. To ensure adherence to licence/permit limits, monitoring would also need to become more stringent than occurs at present. In other words, regulatory and administrative burdens would probably increase for both industry and regulatory agencies but without commensurate environmental gains or improvements in efficiency. This has been the experience in NSW, where the lack of available emissions inventory data has also hampered implementation of a pilot scheme. As a result, the NSW EPA reports that 'the search for a useful pilot application for tradable permits has so far been unsuccessful, but investigation of potential schemes is continuing' (Moore 1994a, 1).

The utility of tradable permits is often misrepresented by economists, who tend to overstate the technical capacities of permit systems and understate the real-world political (and ecological) realities of their implementation. Theoretically, tradable permits encourage industry compliance — and in some cases enhance abatement performance — at lower cost than under traditional licensing schemes. However, in reality, compliance monitoring remains as complex and expensive as for other forms of licensing and regulation and, as Hahn (1991) and others note, may in fact require additional regulatory intervention and administrative costs to ensure that permit requirements are being met and that trades are 'valid'.

Moreover, governments remain responsible for setting and ensuring compliance with the environmental standards to which permits must be 'fitted'. The burden of limiting or cranking back total emissions is still a separate regulatory task — one made more difficult if governments have to 're-acquire' the permits they have issued. Permit systems may be designed to allow programmatic improvements in standards, and to reflect elements of risk and uncertainty in ecological understanding. For instance, governments may withhold a certain percentage of permits to over-compensate for uncertainties in application, limit the duration of permits to allow adjustments over time, and ensure that permits are tailored to spatial and temporal variations in the environment through use of periodic and episodic permits (Tietenberg 1985). However, each of these adjustments significantly lowers the utility of the instrument by 'hampering' free trading. On the other hand, an error in assessing the 'sustainability' of emission or resource use levels means that the permits, having established a 'resource right' or quasi-property right, would have to be 'adjusted' or reacquired at some cost to government and ultimately the community.

Robust scientific understanding is an essential foundation for any ecologically sustainable tradable permit system. Two examples, relating to resource permits for fishing and logging, indicate the problems posed for tradable permit systems by ecological uncertainty. Individual transferable quota (ITQ) systems have been used in Australia in an attempt to manage fisheries. Tradable permits allow harvesting of certain fish and other ocean species. The total sum of the quotas is known as the 'total allowable catch' (TAC), which is intended to be no more than the maximum sustainable yield consistent with the survival of the harvested species (Jubb, Mastoris and van Vliet 1992, 61).

Gentle (1992) and ABARE (1993) have highlighted the problem of conferring property rights in a situation of inadequate environmental knowledge. For instance, the Australian ITQ system for Southern bluefin tuna has failed repeatedly because authorities have consistently over-estimated the size of remaining stocks of this severely depleted species, thereby setting quotas that have continued the process of over-fishing. Property rights and related markets are unable to resolve problems of effective resource management for most commercial fisheries, which currently require greater scientific knowledge and a clearer recognition of the limits of using market mechanisms for managing 'wild species' with natural fluctuations in populations. In 1991, it was estimated that some $20 million would need to be spent on research alone to accurately set TACs for the South East Trawl, with a further $1 million in recurrent monitoring costs (Gentle 1992, 101). Strict regulation and the creation of 'no-fishing' reserves are essential prior components to the main-tenance of fisheries, given profound ignorance of the complexity of marine ecosystems.

Similar issues arise with the transferable licences for harvesting hardwood timber from native forests, introduced in the 1986 Victorian Timber Industry Strategy. The licences are intended to encourage investment and further processing by providing resource security and assisting in the creation of economies of scale. They provide 'tradable quotas' in the sense that licences may be initially auctioned, and then transferred when a mill is sold or amalgamated with another company. In 1987, the strategy's approach to licensing was strongly criticised by the Victorian conservation movement on the grounds that it consolidated harvesting at well above sustainable rates and volumes and locked government into a legal requirement to provide a defined volume per area irrespective of future environmental findings. (Few rigorous environmental surveys had been undertaken in areas to be 'granted' under licence). These views were recently supported by the Victorian Auditor-General (AGV 1993).[17]

Overall, available Australian evidence confirms the view that tradable permit systems do not significantly enhance environmental outcomes or improve pollution abatement performance (e.g. Hahn and Hester 1989). They also appear to be less efficient than pollution charges and taxes in maintaining constant (financial) pressure for pollution abatement and related innovation. In other words, tradable permit systems are a useful device for *politically* managing pollution by lowering costs to industry while *appearing* to increase pressure for abatement, *appearing* to reduce regulatory intervention and encouraging the belief that better environmental outcomes will result than would occur under other regulatory regimes.

## Significant Omissions

Since the OECD surveyed the use of economic instruments by its member countries in 1985, Australia's performance has fallen even further behind that of other comparable nations (OECD 1986, 1994a,b). Australia's lack of innnovation in this area, when confronted by the range of available measures, is highlighted by comparisons with more innovative nations such as the Netherlands, Sweden and the United States (Table 7.3).[18] Clearly, significant differences in administrative, industrial and environmental conditions in Australia (compared with these regions) underlie some of the differences in performance. Nonetheless a number of significant omissions may be observed in relation to nutrient pollution of rivers and streams, clearing of remnant native vegetation and the degradation of habitat for native species, waste generation and disposal, and urban pollution.

For example, there are no *environmental charges on fertiliser use*, despite long-standing recognition of the contribution of fertiliser overuse, in conjunction with clearing and grazing of the riparian zone, to aquatic nutrient pollution. This absence is partly because of the insensitivity of these instruments with respect to equity, partly because of variations in local environmental conditions, but primarily because of the political strength of the rural lobby. By contrast, Sweden has applied a 10 per cent tax on fertilisers and pesticides, with the revenue hypothecated to fund extension activities (notably farmer education). The OECD, on the basis of research conducted in Germany, regards such rates as too low to

**Table 7.3**  A selective country comparison of the application of environmental eonomic instruments (1993)

| Instruments | Australia | Netherlands | Sweden | Norway | USA |
|---|---|---|---|---|---|
| 1.  CHARGES | | | | | |
| *Emission and effluent charges* | | | | | |
| Water pollution | x | x | x | | |
| Air pollution | | x | x | x | |
| Aircraft noise | | x | x | x | x |
| Industrial noise | | x | | | |
| Industrial waste | x | x | | | |
| Municipal waste | | x | | | |
| Manure | | x | | | |
| Soil contamination | | x | | | |
| Nutrients into water | | x | | | |
| Carbon dioxide | | x | x | x | |
| | | | | | |
| *User charges* | | | | | |
| Water pollution | x | x | | | x |
| Industrial waste | x | x | | | x |
| Municipal waste | x | x | x | x | x |
| | | | | | |
| *Product charges* | | | | | |
| Petrol | | x | x | x | x |
| Diesel | | x | x | x | x |
| Sulfur in oil | | | x | x | |
| Electricity | | x | x | | |
| Gas | | x | x | | |
| Coal | | x | x | x | x |
| Fertilisers | | | x | x | |
| Biocides | | | x | x | |
| Batteries | | | x | x | |
| Vehicles | | | x | | x |
| Miscellaneous packaging | | | x | x | x |
| Beverage containers | | | x | | |
| CFCs | x | | | | x |
| Car tyres | | | | | x |
| Chemicals | | | | | x |

**Table 7.3**  (*Cont'd*)

| Instruments | Australia | Netherlands | Sweden | Norway | USA |
|---|---|---|---|---|---|
| **2.  DEPOSIT-REFUND** | | | | | |
| Plastic bottles | | x | x | x | x |
| Glass bottles | | x | x | x | x |
| Metal cans | | | x | | x |
| Batteries | | | | | x |
| Car hulks | | | x | x | |
| Functioning cars (<3.5 tonnes) | | | x | | |
| **3.  TAX INCENTIVES** | | | | | |
| *Tax differentiation* | | | | | |
| Unleaded/leaded petrol | x | x | x | x | |
| Car sales tax (on vehicle performance) | | x | x | x | x |
| Recycled/ordinary paper | x | | | | |
| General profits on forestry related income | | x | | | |
| *Tax credits, rebates, deductions* | | | | | |
| Soil conservation | x | | | | x |
| Revegetation | x | | | | |
| Land held for nature conservation | | x | | | x |
| Recycling | x | | | | x |
| **4.  OTHER** | | | | | |
| *Tradable permit systems* | | | | | |
| Emissions to air | | | | | x |
| Emissions to water | x | | | | x |
| Water resource | x | | | | |
| Fisheries resource | x | | | | |
| CFCs (prod. and consumption) | | | | | x |
| Low emission vehicles | | | | | x |
| Lead in gasoline | | | | | x |
| Wetland mitigation banking | | | | | x |
| Emissions averaging | | | | | x |

**Table 7.3** (*Cont'd*)

| Instruments | Australia | Netherlands | Sweden | Norway | USA |
|---|---|---|---|---|---|
| *Performance bonds* | | | | | |
| Marine emissions | | | x | | |
| Release of hazardous wastes | | | | | x |
| Excessive acid rain emissions | | | | | x |
| Excessive emissions from heavy vehicles | | | | x | |
| TOTAL | 14 | 24 | 26 | 18 | 31 |

*Note*: For federated nations (Australia and USA), results show instruments that have been applied in more than one state.
*Sources*: OECD 1993; OECD 1994a,b; OECD/IEA 1994; and published national data

have any marked effect on behaviour, although a considerable reduction in usage has nonetheless resulted through the associated education program (Moran 1991).

*Performance bonds* have been used in NSW and Queensland to induce mining companies to rehabilitate mine sites (James 1993, 28). However, a broader application of such instruments to natural resource management (e.g. grazing of public land, forestry operations) and industrial activities (e.g. encouraging pollution reduction and risk minimisation with chemicals and waste) (ACF 1994a,b) has not been undertaken.

Several reports and papers have been published in Australia examining *instruments influencing vehicle emissions*. Instruments employed overseas include road pricing, performance-based tax differentiation, mandatory fuel economy requirements and an associated punitive tax, vehicle retirement schemes, and a range of vehicle registration taxes (Jubb, Mastoris and van Vliet 1992; ACF 1994a,b; Moore 1994b). None of these measures are used in Australia. Projections based on current trends indicate that the increasing volume of motor vehicle emissions will cause a serious deterioration in urban air quality over the next two decades. Vehicles are also a significant source of carbon dioxide in most airsheds (some 87 per cent in Sydney) and of other greenhouse gas emissions. Emission control programs and emission standards for new vehicles have been imposed in Australia since the early 1970s. In 1989, responsibility for vehicle standards was assumed by the Commonwealth under the *Motor Vehicle Standards Act*

1989. However, at present, only voluntary targets exist for fuel efficiency of passenger vehicles (a major indicator of emission levels), as adopted by the Federal Chamber of Automobile Industries (FCAI). The FCAI and other road user lobby groups have applied strong pressure to have voluntary measures set at even lower levels than those currently agreed. One of the major problems facing reform in this area is the number of institutional players involved, and the fragmented division of responsibility between the two levels of government. Constitutionally, the Commonwealth has responsibility for most tax measures. However, states can also implement product charges, and impose levies on fuels, registration and vehicle transfers. This gives states both the scope for individual action and also the potential for uncoordinated policy development.

Despite the acknowledged relationship between the clearing of native vegetation on private land, loss of habitat and threats to biological diversity, most states (excepting South Australia and Victoria) and the Commonwealth have failed to respond to the issue of species preservation on private land with adequate regulatory and market-based instruments. Measures to encourage appropriate management and to assist in conservation on private land, including tax incentives for land restoration work (other than tree planting), penalties for degradation by design or neglect, and performance bonds (ACF 1994a,b), are rare.

## Conclusions and Prospects

To date, market-based instruments have played only a minor role in environment policy in Australia, one largely unchanged over the decade from 1984 to 1994. Moreover, the main instruments have been user fees and charges, primarily imposed as revenue-raising measures but often at levels inadequate to ensure that user-pays or polluter-pays policies are met. In addition, despite the long-standing recognition of hidden subsidies and the underpricing of resource rents, measures proposed to increase the economic return to the state and improve the efficiency and environmental sensitivity of natural resource use have been thwarted by industry lobby groups and related state agencies.

Official interest in greater use of economic measures to combat industrial and diffuse urban pollution is growing, together with the threat of deteriorating urban environmental conditions. However, the application of measures in this area still remains astonishingly weak compared with European nations. Where innovation has occurred to date, instruments such as tradable permits have been shown to be of limited applicability due to the size and composition of domestic industries. Market-based instruments have served to increase the economic efficiency of those resource sectors in which they have been applied. However, they have often had uncertain or negative environmental impacts. For instance, the experience with tradable permits for fisheries, forestry and water points to the importance of ensuring a sufficient base of ecological understanding *prior* to the application of these instruments. Without such understanding, the measures not only do nothing to improve environmental conditions but also may consolidate practices that enhance degradation.

Generally, a series of contradictory pressures prevail. In an attempt to diffuse intergovernmental conflict and improve the coordination of environmental policy, the three tiers of government (Commonwealth, state and local) entered into an historic InterGovernmental Agreement on the Environment (IGAE) in 1992 (C'wlth Govt 1992). The IGAE also proposed the creation of a ministerial council, the National Environment Protection Authority (now Council) (NEPC) for the purpose of producing national environmental protection measures. It would be through the NEPC and related ministerial councils that national proposals for new economic instruments would be agreed. Such undoubted gains in environmental policy integration and coordination have, however, been achieved at the expense of bold innovation. (At the start of 1995, even the NEPC is yet to be established.) Although these developments have led to improved communication between states and the Federal Government on issues like common standards, they have also infused discussions with a conservativism that is retarding progress and encouraging a 'lowest common denominator' approach to policy agreements (despite the proposal that NEPC initiatives may be agreed by a two-thirds majority rather than the usual intergovernmental consensus). Significant political tensions survive between the states and Commonwealth over the orientation and implementation of environmental policy. These tensions should, in principle, increase the attractiveness of fiscal measures that can be applied from the national level when the Commonwealth seeks to overcome obstacles of implementation at state level without direct political confrontation.

Meanwhile, the Australian states continue to compete for domestic and foreign investment. In the absence of national coordination of industry development, this has increased the vulnerability of individual states to industry pressure and generally led them to shun environmental taxes and charges on industry as potential disincentives to investment. Indeed, resource charges for primary and manufacturing industries have often been cross-subsidised to enhance locational attractiveness in the hope that other benefits such as employment and other industry-related charges would balance these initial losses. Nevertheless, the deregulatory trend of the 1980s has encouraged environment protection agencies and state and Commonwealth governments to look closely at the realities of implementing market-based measures, in part to meet the increasing need for additional revenue. However, there is an acute awareness within the EPAs of the limits to the rhetoric about market-based instruments: the measures require no less regulation and monitoring than before — and perhaps an increased administrative burden — to work economically. Consequently, without additional resources, some instruments might actually result in a deterioration of environmental conditions.

Finally, sectoral community interests have occasionally expressed public hostility towards the imposition of full-cost pricing of resources or the use of economic instruments as disincentives for resource use for reasons of social equity and because of the regressivity of most environmental charges. Nevertheless, key national environment organisations such as the Australian Conservation Foundation are now advocating a wide ranging reform of the tax system (ACF 1994a,b). Such proposals place greater emphasis on resource-based taxes and incentives, deployed within a strict ecologically based regulatory framework, aimed at improving the efficiency of resource conservation, and waste and pollution minimisation, and imposed with appropriate compensation for low income earners.

Overall, during the coming decade, one can expect Australia to slowly — reluctantly — follow the European trend towards an increased use of market-based instruments. These will be implemented to counter growing urban environmental pressures, to provide new sources of revenue (no doubt accompanied by conflict over whether the funds from these imposts will be fully hypothecated to finance environmental programs or funnelled into consolidated revenue) and to offer financial incentives for environmentally appropriate behaviour in areas that remain beyond the scope of strict regulation, such as the management of biological diversity on private land. However, the adoption of new measures is likely to be varied and uneven across the country until the Federal Government exerts national control over the framing and implementation of these tools of environmental policy.

# Endnotes

1. Under the Australian Constitution, framed in 1901, the Commonwealth government has no explicit legislative power with respect to the environment in areas not under its direct jurisdiction, although it is able to regulate the environment directly through use of its other powers, such as taxation, trade and commerce and external affairs.

2. By 1990, only Victoria and Western Australia had established environment protection agencies. New South Wales had its State Pollution Control Commission, superceded by an EPA in 1992. Other states and territories had a range of state councils and departments with environment protection functions included alongside public works, transport, engineering and water supply. A Commonwealth EPA was created in 1992. Based on a cooperative agreement between the Commonwealth and state governments, it represents an attempt to generate and coordinate nationally uniform environmental standards.

3. At different times, this department has been called the Department of Home Affairs and Environment; Department of Arts, Heritage and Environment; Department of Arts, Sport, Environment, Tourism and Territories; and Department of Environment, Sport and Territories (current title).

4. A prominent example was the 1983 High Court decision that had upheld the Federal Government's right to intervene to protect the Franklin River — part of South West Tasmanian World Heritage estate — from being dammed by the Tasmanian Hydro Electricity Commission, with Tasmanian Government support. Similar instances of federal–state conflict over constitutional rights and environmental management marked the 1980s (Christoff 1994).

5. When, in 1992, Victoria also introduced amendments to its planning regulations to prohibit clearing, no incentives or compensation were made available. No other states have provided strict regulations to control the clearing of native vegetation, which, in 1994, continues at the rate of over 600 000 hectares each year and is responsible for some 24 per cent of national carbon dioxide emissions.

6. These measures were removed from the *Income Tax Assessment Act* in 1983, although ambiguities and loop-holes, which allow the clearing of regrowth, still remain.

7. The two programs are *One Billion Trees*, which, as the name suggests, aims to see one billion trees planted by Year 2000, and the national Landcare movement.

8. The Australian term for those politicians, policy advisers and economists whose predominant ideological goal was the reduction of state intervention and regulation in almost all areas of economic activity.

9. Each of these looked at economic instruments: for example, the IGAE included specific mention of improved valuation, pricing and incentive mechanisms (Cwlth Govt 1992, 14).

10. For example, the construction of a national (coal-based) electricity grid incorporating competing suppliers will see a lowering of power costs, and counter the impact of energy efficiency measures aimed at cutting greenhouse gas emissions.

11. In February 1995, the federal Environmental Minister withdrew his proposal for a carbon levy, which was to be introduced in the 1995 Budget. He did so in response to concerted pressure from industry and unions, hostile and inaccurate media coverage of the economic implications of such a levy, and a clear rejection of the idea — prior to Cabinet discussion — by his ministerial colleagues.

12. In other words, despite the dominance of economic rationalism in other policy areas and the work of proselytisers of privatisation and property rights as the solution to environmental problems (Bennett and Block 1991; Moran, Chisholm and Porter 1991), a more measured consensus has emerged around the notion of government as a limited *facilitator* and *shaper* of the policy environment within which a range of different instruments, including market-based ones, could be applied.

13. Parts of this section draw on a report by David James (1993) to the Commonwealth Department of Environment, Sport and Territories, which is based on responses to a questionnaire by the OECD Environment Directorate on the use of economic instruments.

14. Note, however, that these tables tend to overstate the application of instruments: in many cases, only one or a few states or local governments have adopted the instruments identified in the table as being in use.

15. In other states, container litter reduction and recycling are largely the responsiblity of local government. Enforcement of Litter Acts (usually by local government), community education, voluntary local-council-based recycling (where this exists) and formal and occasional voluntary community programs for litter removal (such as the 'Keep Australia Beautiful' campaign and national Clean-up days) are the main approaches used.

16. There is a danger, however, that in the absence of appropriate environmental research and safeguards, such trading will `relocate' environmental pressures. In other words, reallocation of water from degraded and therefore less productive areas to new, less degraded areas and therefore more productive areas may lead to further environmental degradation in the future.

17. Other factors also serve to undermine gains in resource use efficiency that the strategy and its licensing process might have encouraged. In Victoria (as elsewhere in Australia), substantial subsidies pass to industry through the taxation system, through the underpricing of sawlogs, and the provision of roading and other infrastructure without full cost recovery by the state (Govt Vict, 1983; Parl. NSW 1990; RAC 1991; Rose and Bhati 1992; AGV 1993).

18. As for Tables 7.1 and 7.2, Table 7.3 also overstates Australian developments, which in many cases may be found in perhaps two or three states only.

# References

Auditor-General (AG). (1993) *Implementation of an Interim Greenhouse Response: Department of Primary Industries and Energy, Energy Management Programs*, Audit Report No. 32 1992–93, Australian National Audit Office, Australian Government Publishing Service (AGPS), Canberra.

Auditor-General of Victoria (AGV). (1993) *Timber Industry Strategy*, Special Report No. 22, Government Printer, Melbourne.

Australian Bureau of Agricultural and Resource Economics (ABARE). (1993) *Use of Economic Instruments in Integrated Coastal Zone Management*, Consultancy Report to the Resource Assessment Commission Coastal Zone Inquiry.

Australian Conservation Foundation (ACF). (1994a) *Federal Budget 1994–95: Priorities for the Environment*, Submission to the Federal Government, February, Australian Conservation Foundation, Melbourne.

ACF. (1994b) *Investing in the Future: Federal Budget 1995–96*, Submission to the Federal Government, December, Australian Conservation Foundation, Melbourne.

Australian Environment Council (AEC). (1982) *Report on Litter Control*, Report No. 8, prepared by the Litter Control Committee of the Australian Environment Council, AGPS, Canberra.

Bennett, J. and Block, W. (eds). (1991) *Reconciling Economics and the Environment*, Australian Institute for Public Policy, Perth, Australia.

Bernauer, D. and O'Shea, H. B. (1994) *Pollution Charge Systems: An Information Paper*, Environmental Economics Series, NSW Environment Protection Authority, Sydney.

Carroll, J. and Manne, R. (eds). (1992) *Shutdown: The Failure of Economic Rationalism and How to Rescue Australia*, Text Publishing, Melbourne.

Christoff, P. (1994) 'Environmental Politics' in J. Brett, J. Gillespie and M. Goot (eds), *Developments in Australian Politics*, Macmillan, Melbourne.

Commonwealth Environment Protection Agency (CEPA). (1992) *National Waste Minimisation and Recycling Strategy*, Department of Arts, Sport, the Environment and Territories, Canberra.

Commonwealth Government (C'wlth Govt). (1992) *Inter-Governmental Agreement on the Environment*.

Community Education and Policy Development Group (CEPDG). (1993) *The State of the Environment Report for South Australia 1993*, Department of Environment and Land Management, South Australia.

Department of Arts, Heritage and the Environment (DAHE). (1985) *Economic Development and Sustainable Resource Use*, Environmental Papers, AGPS, Canberra.

Department of Finance (Dept Fin.). (1994) *In Pursuit of Australia's Environment and Resource Goals: The Potential Role of Economic Instruments*, Department of Finance Discussion Paper.

Department of Home Affairs and Environment (DHAE). (1983) *Economics and Environment Policy: The Role of Cost-Benefit Analysis*,

AGPS, Canberra.

Department of Home Affairs and Environment (DHAE). (1984) *Conservation and the Economy: Economic and Environmental Policies for Sustainable Development*, Papers from the Third Conference on the Economics of Environmental Management, sponsored by the Department of Home Affairs and Environment, the NSW State Pollution Control Commission and the NSW National Parks and Wildlife Service, Sydney, September 13–14.

Department of Prime Minister and Cabinet (DPMC). (1989) *Our Country, Our Future*, Statement on the Environment, the Hon. R.J.L. Hawke, A.C., Prime Minister of Australia, AGPS, Canberra, July.

Ecologically Sustainable Development Working Group (ESDWG). (1991) *Draft Report — Energy Production*, AGPS, Canberra, August 1991.

Economic Planning Advisory Council (EPAC). (1992a) *Issues in the Pricing and Management of Natural Resources*, Background Paper No. 16, AGPS, Canberra.

EPAC. (1992b) *Recent Developments in Resource Pricing and Allocation Policy*, Discussion paper submitted to EPAC by the Commonwealth Department of Primary Industries and Energy, AGPS, Canberra, March.

EPAC. (1992c) *Managing Australia's Natural Resources*, AGPS, Canberra, April.

Gentle, D. G. (1992) 'The Price of Fish: The Use of Market Mechanisms in Australian Fisheries Management' in Economic Planning Advisory Council, *Issues in the Pricing and Management of Natural Resources*, Background Paper No. 16, AGPS, Canberra, pp. 95–111.

Government of Victoria (Govt Vict.). (1983) *A Review of Royalty Systems to Price Wood from Victorian State Forests*, Report of the Forests Advisory Committee to the Minister for Economic Development, Melbourne, May.

Grabosky, P. and Braithwaite, J. (1986) *Of Manners Gentle: Enforcement Strategies of Australian Business Regulatory Agencies*, Oxford University Press, Melbourne/New York.

Greiner, N. (1991) Opening Address by the Hon. Nick Greiner MP, Premier of New South Wales, *The New Environmentalism: Applying Economic Solutions in the Real World*, Conference hosted by the NSW Cabinet Office and the NSW Department of Water Resources, March.

Groenhout, R. (1994) *Using Economic Instruments to Control Salinity in the Hunter River*, Environmental Economics Series, NSW Environment Protection Authority, Sydney.

Hahn, R. W. (1991) 'Meeting the Growing Demand for Environmental Protection: A Practical Guide to the Economist's Tool Chest', Paper to *The New Environmentalism: Applying Economic Solutions in the Real World*, Conference hosted by the NSW Cabinet Office and the NSW Department of Water Resources, March.

Hahn, R. W. and Hester, G. L. (1989) 'Marketable Permits: Lessons for Theory and Practice', *Ecology Law Quarterly* 16, 361–406.

Hilmer, F. G, Rayner, M. and Taperell, G. (1993) *National Competition Policy*, Report by the Independent Committee of Inquiry, AGPS, Canberra, August.

House of Representatives Standing Committee on Environment and Conservation (HRSCEC). (1987) *Fiscal Measures and the Achievement of Environmental Objectives*, Report of the House of Representatives Standing Committe on Environment and Conservation, AGPS, Canberra.

James, D. (1993) *Using Economic Instruments for Meeting Environmental Objectives: Australia's Experience*, Environmental Economics Research Paper No. 1, Department of Environment, Sport and Territories, Canberra.

James, D. (1994) *Using Economic Instruments to Control Pollution in the Hawkesbury Nepean River*, Environmental Economics Series, NSW Environment Protection Authority, Sydney.

Jubb, C., Mastoris, I. and van Vilet, R. (1992) *Environmental Regulation: The Economics of Tradable Permits — A Survey of Theory and Practice*, Research Report 42, Bureau of Industry Economics, AGPS, Canberra.

Millington, P. (1991) 'The Water Market: A NSW Case Study', Paper delivered at *The New Environmentalism: Applying Economic Solutions in the Real World* Conference, hosted by the NSW Cabinet Office and the NSW Department of Water Resources, March.

Moore, W. (1994a) *Using Economic Instruments to Control Air Pollution from Stationary Sources*, Environmental Economics Series, NSW Environment Protection Authority, Sydney.

Moore, W. (1994b) *Using Economic Instruments to Control Vehicle Emissions*, Environmental Economics Series, NSW Environment Protection Authority, Sydney.

Moran, A., Chisholm, A. and Porter, M. (eds). *Markets, Resources and the Environment*, Allen and Unwin, Sydney.

Moran, A. (1991) 'Addressing the Limits of Market Solutions' in J. Bennett and W. Block (eds), *Reconciling Economics and the Environment*, Australian Institute for Public Policy, Perth.

Munro, I. (1993) 'Petrol Tax Fuels Old Divisions', *The Sunday Age*, 29 August, p. 2.

Musgrave, W. (1991) 'Property Rights and Water Allocation: Policy, Institutional and Management Issues', Paper delivered at *The New Environmentalism: Applying Economic Solutions in the Real World* Conference, hosted by the NSW Cabinet Office and the NSW Department of Water Resources, March.

Organisation for Economic Cooperation and Development (OECD). (1985) *Environment and Economics*, OECD, Paris.

OECD. (1986) *Economic Instruments for Environmental Protection in the Netherlands*, Unpublished Paper, OECD Environment Directorate, OECD, Paris.

OECD. (1989) *Economic Instruments for Environmental Protection*, OECD, Paris.

OECD. (1993) *OECD Environmental Performance Reviews — Norway*, OECD, Paris.

OECD. (1994a) *Managing the Environment: The Role of Economic Instruments*, OECD, Paris.

OECD. (1994b) *Environment and Taxation: The Cases of the Netherlands, Sweden and the United States*, OECD, Paris.

OECD/International Energy Agency (IEA). (1994) *Climate Change Policy Initiatives — 1994 Update, Volume 1 — OECD Countries*, OECD, Paris.

Owen, A. D. (1991) *Tradable Emissions as a Greenhouse Response Measure*, Greenhouse Studies Report No. 5, Department of Arts, Sport, the Environment, Tourism and Territories, AGPS, Canberra.

Parliament of New South Wales (Parl. NSW). (1990) *Report on the Forestry Commission*, Report No. 52, Public Accounts Committee of the 49th Parliament, December, Sydney.

Paterson, J. (1992) 'Water Utilities and Water Resources' in *Issues in the Pricing and Management of Natural Resources*, Background Paper No. 16, Economic Planning Advisory Council (EPAC), AGPS, Canberra, pp. 67–80.

Pearce, D., Markayanda, A. and Barbier, E. B. (1989) *Blueprint for a Green Economy*, Earthscan, London.

Pigram, J. J., Delforce, R. J., Coelli, M. L., Norris, V., Antony, G., Anderson, R. L. and Musgrave, W. F. (1992) *Transferable Water Entitlements in Australia*, Report to the Land and Water Research and Development Corporation, Centre for Water Policy Research, University of New England, Australia.

Price Waterhouse. (1991) *Carbon Tax as a Greenhouse Response Measure*, Greenhouse Studies Report No. 4, Department of Arts, Sport, the Environment, Tourism and Territories, AGPS, Canberra.

Pusey, M. (1991) *Economic Rationalism in Australia: A Nation-building State changes its Mind*, Cambridge University Press, Melbourne.

Resource Assessment Commission (RAC). (1991) *Forest and Timber Inquiry Draft Report Volume 1*, AGPS, Canberra.

Rose, R. and Bhati, U. N. (1992) 'Pricing of Logs from Native Forests' in Economic Planning Advisory Council, *Issues in the Pricing and Management of Natural Resources*, Background Paper No. 16, AGPS, Canberra.

Senate Standing Committee on Environment, Recreation and the Arts (SSCERA). (1994) *Waste Disposal — A Report of the Senate Standing Committee on Environment, Recreation and the Arts*, Parliament House, Canberra.

Stapleton, J. (1993) 'ALP's Petrol Tax Hits the True Believers', *Sydney Morning Herald*, 24 August, p. 1.

Tietenberg, T. H. (1985) *Emissions Trading: An Exercise in Reforming Pollution Policy*, Resources for the Future, Washington, DC.

Toyne, P. (1994) *The Reluctant Nation: Environment, Law and Politics in Australia*, Australian Broadcasting Commission Books, Sydney.

Ware, J. A. (1985) *Fiscal Measures and the Attainment of Environment Objectives: Scandinavian Initiatives and Their Applicability to Australia*, Department of Arts, Heritage and the Environment, Environment Paper, AGPS, Canberra.

# Part IV

## *Competition and Environmental Performance*

# 8

# Governing at a Distance: Self-regulating Green Markets

## Peter N. Grabosky[1]

## Introduction

Although recently overshadowed by the economy as the major issue of contemporary public concern, the environment remains high on the policy agenda, and is destined to remain so. At the same time, it is becoming widely acknowledged that the capacity of governments to achieve desirable social goals, among them protection of the environment, is not without limits. Continued pressures on governments to reduce public expenditures and to foster a climate favourable to business remain dominant facts of political life. This leads one to ask how non-governmental resources may be mobilised in furtherance of environmental objectives.

This chapter addresses one variety of non-governmental resource: commercial activity within the private sector that is not the subject of direct regulation or the direct application of economic instruments. Such commercial 'third parties', and the influence they exert on and through markets, already have a significant effect on the regulatory landscape and on environmental quality. Their potential contribution is even greater.

The chapter begins with a brief and general discussion of non-governmental interests and their relationship to public policy. In so doing, it reviews recent trends in the devolution of state functions to non-governmental institutions. It then provides an overview of the regulatory landscape for environmental protection, introducing the basic elements of a regulatory ordering, and discussing forms of interaction between institutions and instruments that might comprise such an ordering.

Next, the chapter turns to one corner of this broad canvass — the issue of 'green markets' or environmentally appropriate commercial activity.[2] Notwithstanding the extent of environmental degradation that may be attributed to market failure, it is suggested that there remains considerable potential for harnessing market forces in furtherance of environmental interests. The primary focus will be on 'naturally occurring' market phenomena, and on those occurring as by-products of regulation, as opposed to the direct application of economic instruments (such as effluent charges and licence fees) devised by governments either independently or as an adjunct to command-and-control regulation. It will become apparent that, in some settings, the influence of market forces in furtherance of environmental protection can exceed that wielded by government regulators. The chapter seeks to describe and to explain some of the considerable opportunities that now exist for those of entrepreneurial inclination to profit from environmentalism. In so doing, we shall enjoy the brighter side of the *double entendre* contained in the old adage, 'where there's muck, there's money'.

The chapter concludes with a discussion of what particular institutional orderings might best enhance the constructive operation of market forces in furtherance of environmental interests.

## New Technologies of Government

Before the rise of the modern state, many functions that came to be regarded as core responsibilities of government were carried out by non-governmental institutions or individuals. As the state grew in power and scope, it assumed an increasing number of functions such as welfare, criminal justice, and education. But even at the high water mark of state influence, governments were hardly monopolists of social control and conflict resolution. Rather, governments shared many functions with various non-state institutions, both formal and informal.

The idea that governance can be subtle or indirect is very old indeed; the ancient Chinese philosopher Lao Tzu observed that the wisest leader is one who does not appear to be governing, but makes use of the efforts of others. By fostering the belief among subjects that they are self-determining, the sage ruler 'accomplishes without having to act' (Lao Tzu 1963, 108).

Law, too, had its analogues outside the public sector. Observers such as Ehrlich (1912), who came to be known as 'Legal Pluralists", saw law as but the top stratum from which a web of quasi-legal rules and controls ordered everyday life. More recent scholars began to focus on the inter-relationship between state law and private forms of social control and conflict resolution (Fitzpatrick 1984).

One of the seminal thinkers of the late 20th century, Michael Foucault, observed that the real practice of government was not through the imposition of law, but rather working with and through the constellation of interests, institutions and inter-personal relations that are part of civil society (Foucault 1991). Burchell adds further texture to Foucault's outline when he refers to 'governing in accordance with the grain of things' (1991, 127) and the role of the state in guiding conditions so that interests may converge in furtherance of the public good.

Teubner (1983) has spoken of how, instead of imposing direct substantive controls on behaviour, states might structure mechanisms for self-regulation. He refers to the fostering of a 'regulated autonomy' based largely on private orderings. The state facilitates the development of these self-regulating systems rather than engaging in direct intervention.

Rose and Miller (1992) refer to this as 'governing at a distance', using 'new technologies of government', which harness energies resident outside the public sector in furtherance of public policy:

> The question is no longer one of accounting for government in terms of the 'power of the state', but of ascertaining how, and to what extent, the state is articulated into the activity of government: what relations are established between political and other authorities; what funds, forces, persons, knowledge or legitimacy are utilised; and by means of what devices and techniques are these different tactics made operable
>
> (1992, 177).

This line of argument has been popularised in the very influential North American book *Reinventing Government* (Osborne and Gaebler 1992).[3] Recognising that government as traditionally configured has its constraints and limitations, the authors advocate that governments adopt the role of facilitator and broker, rather than that of commander. They suggest that governments 'steer' rather than 'row', and that they structure the marketplace so that naturally occurring private activity may assist in furthering public policy objectives. Osborne and Gaebler use the term 'leverage' to refer to this approach (1992, 280).

*The Shrinking State*

This idea of a 'hybrid space of government' combining public and private energies (Burchell 1991, 141) is receiving increasing recognition just as the traditional activities of the state have begun to be called into question. Recently, Western industrial societies have experienced a contraction in the role of the state (Crook, Pakulski and Walters 1992, ch 3). Inspired in part by ideology, in part by chronic fiscal constraint, and in part by a recognition that some functions normally performed by the state can be performed by non-governmental actors more effectively and at less cost, this transfer of state functions has taken numerous forms.

In some instances, state responsibilities have been shed upwards. Most nations today are bound by numerous international covenants and treaties that establish standards and define appropriate conduct in realms as diverse as the interdiction of illicit drug traffic and the protection of migratory birds.[4] Member nations of the European Community (EC) are bound by EC regulations. Other institutions such as the World Bank exercise considerable control over national economies.

In the domestic realm, the commingling of public and private resources in furtherance of social control has been accorded extensive treatment.[5] In one type of public–private interface, the state may conscript private institutions to perform functions in furtherance of public policy. In Australia and a number of other Western nations, banks are required by law routinely to report transactions over a certain threshold, and those transactions that are of a suspicious nature irrespective of their amount, to a governmental authority. Thus have banks become instruments of policy to combat tax evasion, drug traffic, and money laundering generally. Similarly, immigration authorities routinely require that international airlines screen passengers to ensure that they possess valid travel documents (Gilboy 1992).

In some cases, the state may simply abdicate its activities, and leave them to markets to provide. The demise of government business enterprises, from transportation, to insurance, to publishing are but three examples. In other instances, private activity will emerge to meet a need that has been neglected by governments. Early efforts on behalf of victims of sexual assault and domestic violence were provided by 'grass-roots' collectivities, precisely because public agencies of health, welfare and criminal justice were regarded as unresponsive to victims' needs.

Another form of governmental devolution is that of contracting to private enterprise functions previously performed by public agencies. Here one sees activities previously regarded as quintessential state responsibilities, such as the management of prisons, now often performed by the private sector.

The devolution (or upward transfer) of state functions may also occur by mutual agreement between public and private sectors. Through agreements of varying degrees of formality, international air carriers cooperate with immigration authorities in processing and repatriating undocumented aliens (Gilboy 1992), and customs authorities enlist the assistance of major importers to report activities that may indicate movement of contraband.

Governments may invite routine contributions by private interests to public forums. To be sure, this in part reflects democratic principles, and the need to maintain legitimacy. But one may also regard the contributions of interest groups as information resources, which might lie beyond the normal inclination or capacity of public authorities to generate.[6]

What, then, are the implications of the above trends for environmental protection?

## On Regulatory Orderings for Environmental Protection

Although it is not uncommon to think of environmental regulation as the exclusive province of government, Shearing (1993) reminds us that the function of corporate social control is shared by a variety of institutions in the public, private, and non-profit sectors.[7] Indeed, in light of the above discussion of governmental technologies, it could be argued that some of these control functions are performed more effectively, more efficiently, and with greater legitimacy (from the standpoint of the regulatee) by non-governmental institutions, than by government agencies.

A given regulatory domain, or 'policy space' (Harter and Eads 1985), will contain a variety of institutions, each possessing a set of resources or instruments. At a general level within the domain of environmental protection, these may be categorised as follows:

1. Command-and-control regulation by government authorities, including the mandating of standards and licensing conditions, and the enforcement of non-compliance.
2. Fiscal and monetary policy by government authorities, including the use of taxes, charges, and incentives.
3. Government-based information-based strategies, such as 'community right to know' legislation.
4. Third party activity by citizens' interest groups and individuals, including public information, interest articulation, liti-

gation, information, and oversight of public and private sector activity.

5.   Activity by commercial third parties, including banks, insurance companies, institutional investors, the environmental services industry, and others exerting influence through the market.

6.   Self-regulatory activity, including standards developed by the private sector, monitoring strategies such as environmental audit, and internal compliance programs.

7.   Property rights, or privatisation, where environmental resources are sold to the highest bidder, and their management left to private decision making.

These categories are not mutually exclusive. For example, tradable emissions permits entail the combination of regulatory standards and property rights. Self-regulatory activity may enlist the participation of citizens and/or commercial third parties.

The fact that state regulatory agencies do not exist *in vacuo*, but rather in a framework of mutually constitutive interaction with non-governmental institutions and actors, suggests that to focus on a single institution, in whatever sector, gives one a limited perspective on the regulatory process. Indeed, one of the most neglected areas of regulatory analysis is the interaction between sets of instruments within and between the general categories specified above.[8]

## On the Complementarity of Regulatory Institutions and Instruments

The interaction of regulatory institutions, and of the instruments they command, may take numerous forms. The following section presents a typology of interactions, and offers some tentative illustrations from the domain of environmental protection.

*Neutralisation*
The term neutralisation refers to the effect of one institution in negating or diluting the effects of another. Criticism voiced by a citizen's group about the polluting behaviour of a large industrial corporation may be neutralised by a public relations campaign on the part of the company, which portrays itself as a paragon of environmental stewardship.[9]

*Catalysis*
The term catalysis refers to the effect of a given institution or instrument in initiating a reaction between two others. As will be

discussed in greater detail below, consumer demand for environmentally appropriate products may inspire retailers to exert considerable influence on manufacturers to conform to 'green' specifications.

## Inhibition

Inhibitors are the opposite of catalysts. For example, it might be argued that the law of libel, by deterring criticism of a particular polluter or of a regulatory authority, inhibits the influence that an environmentalist organisation may otherwise have in pressing for more stringent regulatory enforcement against polluters.

## Activation

By activation, we refer to a situation whereby a particular institution or instrument is requisite to the functioning of another. The activating condition may be required in advance of, concurrently with, or following use of the other instrument.

Regulations regarding product safety and environmental protection in Sweden have inspired technological innovation and competitive advantage in a number of industries; similar efficiencies have been achieved in the Netherlands (Huppes and Kagan 1990, 225; Porter 1990, 648). The regulations may be regarded as activators if the innovations would not otherwise have occurred.

## Redundancy

Redundancy occurs when one institution duplicates the activities of another. One might envisage, for example, a federal agency and a state authority each undertaking a lifecycle analysis of the same brand of washing machines. Redundancy may occur across jurisdictions in a federal system, or it may reflect duplication of effort by public agencies and private interests.

## Synergy

The term synergy refers to interactions in which each instrument enhances the effect of the other. The combined action of the two instruments is thus greater than that of their independent contributions added together (Russell 1988, 268). The institution of 'eco-labelling', or formal certification of products as being environmentally preferable, facilitates environmentally conscious purchasing behaviour, and amplifies the influence of consumers. The exercise of consumer purchasing power in turn enhances the legitimacy and credibility of the eco-label.

## Complementarity

Here we refer to circumstances where one institution functions to fill a gap left by the absence or inactivity of another. In the United

States, the expansion of citizen litigation under the *Clean Water Act* in response to the perceived relaxation of enforcement by the EPA constitutes one example (Boyer and Meidinger 1985).

In recent years, marine insurance underwriters have been concerned about inadequate government inspection of maritime vessels, particularly those flying 'flags of convenience'. To compensate for this regulatory shortfall, and to ensure that the vessels they insure are indeed seaworthy, underwriters have engaged their own marine surveyors to inspect the vessels of prospective clients.

## The Genesis of Market Opportunities for Environmental Protection

To what extent can market forces arising from individuals' social preferences produce environmentally beneficial consequences? Economists maintain that reliance on markets is more likely to result in cost-effective outcomes than solutions imposed by command-and-control requirements (see Schultze 1977; Moran 1990, 11; and Moran and Hahn in this volume).

Market opportunities arise from a number of influences. As noted above, command-and-control regulation, by prohibiting, specifying or discouraging certain practices, may inspire a quest for more environmentally appropriate alternatives. Impending restrictions on the use of CFC aerosol propellants stimulated a search for substitutes; limits on permissible levels of lead in petrol encourage the development of unleaded petrol and alternative automotive fuels.

Herein lies a significant irony: command-and-control regulation, often regarded as an economic burden, may actually create commercial opportunities. Regulation, rather than stifling economic activity, can trigger innovation, and thereby produce a competitive advantage to the innovator (Porter 1990, 585–88; Braithwaite 1993; Jacobs 1993). It is by no means coincidental that the world's leading exporters of pollution control products are those OECD countries with the most stringent environmental regulations; Japan leads in air pollution control, Germany in water pollution abatement technology, the Netherlands in soil remediation and the United States in the management of toxic waste (OECD 1992, 19).

A range of impending directives and standards to be introduced by the European Community will further stimulate the environment industry. New industries have also emerged to assist production engineers in assessing the relative environmental impacts of particular materials and processes.

Market opportunities are also created as a result of changing consumer preferences. Growing public sensitivity to environmental issues is reflected in consumer behaviour. Consumers who are environmentally aware are inclined to purchase products that they perceive to be environmentally appropriate, and to favour products of manufacturers who have otherwise demonstrated concern for the environment. Companies that are in a position to demonstrate their credibility as environmentally responsible corporate citizens, and thereby benefit from consumer preferences, will thus enjoy a competitive advantage (Stewart 1992). Indeed, consumer preferences may be more exacting than regulatory requirements. In the words of one Swedish pulp and paper operator, 'it would be easy if we only had to cope with the regulators: It is the consumer's pressure that changes us most' (Beaucamp and Girgensohn 1992, 24).[10] Substantial public relations and marketing advantages can flow from a legitimately earned reputation as an environmentally responsible company.

The influence of consumer preferences also extends to the financial industry. We discuss below how financial institutions are concerned about the image (and liability) of their corporate borrowers. It will also be noted that banks, in their pursuit of competitive advantage, are becoming increasingly sensitised to the importance of projecting a green image with regard to their own retail operations (Mechlin 1993).

Collaboration between companies can lead to mutual advantage. The United States computer manufacturer Digital Equipment converted 15 tons of recycled computer plastic into roof tiles for two McDonald's restaurants in Chicago. Both companies are able to boast an enhanced 'green image'.

Failure to anticipate changes in consumer demand can be costly indeed. The United States automobile industry paid a heavy price for its neglect of emerging preferences for more fuel-efficient vehicles. The more prescient Japanese industry seized the competitive advantage at the time of the 1973 oil crisis, an advantage it has continued to enjoy for two decades.

A third factor influencing market opportunity is the profit potential arising from technology-driven efficiency. More efficient production can also be cleaner production. In many manufacturing processes, consumer preferences are gratuitous, since efficiencies in production are inherently green. For example, improvements over the years in smelting technology have enabled more efficient processing of ore, which incidentally achieves reduction in emissions.

Simple efforts to reduce waste in organisations can combine favourable environmental impact with significant profitability (Schmidheiny 1992). Not only can waste minimisation programs appeal to downstream purchasers and to an environmentally conscious public, they can also achieve substantial cost reduction. As a result of its 'Pollution Prevention Pays' program, the 3M Corporation claims to have saved US$500 million over 15 years (Berle 1991, 213).

The influence of regulation, consumer preferences, and process-driven opportunities have produced at least seven emerging trends in environmentally appropriate commercial activity.

*1.    Consumer Preferences for Environmentally Appropriate Products: Scrutiny of Suppliers and Buyers*

The power of consumer preference is by no means wielded solely by the ultimate purchaser. Companies affect each others' behaviour. Purchasers influence suppliers; in industry, the interchange between buyers and suppliers generates incentives to innovate (Porter 1990, 590).

Large retailers are in a position to register their product and process preferences with suppliers, and the awesome purchasing power that large retailers command often carries considerable influence. The influence of the retail sector in driving innovation is widely recognised (Porter 1990, 502, 523). Suppliers' practices can bear on a retailer's public image, and buyers are increasingly sensitive to the risk of being tainted by a supplier's questionable environmental performance. To this end, buyers are tending increasingly to scrutinise products from a 'cradle to grave' perspective, noting such considerations as energy efficiency in manufacture, minimisation and responsible disposal of waste, economical use of materials in packaging, and recyclability of product (Stuart 1992). Anticipated purchasing power may also influence product design. Thus are producers of raw materials and manufacturers of basic ingredients such as cold rolled steel, normally beyond the reach of the average consumer, subject to the discipline of environmentally conscious purchasing.

In 1990, McDonald's Restaurants began a program to purchase $100 million worth of products made from recycled materials each year. The British retail chemist Boots has set a goal to reduce the volume of packaging of its merchandise by 75 per cent by 1997 (Reuters 1992a). Another firm in the United Kingdom requires every supplier to have a company environmental policy, affirmed by an audit (Stuart 1992). In addition, it has developed a comprehensive questionnaire to obtain information from prospective suppliers. Successful suppliers are required to sign codes of conduct and to manage their activity in accordance with specified principles. Non-compliance may lead to the buyer obtaining a new source of supply.

Similarly, British Telecom encourages prospective suppliers to explain their own environmental programs, and encourages them to be responsible for their products' environmental impact. A company questionnaire seeks information from prospective suppliers on the use of recycled materials in their products, and the potential for reuse and recycling of products. It further seeks to identify any environmental hazards that may arise during the course of the product's life, energy consumption entailed in manufacture, and the supplier's plans for improving its overall environmental performance. British Telecom also encourages supplier buy-back of products after their normal life.

While larger suppliers command the resources and organisational infrastructure to develop environmental management programs, their smaller counterparts may not. Confronted with detailed requirements specified by the purchaser, small business may be unable to compete in the market. There are nevertheless other green purchasing strategies that may help the smaller supplier.

A more cooperative approach to prospective suppliers is that taken by the Body Shop cosmetics retailer, which assists suppliers in self-assessment, and works with them to improve their environmental performance. At other times, the Body Shop can be more adversarial, and more demanding. Recently, it advised a supplier that the company would consider increasing its purchases if the supplier were to adopt a formal environmental policy, publish a comprehensive audit report, and end 'unnecessary confontation with environmental groups' (Greenpeace 1993).

Wal-Mart, a large retailer in the United States, encourages its suppliers to reduce overpackaging, and actively seeks environmentally preferable changes to their products (Elkington, Knight and Hailes 1992, 126). The retailer then actively publicises their achievements (Berle 1991, 143). The company is even developing prototype 'green' stores, which would be designed and managed consistent with principles of low energy consumption, low waste generation, and recyclability (Platt 1992). By calling public attention to their environmental policies and practices, retailers perform an educative function that extends well beyond the conventional marketing role (Schmidheiny 1992, 112). This in turn can help to shape future consumer preferences.

Scrutiny of suppliers is hardly the sole province of retailers. Manufacturers are also in a position to influence supplier behaviour. Volvo, for example, asks that its suppliers comply with its environmental standards.

Even financial institutions may work to improve the environmental performance of their suppliers. One large bank, in its invitations to tender for the supply of a variety of goods and services, asks whether the prospective supplier has an environmental policy, whether it has environmental management systems in place, and inquires about the company's philosophy of compliance with environmental regulations (Lury and Hatfield 1992).

Governments themselves are significant consumers of goods and services, and wield great potential influence in the market (Porter 1990, 127). They may therefore exercise their very considerable purchasing power in furtherance of environmental objectives. Just as large retailers can demand environmentally appropriate products from their suppliers, so too can governments. Government purchasing power, no less than that of large buyers in the private sector, can stimulate innovation. By contributing to the demand for such products as recycled paper, governments may nurture a market, strengthen demand for new products, and assist emerging industries.

In 1992, the Australian Government, which spends about $10 billion each year buying goods and services, announced an environmental purchasing policy (Australia 1992). The policy seeks to identify and to promote environmentally sound products and to raise the awareness of buyers. In addition, it seeks to encourage industry to develop new products that are environmentally responsible, and to redesign existing products to reduce adverse environmental impact.

As is the case with private sector purchasing, government buyers may impose 'green standards' or work with suppliers in a more cooperative way to encourage them to improve their environmental performance. Although each approach may have its merits in particular settings, a more genuine market solution would entail appraising the suppliers of the desired environmental outcome, and allowing innovation to produce a product solution.

The opportunity also exists for government buyers to team up with other buyers in the private and public sectors to increase their influence in furtherance of greener products and processes.

The very existence of supplier assessment sends signals to the marketplace. As upstream environmental vetting becomes more common, these signals will be amplified. Of course, prospective suppliers are always free not to cooperate with 'green' purchasing policies. But in defying market forces, they run the risk of losing a competitive edge.

Market influence is by no means limited to the purchaser. Suppliers are also in a position to influence 'downstream' use of their products. The 'Product Stewardship' program in the chemical industry embraces concern well beyond initial design and manufacture of products, to include their sale, distribution, use and ultimate disposal. This entails informing customers about known product hazards, and providing advice on proper use, handling and disposal. In some instances it entails actual monitoring by the manufacturer of customer use (Morris 1991; Elkington, Knight and Hailes 1992, 120).

Indeed, it has been suggested that opportunities exist for chemical industry firms to provide commercial consulting services, and to profit by marketing their knowledge and expertise to downstream customers. Any reduction in profit to the manufacturer resulting from the customer's more efficient use of the product could be offset by revenues from consultancy services (Wheatley 1993).

To be sure, product stewardship programs are not entirely grounded in altruism. Misuse or improper disposal of a product may result in significant harm to the public or to the environment; this in turn may produce legal action, adverse publicity and, ultimately, financial loss for the manufacturer. But here again we see the potential for market forces contributing to environmental improvement.

To cite yet another example of the greening of commercial relations, companies are now advised to choose their waste management contractors carefully. 'Don't hesitate, even after giving a waste management firm your business, to monitor periodically, and even to audit their waste management practices. A reputable firm with nothing to hide will welcome such scrutiny by its customers' (Kamlet 1992, 37). Companies are encouraged to require accurate disposal records from their waste disposal contractors.

The purchase of environmentally preferable goods and services entails implicit rejection of less acceptable alternative products. At times, this rejection can become explicit. The boycott, or concerted avoidance of certain purchases, may be mobilised against products or producers deemed to be environmentally harmful.[11]

One recent example of a consumer boycott in furtherance of environmental protection is the boycott of Norwegian fish products organised in 1993 by Greenpeace in protest against that nation's resumption of whaling. Boycott organisers maintained that the loss of foreign markets significantly exceeded the commercial value of Norway's whale catch.

Aside from their questionable legality in some jurisdictions, the boycott can be a double-edged sword. In 1989, representatives of the United States timber industry called for the boycott of a brewer who sponsored a controversial television documentary on forests that had been produced by the National Audubon Society (Fahey 1992, 679).

## 2.    'End-of-Pipe' Pollution Abatement Technology

Environmental concerns have given rise to entire new industries, each with significant market opportunities. Innovations in pollution abatement tend to be driven by regulation. By contrast, process modification technologies such as energy efficient plant and equipment tend to be profit driven.

The main types of pollution abatement innovation concerns water and effluents treatment, waste management, air quality control, land reclamation and noise reduction. The pollution abatement industry serves a worldwide market estimated in 1992 at US$200 billion dollars per year. Already larger than the aerospace industry, this market is expected to grow at 5.5 per cent per year through the turn of the century (OECD 1992, 4).

(i) *Water pollution*    Public protest over the pollution of Sydney's beaches in the late 1980s (Beder 1989) was perhaps the most visible example of citizen concern over water quality in recent Australian history. One might cite German reaction to pollution of the Rhine by chemical industry spills for an overseas comparison.

Municipal water and wastewater treatment facilities and effluent treatment for manufacturing industry constitute a significant market opportunity. Primary treatment equipment such as filters exist to remove solid particles; secondary treatment equipment, such as chlorination and biological treatment, addresses bacteria, and tertiary equipment such as chemical recovery systems and reverse osmosis addresses chemical or metal compounds.

Problems of leakage from underground storage tanks, which exist by the hundreds of thousands around the world, have inspired innovations in monitoring technology and in improved tank construction. The challenge of remediating groundwater contamination has inspired the development of monitoring systems and methods to remove contaminants.

(ii) *Waste management*    Growing recognition of the problem of toxic waste has led to the development of specialised handling equipment, and disposal technologies such as chemical and biological degradation methods and incineration systems. One sees the emergence of entire new industries involved with the collection, transport, treatment and disposal of wastes. Commercial opportunities exist for the development of incineration, reuse and recycling methods, and techniques for the neutralisation of waste products.

Landfill space in Australia, and in most other western industrial societies, is in short supply. It has been estimated that at current rates of waste generation, and barring further development, landfills in Australia's major metropolitan areas will be used up soon after the turn of the century (Australian Bureau of Statistics 1992). Such pressures suggest an obvious market for alternative waste disposal services. Declining landfill space around the world has stimulated the development of incineration techniques and improved landfill management methods, including the use of impermeable lining materials and techniques of leachate collection.

It is increasingly acknowledged that recycling will become an important part of the future global economy. Firms in the forefront of developing recycling technology and those in the development of recyclable materials or the production of recyclable products are well positioned to exploit future market opportunities. European automobile manufacturers, for example, have begun to produce vehicles that are 100 per cent recyclable.

(iii) *Air pollution control* Air quality control equipment exists to remove pollutants from a gaseous stream, or to reduce their concentration prior to discharge. Air pollution control equipment may be designed to affect particulates such as dust and ash, gases such as carbon monoxide and sulfur dioxide and liquids or liquid fumes.

Market opportunities for environmental protection have not been overlooked by some of the largest companies in those industries in which one might expect to find awareness of pollution control problems — chemical, engineering and electronics. In recent years, Dupont has established a subsidiary company for toxic waste management services. Dow, Bayer and Hoechst are developing methods for recycling plastic.

Profit and environmental protection, far from being mutually exclusive, can be part of the same package. Improved production technologies generate fewer pollutants and make more efficient use of materials and energy. The relative merits of investing a given amount in pollution abatement technology and investing in new production facilities that would achieve more efficient production and generate less waste should be obvious.

*3. Process Modification Technologies that Conserve Raw Materials and Energy and Minimise Waste*
According to the OECD, market opportunities are shifting from 'end of pipe' abatement technologies to manufacturing process technologies. The design of production systems that are both environmentally appropriate and more efficient will generate even greater competitive advantage. Integrated technologies for feedstock and process modifications that combine low energy con-

sumption with low emissions are the most desirable. The emphasis of such an approach is on pollution prevention through production efficiency, rather than abatement. This industry will develop and exploit opportunities in energy conservation, and in environmentally appropriate materials and production processes. The company that can claim to be first with the greenest manufacturing technology will be ahead of the market.

Governments have actively sought to inspire the development and dissemination of clean technology. The Victorian Government's Clean Technology Incentive Scheme provides grants to businesses for the introduction of innovative technologies to reduce waste (OECD 1992, 28). The Australian Government makes 10-year interest free 'cleaner production' loans to eligible companies. In Norway, subsidies to the pulp and paper industry have encouraged the introduction of new, cleaner production processes (Cramer et al. 1990, 49).

*4. Renewable Energy Systems*
A number of energy technologies exist as alternatives to fossil fuels. Some are already commercially viable, albeit on a small scale. Others have considerable potential that could be realised when technological developments permit.

The most common technology is solar power. Solar collectors for water heaters have become a common feature on the roofs of Australian houses. Telecom Australia has been using solar photovoltaic technology to power remote area telephone systems for nearly two decades. Prototype motor vehicles powered by solar energy have crossed the Australian continent; further refinements in the technology of collection and storage will extend the potential for solar energy considerably.

Although hydroelectric power generation on a massive scale tends to require a degree of environmental devastation, less intrusive technologies of micro-hydroelectric power generation entail no such cost. Small generators may be constructed on the banks of rapidly flowing streams, and the resulting power may be sufficient to support a small village. Such technology already exists, with considerable potential application in developing nations.

The windmill is a common feature of Australian rural landscapes. But the potential for wind energy extends well beyond pumping water. Wind energy technology has developed to the extent that it complements conventional electric power generation in some locations.

Other forms of alternative energy include biomass, where organic matter is either burned or used in the production of alcohol or gas fuels; geothermal, where the earth's internal heat is harnessed as a source of energy; and wave or tidal power, where water movements can be used to drive turbines for the generation of electricity.

### 5.  Green Institutional Investors

Environmental performance is increasingly regarded as an indicator of business health. Good environmental management reflects good management in general. To the extent that this perception is shared by financial markets, pressure on companies to improve corporate environmental citizenship will be that much greater.

Recent years have seen the emergence of specialised environmentally conscious investment funds (Smith 1990, 175–76). Such green institutional investors avoid companies and industries with poor environmental reputations, and specialise in environmentally reputable companies. Beyond the influence of specialised 'green funds', the potential influence of large institutional investors in this regard can be substantial. In 1991, the 20 largest pension funds in the United States controlled over $620 billion in assets. In a number of United States jurisdictions, state pension fund managers are required to give preference in their investment decisions to companies in compliance with the Valdez Principles (Elkington Knight and Hailes 1992, 71). One trustee of the New York City Employees Retirement System, with $21 billion in assets, was quoted as saying 'We hold the view that when corporations treat the environment badly, they treat their investors badly — by subjecting the company to harmful publicity and by exposing themselves to enormous liability. The pension funds have become activists in protecting our investments by working to protect the environment' (Reuters 1992b). Market influence is further enhanced by regulatory requirements that shareholders and financial markets must be kept informed of potential environmental liabilities.[12]

### 6.   Banking and Insurance Companies as Co-producers of Regulation

In addition to their activities as institutional investors, banks and insurance companies are in a position to exercise considerable influence over their clients. Lenders and insurers now recognise the risk to their own commercial well-being posed by questionable environmental practices on the part of a borrower or policyholder. Beyond the lender's obvious interest in the commercial viability of the borrower, banks must now be concerned about the environmental risks posed by any assets they might hold as security for a loan. In the event of foreclosure, banks could end up owning a liability rather than an asset. The pressures that the banking and insurance industries can exert in furtherance of environmental citizenship can be considerable. Schmidheiny (1992, 64–65) predicts that an environmental audit report is likely to become an integral part of a loan application, and that companies with an unfavourable record of environmental compliance 'will find it increasingly difficult and expensive to get insured'.[13]

### 7. *Environmental Services Industry*

The OECD predicts that the market for environmental services will exceed that for equipment in the years ahead, and predicts that the environmental services industry, which delivers such auxiliary products as environmental monitoring, auditing, risk management and product testing, will become one of the growth industries of the 1990s, with growth estimated to be in excess of 7 per cent per year (OECD 1992, 14).

One of the more dynamic new industries is the provision of engineering services to assist in the selection and implementation of the improved process technologies referred to above.

## The Environmental Adaptability of Business

Those companies that can anticipate consumer preferences and regulatory trends are in an advantageous position. Businesspeople with anything more than a very shortsighted view towards next quarter's profit figures will see significant opportunities in environmental stewardship. The framework of environmental regulation entails as many if not more opportunities than it does obstacles. Pressure from government, the public and other commercial actors can be converted to commercial advantage.

Business culture reflects the wider culture within which it resides. In those societies where environmental awareness is relatively high, such as The Netherlands, businesses tend to integrate environmental considerations into all aspects of their operations. The Australian business community has been encouraged to emulate the Dutch, who have succeeded admirably at capitalism for most of the past 500 years, and incorporate environmental issues into their overall strategy development (Beaucamp and Girgensohn 1992).

It should also be recognised that, at least in Western industrial societies, pressures that emanate from the market are likely to be regarded as more legitimate, and thus likely to encounter less resistance, than directions issued by governments. As noted above, in some industry sectors, firms exert greater pressure on each other than governments could ever wield.

One of the ironies of life is that just as market failure has produced environmental despoilation, so too can market forces provide efficient means of environmental protection. The challenge is how best to intervene to prevent the former and how best to nurture the latter.

Markets need not necessarily produce 'zero-sum' solutions where the economy benefits at the expense of the environment, or vice versa. Indeed, markets often produce 'win–win' situations, the development of products or processes that are both greener and more efficient. Companies that can foresee environmental trends will be best situated to exploit them. The governing paradigm of economies, the logic of the market, holds that individuals independently pursuing their private interests will produce outcomes in the public interest.

We noted above how small business may be disadvantaged by the lack of organisational resources with which to conform to 'green' buyer requirements. Similarly, the cost of abatement technology or environmentally responsible waste management services may be prohibitive. Particularly during periods of recession, economic survival may be the dominant concern. It may be difficult to 'think green' when one is confronted by a rising tide of red ink. Nevertheless, adversity or constraint can be an energising force for innovation (Porter 1990, 282). The incorporation of environmental considerations into general business strategy may have a radiating effect throughout the entire economy (Cramer et al. 1990, 51).

## Conditions that Foster Green Markets

Like any other instrument for environmental protection, markets are no panacea. Markets in the environmental industry may still be vulnerable to failure. Profit-driven behaviour may still result in cutting corners or opting for a cheaper and dirtier alternative. Markets may not always be conducive to recycling. As demand for recyclable material is driven in turn by consumer demand for products made from recyclable material, the value of materials recovered must exceed the cost of collection and processing.

For this reason, markets should be regarded as but one strand, albeit a significant one, in the web of orderings for environmental protection. Non-market institutions can act to foster and strengthen markets; market forces themselves complement other institutions.

What kind of institutional ordering might one envisage in order to enhance the effect of market forces in furtherance of environmental protection?

Government influence on markets extends well beyond command-and-control regulation or the use of fiscal and monetary policy, although the entrepreneurial opportunities that flow from regulation have been widely recognised. We noted above the influence that government purchasing policies may have on establishing and maintaining markets and in fostering environmentally appropriate industry practices.

*Incentives and Technical Assistance*

There are still other ways in which governments can send strong signals to the marketplace. Although the market for environmental protection products may thrive even in the face of a 'hands off' policy by government, state intervention may stimulate innovation and demand. Here we refer not to the stimulus that may be provided by strict regulatory standards, 'green' taxes, or to the influence of government purchasing power, discussed above, but to other non-coercive involvement such as the provision of information and the sponsorship of research and development. We have noted the selective use by governments of subsidies to encourage cleaner process technology. Nations whose governments regard environmentally appropriate technology in strategic terms stand to benefit both environmentally and economically.

One of the more significant barriers to the diffusion of clean technology can be simple ignorance. Small firms, in particular, may be unaware of developments that could enhance their competitive position. Although the purveyors of green technologies may be competent in the marketing of their products, they may well benefit from governmental assistance.

The provision of information and technical assistance to industry is a common feature of industrial policy in advanced societies. By raising industry awareness of environmental issues, and by offering assistance to industry in achieving technical solutions to a variety of environmental problems, governments can contribute to both economic development and environmental improvement. Assistance may be informational, or may entail a form of financial subsidy. The Swedish National Board for Industrial and Technical Development offered an award for the development of an energy-efficient refrigerator; included in the package was a guarantee to purchase a given number of units, and subsidies to reduce the price of the product (Schmidheiny 1992, 238).[14]

Assistance to industry in furtherance of green productivity can thus be made a core element of industry policy. Environmental care can become an integral part of business strategy. The Netherlands Ministry of Economic Affairs provides information, assistance, training, and establishes regional demonstration projects for firms throughout the Dutch economy (Cramer et al. 1990).

For other illustrations of industrial policy and its environmental implications, one may look to Japan. There, the Ministry of International Trade and Industry (MITI), by commissioning reports that are given substantial publicity and by undertaking high profile campaigns, can prod industry to improve its environmental performance. This is characteristic of government–business relations in Japan, a style often described by the term 'administrative guidance'.

International organisations are also in a position to provide environmentally appropriate industry assistance. We have already referred to the OECD report on trends in the environment industry. The United Nations Environment Program (UNEP), through its cleaner production program established in 1989, seeks to increase awareness of cleaner production techniques around the world. It maintains an International Cleaner Production Information Clearing House (ICPIC) to promote the use of safe and clean technologies. UNEP publishes technical reviews and guidelines and convenes training courses and conferences.[15] Their efforts are particularly important in fostering environmentally appropriate technology transfer to developing nations in order to minimise the environmental impact of such industries as metal finishing, tanning, textiles and pulp and paper.

Government investment in environmentally oriented research and development (R&D) may help the growth of an environmental protection industry. The strength of the United States aerospace industry in the decades since the Second World War owed a great deal to government R&D. Although driven primarily by considerations of national defence, economic benefits were obvious. Environmental R&D could be given a similar stimulus in Australia, as it has in Japan, where the powerful MITI has established a Research Institute of Innovative Technology of the Earth (RITE) to coordinate research on environmentally appropriate technologies. Australia's Waste and Environmental Management Technology Program (WEMT) was funded at $A12 million over 3 years, as part of a larger Industry Research and Development Program (OECD 1992). Nevertheless, environmental protection accounted for only 1.3 per cent of Australian government research expenditure in 1992. This figure is relatively low in comparison with other advanced industrial societies; the comparable German figure exceeds 3 per cent.

*Information*
The basis of a market is information. Still another contribution

that governments can make to enhance the influence of markets is to ensure that those markets are properly informed. Market failure often results from lack of information (Levacic 1991). By requiring a manufacturer to disclose the contents of a product, the exercise of consumer preferences is facilitated. Efforts from whatever sector to enhance the availability and quality of information about products will contribute to greener markets.

There are circumstances in which governments may compel disclosure of information relating to environmental implications of products and processes. Alternatively, such disclosure may be required by actors upstream or downstream in the course of a commercial transaction.

Governments may also play a role in ensuring the integrity of information made available to the marketplace. More generally, they can create and enforce laws that are conducive to the functioning of a healthy marketplace (Hayek 1991, 197).

The influence of markets may be further enhanced by the existence of criteria for the assessment of environmental compatability. A product that can boast of a 'Green Seal' or 'Eco-label' is likely to enjoy a decided advantage in today's market.

Claims of 'environmental friendliness' are easily made; not all are valid. The development of nationally or internationally recognised certificates of environmental appropriateness can reduce the risk of deceptive, misleading, ambiguous or trivial claims. Governments can contribute to the development of labelling standards, to the accreditation of eco-labelling schemes, and thus to the legitimacy of markets for environmentally appropriate goods and services (OECD 1991; Van Goetham 1992).[16]

The proliferation of such criteria within nations, and across international collectivities such as the European Community, has given rise to differences of opinion over the rigor and appropriateness of various schemes. Significant regional variations may exist in the ability of the ecosystem to absorb a given environmental impact. While CFC emissions are harmful to the biosphere, the impact of phosphates may be more selective.[17]

*Recognition*

Governments and the private sector may also develop awards programs to encourage green business in general, to highlight new products that are the most ecologically innovative, or publicly to praise suppliers that have made singular contributions to the environment.

The United Nations Environment Program (UNEP), in cooperation with the European Community, sponsors 'The European Better Environment Awards for Industry', and confers awards in the categories Good Environmental Management, Clean Technology, Eco-Product and Environmental Technology Transfer. The Confederation of British Industry, as part of its 'Environment Means Business' program, sponsors Better Environmental Awards for Industry. These include a category devoted to encouraging technology transfer to developing nations. Such awards, and the publicity that accompanies them, can be a significant incentive to innovation and a boon to marketing.

*Interest Groups and Green Markets*
Interest groups are well situated to help to create and enhance environmentally beneficial markets. Through their educative role, interest groups help to raise public awareness and can play a crucial role in shaping consumer preferences.

Interest groups are in a position to engage in strategic collaboration with industry, and thereby directly contribute to improvement in corporate practices. Such collaboration may be general, with an entire industry or with a particular industry association. In some cases, they may assist firms in developing environmentally beneficial products or procedures. The Environmental Defense Fund, for example, has assisted McDonald's restaurants in developing its recycling program (Elkington, Knight and Hailes 1992, 16; Schmidheiny 1992, 88). Greenpeace collaborated with German appliance manufacturers to produce a CFC-free refrigerator. A public utility and an environmental group in the United States have collaborated in an energy demand reduction program involving financial incentives to encourage consumer conservation.[18] In 1993, the Australian Conservation Foundation launched a 'Green Home' and gave official recognition to its architects, suppliers and builders. One may expect a proliferation of collaborative ventures between interest groups and industry (Schmidheiny 1992, 86, 189).[19]

Environmental groups play an important educative role, calling public attention to specific environmental issues, themselves generating information about products in the market, monitoring that information and suggesting appropriate consumer behaviour.

Interest groups may play a constructive role by identifying and publicly criticising environmentally deleterious market failures. Within the constraints posed by laws of libel, they are also in a position to maintain vigilance against spurious marketing claims (Sethi 1990; Schorsch 1990). Indeed, one organisation makes 'Green Con' awards (Commoner 1990).

Alternatively, by recognising and publicly bestowing praise for good environmental citizenship, interest groups help industry to achieve a competitive advantage.

*Third Party Commercial Interests and Green Markets*
In addition to the influence of purchasing power, product stewardship, and the exercise of environmentally sensitive investment,
lending and insurance decisions, there are other means by which
commercial third parties may contribute to 'green markets'.
Within the burgeoning environmental services industry there are
those who advocate more open environmental reporting, and offer
to assist clients in 'coming clean' (Deloitte Touche Tohmatsu
International 1993).

# Conclusion: Some Principles for Governing at a Distance

If ever it served a useful purpose, the simplistic dichotomy of
environmental libertarianism, on the one hand, and command-
and-control environmental regulation, on the other, would appear
no longer to do so. Neither of these polar opposites is technically
achievable, politically feasible, or indeed, environmentally
desirable.

However, between the extremes of the 'directing state', which
keeps environmental policy tightly reined, and the 'minimalist
state', which drops the reins altogether, lies a continuum along
which the degree and nature of state intervention will vary. It is
along this continuum that one finds the 'facilitating state' (Offe
1972; Habermas 1976; Dandeker 1990) where individual and
commercial autonomy are encouraged to flourish and, where
necessary, interests are gently guided towards environmentally
preferable outcomes. The form of this facilitation will differ within and between jurisdictions, depending on industry structure,
environmental considerations, and the relative capacities of
government, industry, and third parties.

In democratic societies, governments are and will remain
accountable for environmental quality. Current and future
environmental awareness in these societies appears to make
abdication of governmental responsibility for the environment
most unlikely. At the same time, political and financial constraints
appear to dictate that the public sector will become a less
dominant force in environmental protection.

This may be a good thing, in terms both of democratic theory
and environmental outcome. Environmental policy is now and
will remain the product of a hybrid regulatory ordering, involving
public and private institutions. A given environmental problem
will lend itself to a particular institutional solution. In certain
circumstances, spontaneous commercial activity may be a more

effective avenue to achieve a desired policy end. In other settings, governments may, through incentives or other indirect means, contribute to a climate within which non-governmental instruments and institutions function more effectively in furtherance of public policy. The key question facing democracies as they enter the 21st century is how to facilitate those commercial activities that are most appropriate to given policy goals, what combination of market and bureaucratic instruments of allocation and coordination to select, and how to ensure the accountability of those activities.

Despite the promise of green markets, green technology, and their anticipated environmental benefits, they should be embraced with a degree of caution. In practice, markets are not always democratic institutions. Not all markets perform as textbook accounts would have them (Kettl 1993, 127). No consumer is omniscient; the chain of production is such that a cradle-to-grave perspective may be obscured. Consumers are not all models of rational decision making and, in any event, market imperfections may deny them effective choice. In certain circumstances, markets can even be more coercive than governments, and private surveillance more penetrating than that brought to bear by the state.

Nor are they necessarily ideal instruments of environmental policy. Markets, at least until recently, have not been kind to the environment. Some of the orderings that we envisage, such as those relying on environmental audit, may be no more successful in producing environmentally responsible conduct than were financial audits successful in preventing the corporate excesses of the 1980s. Some observers have suggested that the upstream influence of large purchasers of agricultural products can contribute not to stewardship of the land but rather to environmentally irresponsible use of pesticides, fertiliser and irrigation water (Burch, Rickson, and Annels 1992).

Democratic political institutions are also less than perfect mechanisms for translating citizen preferences into public policy, or for achieving ideal environmental outcomes. In addition to the political and financial constraints noted above, the political marketplace may be dominated by intense and well-resourced interests, to the detriment of the wider public.

Ideally, the imperfections in politics and markets will be cross-cutting, in a manner that will permit the strengths of one to compensate for the deficits of the other. Such complementarity is an essential characteristic of hybrid regulatory orderings.

The electoral accountability of governments, combined with the accountability of the market to consumers, can lead to a more truly representative environmental policy. Participation in the marketplace can complement conventional political participation for members of the public. Consumers can 'vote' for the environment by giving direct expression to their preferences. The injunction to think globally and act locally would apply nowhere if not in the marketplace.

Moreover, the legitimacy of environmental policy is likely to be greater when governments shape incentives rather than command, and when environmental controls are imposed by markets, rather than by bureaucrats.

When the 'democracy' of the market and political democracy complement each other, the likelihood of environmentally appropriate outcomes is greater. Meanwhile, both public and private spheres can play educative roles so that the democratic performance of each can be improved.

Political capital is no less exhaustible than are financial resources. Both should be expended judiciously. Governments squander either at their peril. When policy goals may be achieved more efficiently through reliance on non-governmental means, public resources should be spared. Governments should reserve their political capital for those issues not otherwise amenable to market solutions.

When non-governmental institutions are able to perform a function better than can a public sector agency, governments should defer to them. When they can be assisted to do it better, governments should assist them. The judicious use of incentives may lead to a higher pay-off than would a direct investment of public resources.

Earlier, we observed that certain industrial/environmental settings are more amenable to control by 'green' market forces than others. The same would hold true for instruments of self-regulation. Where conditions conducive to environmentally appropriate commercial activity exist or can be made to exist, the ideal ordering will be self-regulatory or market-based. By contrast, where market forces are unable to reach a particular environmental problem, the regulatory ordering must be more bureaucratic.

What, then, would an ideal regulatory ordering for environmental protection look like? Consider an industry comprised of very large companies, protective of their individual and collective reputations, with sophisticated environmental compliance policies in place. Such an industry would require very little in the way of regulatory scrutiny by command-and-control agencies. The occasional attention of environmentalist groups would provide more than enough impetus to maintain a rigorous self-regulatory regime. Here governments can largely defer to private orderings to bring about compliance.

By contrast, consider an industry comprised of small companies, with little or no concern over public image, no shared identity, and normally ignored by environmental interest groups. Assume that members of the industry command insufficient resources to support meaningful self-regulation. Companies in this industry would require greater vigilance by traditional command-and-control regulators, reinforced by the guiding and occasionally coercive influence of insurers and lending institutions. Here, governments share control functions with certain commercial third parties.

It would appear that the domain of environmental protection provides an excellent proving ground for new technologies of government as we approach the 21st century. The interests of industry can be guided at a distance by governments, and further conditioned by commercial and non-commercial third parties, to produce outcomes more advantageous than might ever be achieved by directions imposed from above. Organisational leverage may enable governments to achieve environmental outcomes that industry could not achieve if left to its own devices.

Although many radical ecologists are likely to remain skeptical, one might argue that increasing public environmental awareness is producing a new kind of participatory regulation through the market place. This exercise of personal and corporate autonomy may have the potential to produce outcomes superior to those achieved thus far by traditional methods.

# Endnotes

1. This chapter was prepared in the context of a larger research program that the author is conducting in collaboration with Neil Gunningham of the Australian Centre for Environmental Law, Australian National University. The author is grateful to the ANU Urban Research Program for its support, and to the Institute of Comparative Law in Japan at Chuo University for the use of its facilities during revision of the manuscript. In addition, the author wishes to acknowledge the helpful comments of Tim Bonyhady, John Braithwaite, Robyn Eckersley, Bob Goodin, and Max Neutze on earlier versions of this essay.

2. The focus of this essay is self-consciously pragmatic; it addresses some commercial activity that may produce positive benefits for the environment, and other activity that might be regarded as minimising environmental harm. The term 'environmentally appropriate' is used throughout as an alternative to the oft-abused and loosely used 'environmentally friendly'.

3. The book was praised by Governor Clinton of Arkansas prior to his election as President of the United States, and subsequently served

as a model for vice President Gore's report on reform of the US federal public sector (Gore 1993).

4. See, for example, Chayes and Chayes (1991).

5. The collection of essays by Shearing and Stenning (1987) and in particular by Marx (1987) is richly illustrative. See Johnston (1992) and Grabosky (1992).

6. The institutionalised participation of business and labour in public policy is the essence of European corporatism. Australian models of tripartism include regimes for the regulation of occupational health and safety, and environmental protection. Here, governments may provide direct grants to interest groups to facilitate their contributions to policy. On regulatory tripartism generally, see Ayres and Braithwaite (1992).

7. Commercial activity is subject to a variety of coordinating influences, most of which are non-governmental. See Thompson et al. (eds) (1991).

8. The few scholars who have focused on regulatory systems as systems, and on the interaction of their components and instruments include Harter and Eads (1985) and Bressers and Klok (1988).

9. The term 'greenwash' has been used to refer to unjustified claims of environmental friendliness. See Greenpeace (1992).

10. According to the British Secretary for the Environment, 'The penalties for poor environmental performance that the financial world will exact are likely to be far more swift and certain than anything governments have been able to achieve' (Howard 1992).

11. For discussions of various aspects of consumer boycotts, see Harper (1984); Joyner (1984); Smith (1990); Friedman (1991); Fahey (1992).

12. For a less optimistic perspective on the effects of ethical investing, see Dowie (1993).

13. One prospective lender requires a comprehensive assessment of all risks associated with a proposed loan; a 17-page environmental compliance checklist comprises part of the loan application (Schmidheiny 1992, 258). Canadian banks have begun to require detailed information from prospective commercial borrowers regarding all aspects of the latter's environmental exposure (Deloitte Touche Tohmatsu 1993, 40).

14. While subsidies may be appropriate to assist the development of some products, they are generally regarded as inferior instruments, which in time will induce a dependent orientation and will operate to suppress innovation (Porter 1990, 640).

15. See, for example, any issue of the UNEP periodical *Industry and Environment*.

16. It should be noted that eco-labelling, as with other forms of certification and accreditation, need not be exclusive to the public sector. Private sector and hybrid public-private programs exist in a number of settings. See Cheit (1990) and Grodsky (1993).

17. Assessing the full environmental implications and the relative merits of competing products is not always a simple task. For some of the

difficulties surrounding eco-labelling programs, see Howett (1992); Grodsky (1993) and Israel (1993).
18. Cynics will observe that there is a limit to which a commercial enterprise can advocate reduced consumption of its product. The commercial viability of such demand reduction strategies depends on the extent to which efficiencies may be realised upstream.
19. Another example: the Californians Against Waste Foundation encourages fast food restaurants and their suppliers to create markets for environmentally appropriate products by exercising their purchasing power (Reuters 1993).

# References

Australia, Department of Administrative Services. (1992) *Environmental Purchasing Policy*, Australian Government Publishing Service (AGPS), Canberra.

Australian Bureau of Statistics (ABS). (1992) *Australia's Environment: Issues and Facts*, AGPS, Canberra.

Ayres, I. and Braithwaite, J. (1992) *Responsive Regulation: Transcending the Deregulation Debate*, Oxford University Press, New York.

Beaucamp, A. and Girgensohn, T. (1992) 'Environmental Based Consumption', *Business Council Bulletin* Jan–Feb, 22–27.

Beder, S. (1989) *Toxic Fish and Sewer Surfing: How Deceit and Collusion are Destroying our Great Beaches*, Allen and Unwin, Sydney.

Berle, G. (1991) *The Green Entrepreneur*, Liberty Hall Press, New York.

Boyer, B. and Meidinger, E. (1985) 'Privatising Regulatory Enforcement: A Preliminary Assessment of Citizen Suits Under Federal Environmental Laws', *Buffalo Law Review* 34, 833–964.

Braithwaite, J. (1993) 'Responsive Regulation for Australia' in P. Grabosky and J. Braithwaite (eds), *Business Regulation and Australia's Future*, Australian Institute of Criminology, Canberra.

Bressers, H. and Klok, P. (1988) 'Fundamentals for a Theory of Policy Instruments', *International Journal of Social Economics* 15(3–4), 22–41.

Burch, D., Rickson, R. and Annels, H.R. (1992) 'Agribusiness in Australia: Rural Restructuring, Social Change and Environmental Impacts' in K.J. Walker (ed.), *Australian Environmental Policy*, New South Wales University Press, Sydney.

Burchell, G. (1991) 'Peculiar Interests: Civil Society and Governing "The System of Natural Liberty"' in G. Burchell, C. Gordon and P. Miller (eds), *The Foucault Effect*, Harvester–Wheatsheaf, Hemel Hempstead.

Chayes, A. and Chayes, A. (1991) 'Compliance Without Enforcement: State Behavior under Regulatory Treaties', *Negotiation Journal* 7(3), 311–30.

Cheit, R. (1990) *Setting Safety Standards: Regulation in the Private and Public Sectors*, University of California Press, Berkeley.

Commoner, B. (1990) 'Can Capitalists be Environmentalists?', *Business and Society Review* 75, 31–35.

Cramer, J., Schot, J., van den Akker, F. and Mass Geesteranus, G. (1990) 'Stimulating Cleaner Technology Through Economic Instruments', *Industry and Environment* 13(2), 46–53.

Crook, S., Pakulski, J. and Waters, M. (1992) *Post Modernisation: Change in Advanced Society*, Sage Publications, London.

Dandeker, C. (1990) *Surveillance, Power and Modernity: Bureaucracy and Discipline from 1700 to the Present Day*, Polity Press, Cambridge.

Deloitte Touche Tohmatsu International. (1993) *Coming Clean: Corporate Environmental Reporting*, Deloitte Touche Tohmatsu International, London.

Dowie, M. (1993) 'Feel-Good Investing: Clean, Green and Guilt-Free Funds', *The Nation* April 26, 550–56.

Ehrlich, E. (1912) *Fundamental Principles of the Sociology of Law*, Harvard University Press, Cambridge.

Elkington, J. and Knight, P. with Hailes, J. (1992) *The Green Business Guide*, Victor Gollancz, London.

Fahey, P. (1992) 'Advocacy Group Boycotting of Televison Advertisers, and its Effect on Programming Content', *University of Pennsylvania Law Review* 140, 647–709.

Fitzpatrick, P. (1984) 'Law and Societies', *Osgoode Hall Law Journal* 22, 115–38.

Foucault, M. (1991) 'Governmentality' in G. Burchell, C. Gordon and P. Miller (eds), *The Foucault Effect*, Harvester–Wheatsheaf, Hemel Hempstead.

Friedman, M. (1991) 'Consumer Boycotts: A Conceptual Framework and Research Agenda', *Journal of Social Issues* 47(1), 149–68.

Gilboy, J. (1992) *Government Use of Private Resources in Law Enforcement*, ABF Working Paper No. 9203, American Bar Foundation, Chicago.

Gore, A. (1993) *From Red Tape to Results: Creating a Government that Works Better and Costs Less*, US Government Printing Office, Washington.

Grabosky, P. (1992) 'Law Enforcement and the Citizen: Non-Governmental Participation in Crime Prevention and Control', *Policing and Society* 2, 249–71.

Greenpeace. (1992) *Greenwash*, Greenpeace, London.

Greenpeace. (1993) 'Body Shop Places Albright and Wilson on Environmental Probation', *Greenpeace Business* No. 6(6) March.

Grodsky, J. (1993) 'Certified Green: The Law and Future of Environmental Labeling', *Yale Journal on Regulation* 10(1), 147–227.

Habermas, J. (1976) *Legitimation Crisis*, Heinemann, London.

Harper, M. (1984) 'The Consumer's Emerging Right to Boycott: NAACP v. Claiborne Hardware and its Implications for American Labor Law', *The Yale Law Journal* 93(3), 409–54.

Harter, P. and Eads, G. (1985) 'Policy Instruments, Institutions, and Objectives: An Analytical Framework for Assessing "Alternatives" to Regulation', *Administrative Law Review* 37(3), 221–58.

Hayek, F. (1991) 'Spontaneous ("grown") Order and Organised ("made") Order' in G. Thompson, J. Frances, R. Levacic and J. Mitchell (eds), *Markets, Hierarchies and Networks: The Coordination of Social Life*, Sage Publications, London.

Howard, M. (1992) Address to conferences on 'European Business and the Environment — The Future', Borschetle Centre, Brussels, Belgium, 19 Nov. 1992. *Reuters News Service* 19 Nov. 1992.

Howett, C. (1992) 'The "Green Labelling" Phenomenon: Problems and Trends in the Regulation of Environmental Product Claims', *Virginia Environmental Law Journal* 11, 401–61.

Huppes, G. and Kagan, R. (1990) 'Market-Oriented Regulation of Environmental Problems in the Netherlands', *Law and Policy* 11(2), 215–39.

Israel, G. (1993) 'Taming the Green Marketing Monster: National Standards for Environmental Marketing Claims', *Boston College Environmental Affairs Law Review*, 20(22), 303–33.

Jacobs, M. (1993) 'Growth, Industrial Policy and Regulation-Led Innovation: Some Thoughts on Macro-Environmental Economics', Occasional Paper No. 6, Institute of Ethics and Public Policy, Monash University, November.

Johnston, L. (1992) *The Rebirth of Private Policing*, Routledge, London.

Joyner, C. (1984) 'The Transnational Boycott as Economic Coercion in International Law: Policy, Place and Practice', *Vanderbilt Journal of Transnational Law* 17(2), 206–86.

Kamlet, K. (1992) 'Environmental Management: The Ten Commandments', *Internal Auditor* 49(5), 36–44.

Kettl, D. (1993) *Sharing Power: Public Governance and Private Markets*, The Brookings Institution, Washington.

Lao Tzu. (1963) *Tao Te Ching*, translated by D.C. Lau, Penguin Books, Harmondsworth.

Levacic, R. (1991) 'Markets and Government: An Overview' in G. Thompson, J. Frances, R. Levacic and J. Mitchell (eds), *Markets, Hierarchies and Networks: The Coordination of Social Life*, Sage Publications, London.

Lury, K. and Hatfield, S. (1992) 'Recycling Computer Products: More Enlightened Attitude from both Suppliers and Customers Needed for Success', *Reuters News Service* 24 September.

Marx, G. T. (1987) 'The Interweaving of Public and Private Police in Undercover Work' in G. Shearing and P.C. Stenning (eds), *Private Policing*, Sage Publications, Beverly Hills.

Mechlin, S. (1993) 'Savvy Bankers Remember Mother Nature', *Reuters News Service* 12 February.

Moran, A. (1990) *Protecting the Environment Using Market Mechanisms*, ACC–Westpac Economic Discussion Papers, No. 2, Australian Chamber of Commerce and Westpac Banking Corporation, Canberra.

Morris, G. (1991) 'Responsible Care: Amoco', *Chemical Week* 17 July, 74.

Offe, C. (1972) 'Advanced Capitalism and the Welfare State', *Politics and Society* 2(4), 479–88.

Organisation for Economic Co-operation and Development (OECD). (1991) *Environmental Labelling in OECD Countries*, OECD, Paris.

Organisation for Economic Co-operation and Development (OECD). (1992) *The OECD Environment Industry: Situation, Prospects and Government Policies*, OECD, Paris.

LIVERPOOL JOHN MOORES UNIVERSITY
LEARNING SERVICES

Osborne, D. and Gaebler, T. (1992) *Reinventing Government*, Addison Wesley, Boston.

Platt, N. (1992) 'The Rise of the Eco-Consumer Has Big Business Seeing Green', *Reuters New Service* 25 May.

Porter, M. (1990) *The Competitive Advantage of Nations*, Macmillan, London.

Reuters. (1992a) 'Its Green for Go in Boots the Chemist', *Reuters News Service* 13 June.

Reuters. (1992b) 'N.Y. City Fund Wants Green Stance from 4 Companies', *Reuters News Service* 10 December.

Reuters. (1993) 'Fast Food Environmental Summit Lays Groundwork for Increased Communication and Cooperation', *Reuters News Service* 15 January.

Rose, N. and Miller, P. (1992) 'Political Power Beyond the State: Problematics of Government', *British Journal of Sociology* 43(2), 173–205.

Russell, C. (1988) 'Economic Incentives in the Management of Hazardous Wastes', *Columbia Journal of Environmental Law* 13, 257–74.

Schmidheiny, S. (1992) *Changing Course: A Global Business Perspective on Development and the Environment*, MIT Press, Cambridge, Massachusetts.

Schorsch, J. (1990) 'Are Corporations Playing Clean with Green?', *Business and Society Review* 75, 6–9.

Schultze, C. (1977) *The Public Use of Private Interest*, The Brookings Institution, Washington.

Sethi, S. (1990) 'Corporations and the Environment: Greening or Preening?', *Business and Society Review* 75, 4–5.

Shearing, C. (1993) 'A Constitutive Concept of Regulation' in P. Grabosky and J. Braithwaite (eds), *Business Regulation and Australia's Future*, Australian Institute of Criminology, Canberra.

Shearing, C. and Stenning, P. C. (eds). (1987) *Private Policing*, Sage Publications, Beverly Hills.

Smith, M. (1990) *Morality and the Market: Consumer Pressure for Corporate Accountability*, Routledge, London.

Stewart, R. (1992) 'Models for Environmental Regulation: Central Planning Versus Market Based Approaches', *Boston College Environmental Affairs Law Review* 19(3), 547–62.

Stuart, G. (1992) 'Marketing Reports on Environmental Concerns in the Packaging Industry', *Reuters News Service* 20 August.

Teubner, G. (1983) 'Substantive and Reflexive Elements in Modern Law', *Law and Society Review* 17(2), 239–86.

Thompson, G., Frances, J., Levacic, R. and Mitchell, J. (eds). (1991) *Markets, Hierarchies and Networks: The Coordination of Social Life*, Sage Publications, London.

Van Goetham, A. (1992) '"The European Eco-Label" — Features from Europe Environment', *European Information Service*, Brussels, December.

Wheatley, A. (1993) 'Firms Start to Warm to the Environment', *Reuters News Service* 7 March.

# 9

# *Global Competition and Environmental Regulation: Is the 'Race to the Bottom' Inevitable?*

Gordon L. Clark

## Introduction

The relationship between international competitiveness and environmental standards is contentious and fraught with many uncertainties (GATT 1992). For some firms and industries, national environmental standards are considered a threat to their international competitiveness. For others, nation-based environmental standards are a threat to liberalised, global free trade. A common working hypothesis is that firms located in countries with high environmental standards are economically disadvantaged compared with firms located in countries with low environmental standards. Investment is thought to flee nations with high standards, since low standards or non-enforced standards represent, in effect, a subsidy to firms that produce and export from these locations.[1] Moreover, high standards may be a barrier to free trade if they deny imported products a local market by virtue of the peculiarities of domestic environmental regulations. One way or another, or so it is supposed, rational economic policy makers are drawn to the lowest common denominator; local environmental standards are at risk in a world of international economic competition (Office of Technology Assessment 1992).

The global environmental implications of a 'race to the bottom' are well appreciated, at least in theory. The potential for 'pollution havens' (countries specialising in the production and storage of pollution) is also well appreciated, supported in principle by some officials of the World Bank even if disputed as a practical reality (Birdsall and Wheeler 1991). Thus, moves towards setting international environmental standards and moves towards the international harmonisation of existing standards are indicative of the importance of cooperative solutions to what appear to be (analytically speaking) country-to-country 'prisoner dilemma' situations (see Stein 1990). Even so, there are profound issues of national sovereignty that may not be easily reconciled within a new (environmental) world order. The possible linkage of a post-Uruguay General Agreement on Tariffs and Trade (GATT) round of negotiations with respect to the environment may be of minor significance compared with the racial and ethnic rivalries emerging from the 'new' states of eastern Europe. Will the new international order be one of cooperation and interdependence suited to environmental policy harmonisation or will self-interest dominate (Kennedy 1991)?

With respect to the relationship between industry competitiveness and environmental standards, the 'race to the bottom' should not be thought to be the only plausible (and inescapable) conclusion. To suppose so is to implicitly equate the interests of nation-states with the interests of private corporations. Some environmentalists, while rightly concerned with the global implications of devalued national and international environmental standards, gloss over the possibility that private corporations may have interests very different from those of their host nation-states. As I shall argue here, reflecting the experience of Australian multinational minerals and resource companies, there are reasons to believe that these companies are joined together in a 'race to the top' with respect to their environmental performance. If so, we need to rethink the design and implementation of national environmental policies and reassess the virtues of harmonising national policies and promulgating uniform international standards. This chapter focuses on firm-based incentives that enhance long-term environmental quality.

This argument does not imply that market solutions are always superior to conventional command-and-control regulation of the environment (compare Moran, Chisholm and Porter 1991 with Hahn and Stavins 1991). Nor does this argument necessarily or readily apply to other sectors and firms. The basis of the argument is empirical; its scope is constrained by the context of the analysis — multinational minerals and resource companies. It must also be observed that identified environment-enhancing incentives do exist within a certain economically 'sustainable industry configuration' (Baumol, Panzer and Willig 1988, 5). As that configuration changes, we should see changes in the ways in which underlying economic incentives affect firms' environmental performance. If, as now appears to be the case, the inherited industry configuration is threatened by new entrants, a new price regime and competitive pressures, we should also expect that the environment-enhancing qualities of inter-firm competition may change.

## Minerals and Domestic Environmental Policy

To begin, it is important to understand the nature of domestic environmental regulation, particularly with respect to the interests of the large minerals companies. This is a necessary, preliminary step before tackling the issue of firm behaviour and international competitiveness. An appreciation of the domestic regulatory context is important for two reasons. First, it highlights the significance of environmental regulation for Australian minerals companies, placing those firms within a multi-jurisdictional setting; and, second, it helps us to understand what is important and unimportant for minerals companies about regulation as a social practice.

The Australian minerals industry is involved in mining and processing an extensive range of minerals including nickel, iron ore and coal as well as precious and semi-precious metals like gold, silver and uranium. While there is a close link between minerals production and the domestic steel, auto, and aluminium industries, the industry is largely export oriented. In terms of the volume and value of shipped minerals, the industry is quite dependent on the Japanese and Korean (in that order) metals industries. Australia is the world's leading coking coal exporter and the second most important (after Brazil) exporter of iron ore (Hilly 1989). If Japan and Korea are now the hearth of global industrial production, Australia is their quarry. With a few exceptions, where there is an overlap between mineral production and domestic consumption, exported minerals are normally unprocessed. It is difficult to demonstrate that Australian minerals firms have any comparative advantage in the value-added processing of materials prior to their export overseas (Lloyd 1991).

In terms of gross domestic product, the minerals industry contributes about 5 per cent per year, down somewhat since the mid-1980s and certainly much less than manufacturing and finance and business services. It is also an efficient industry by world standards, one that has dramatically improved labour productivity over the past decade. However, in terms of its direct contribution to employment, the industry is relatively insignificant. Nevertheless its contribution to Australia's overall standard of living is profoundly important. In Table 9.1, the data show the industry to be the nation's single most important foreign exchange earner, with almost 40 per cent of the value of all exports attributable to this one sector. Given Australia's accumulated foreign debt and continuing balance of payments problems, the nation's welfare is intimately connected with the export performance of the large mineral companies. It is also apparent from the data how vulnerable Australia would be to the introduction of any global environmental policy such as a uniform carbon tax (see London Economics 1992).[2]

**Table 9.1**  Australian exports by sector and current account balance 1987/1988 to 1991/1992 ($A current prices)

| Sector | 1987–88 ($m) | 1988–89 ($m) | 1989–90 ($m) | 1990–91 ($m) | 1991–92 ($m) |
|---|---|---|---|---|---|
| Rural | 15 437 | 16 185 | 15 469 | 14 198 | 15 797 |
| Minerals | 19 605 | 21 058 | 24 845 | 27 864 | 28 175 |
| Other merchandise | 6 473 | 6 651 | 8 250 | 10 093 | 10 916 |
| Services | 9 786 | 10 999 | 11 760 | 13 224 | 14 146 |
| *Total exports* | *51 301* | *54 893* | *60 324* | *65 379* | *69 034* |
| Current accounts | *12 327 | *18 494 | *21 581 | *15 629 | *11 861 |
| % GDP | 4.2 | 5.4 | 5.8 | 4.1 | 3.1 |

* Preliminary figures
'Rural' includes cereal grains, forest products, meat, sugar, wool ...; 'Minerals' includes coal, coke, iron ore, bauxite, gold ...; 'Other merchandise' includes manufactured products (steel, etc.); 'Services' includes tourism, finances, banking, transport.

*Source: Agricultural and Resources Quarterly* 4(3) 1992, 410 and 419; 3(3) 1991, 417; and 1(2) 1989, 239 (Canberra).

Any inventory of Australian environmental regulation would return with evidence of internationally recognised legislation and institutions. Over the past 20 or so years, Australia has copied and implemented many US policy initiatives (notably environmental impact assessment), policy-related institutions (notably environmental protection agencies), and environmental standards (such as those related to hazardous wastes). But unlike those of the US, until very recently most of these initiatives have been at the state level rather than at the federal level. The particular constitutional distribution of powers between the states and the federal government has resulted in state-based, differentiated environmental regulation. Coordination between the states on environmental matters has been limited; differences between the states in terms of industry structure, urban concentration, and patterns of growth have resulted in very different environment and development coalitions. Moreover, following the unprecedented growth in public environmental concern throughout the decade of the 1980s, the Federal Government demonstrated an increasing preparedness to exercise its constitutional powers to over-ride state development approvals in a series of major environment/development conflicts.[3]

Only recently has the Federal Government adopted a more conciliatory and integrated approach to environmental policy, principally through the Intergovernmental Agreement on the Environment (IGAE), signed by the Australian Heads of Government in 1992. As an exercise in 'cooperative federalism', the IGAE seeks to reduce federal–state environmental conflict and foster a more streamlined approach to environmental management in Australia by the federal, state and local governments (ANZECC 1991; IGAE 1992). It is also intended to provide a clearer definition of the responsibilities and interests of the three tiers of government across a wide range of environmental policy and management issues in order to provide greater certainty for business, minimise duplication of government decision making and improve environmental protection. The IGAE also laid the framework for the development of national ambient environmental standards and guidelines, to be set by a new intergovernmental ministerial council now known as the National Environmental Protection Council (NEPC). The Federal Government's coordinating role is being overseen by a newly created Commonwealth Environmental Protection Agency.[4] It remains an open question whether these recent moves towards national environmental standards will exert an upward pressure on standards in Australia. Given that ministerial councils generally work on a consensus basis (and any member can exercise a power of veto), it seems more likely that the decision-making process will not lead to 'world best practice'.

Nonetheless, green groups have tended to advocate a stronger federal role in environmental policy because of competition between the states for investment and a fear that in the right circumstances, such as the dominance of a state by a pro-business political coalition, competition could easily degenerate into a 'race to the bottom'. Through reduced environmental standards, lax enforcement of existing state standards and requirements, and more favourable access to crown land, it is feared that one state could force other states dependent on the mineral industry to reduce their standards. One state could thus propel all states to the lowest environmental common denominator matching, in essence, the role of Delaware with respect to the claimed 'deterioration of [US] corporate standards' (Cary 1974, 663). And yet, notwithstanding the rhetorical appeal of the analogy, minerals companies have also advocated a stronger, albeit constrained, federal role in environmental regulation. The major minerals companies fear the power of urban-based green coalitions, who are perceived to be able to scuttle development projects.[5] Rather than benefiting from a 'race to the bottom', minerals companies argue that they face a never-ending competition for influence over environmental policy and its implementation, made especially difficult by the various interests and different circumstances of the states.

As a matter of political fact, this reality is hardly unique. Although problematic for the minerals industry, it is a political reality that is apparent for many other issues and constituencies (e.g. industrial relations, housing and health care). More problematic, however, are three aspects of state-based minerals industry-related environmental policy making that cut against the integrity of the policy process in general. First, some states' environmental policies lack transparency. The boundaries of policies, the meaning of policies, and the process by which those policies are applied, all lack sufficient detail and definition to be predictable in specific cases. Second, lack of transparency combined with the bureaucratic practices of state-based environmental agencies can translate into the exercise of administrative discretion that harms project developers relative to third-party objectors. This may mean either that projects are delayed without adequate due process, or project developers are caught up in wider political conflicts over the relative powers of agencies. Third, in effect, lack of transparency combined with bureaucratic discretion may serve to advantage incumbent firms over new entrants — something that may be desired in its own right (the product of local political and industrial coalitions), or something that is incidental to wider considerations (retention of the jobs associated with existing development projects).

The general problems associated with state-based policy making are shared by many other countries. However, the limited role and scope of judicial review of public decision making in Australia means that affected companies (and individuals) have very few opportunities to appeal against decisions (compare Edley 1990). Furthermore, the fact that the minerals sector directly employs few people, most of whom are located at isolated production sites, means that the limited political significance (in terms of their negligible impact on political parties' electoral fortunes) of the industry does not match the significance of the industry in terms of its contribution to some states' revenue (see ABARE 1990 for state revenue data). The extent to which states favour incumbent firms over new entrants may simply be because of the dominance of inherited elite networks. Many commentators (mining companies and green activists alike) believe that only the Federal Government has an immediate stake in the development process, in particular, the contribution of mineral firms' exports to the nation's balance of payments. Its electoral fortunes are dependent on middle-class concerns for a stable and strong currency.[6]

Despite the recent moves towards a more coordinated national environmental policy regime, there are still instances where states do discount local environmental standards to attract investment, just as there are instances where firms take advantage of the competition between the states for concessions. These instances seem more related to short-term opportunism than a guiding, long-term corporate philosophy.[7]

The federal response to the competition between the states is more consistent with Romano's (1990) 'transaction cost' explanation of inter-jurisdictional corporate regulation rather than Cary's 'race to the bottom' or Fischel's (1982) 'race to the top'. The government's predominant interest appears to be in maintaining a comprehensive system of environmental regulation that combines substantive expertise with comprehensive jurisdictional powers and predictability mediated by political and bureaucratic agents who have a stake in the continuing vitality of the industry. If a state were to set out to dominate the minerals-related domestic environmental policy process, it is unlikely that it could do so by instigating a 'race to the bottom'.

## Economic Incentives and Environmental Performance

In the context of the Australian minerals industry, there are reasons to suppose that mineral companies have an interest in a policy regime that sustains the minerals development process over the long term rather than a policy regime that offers short-term advantage in a particular state jurisdiction. One reason for this longer term interest is the national and international operational scope of firms in the industry. While dependent on the particular location of resources for their sites of production, the Australian industry is a national industry dominated by very large, multinational firms with national and international shareholders. In any event, short-term incentives in one jurisdiction would be difficult to take advantage of, given the scale of sunk costs in existing projects (Clark 1994), and the long-term imperatives of economic competition between companies operating in Australia and overseas. For these companies, there is a set of internal (to the firm) and external (in the market and industry) incentives, quite distinct from domestic policy considerations, that promote a 'race to the top' in terms of firms' comparative environmental performance. Here, the 'race to the top' is set in a world in which firms compete on the basis of market-driven (higher and higher) environmental standards and rewards.

Given the export oriented nature of the industry, there is an intimate connection between firms' environmental performance and their international competitiveness. Michael Porter (1991), who is cited in Schmidheiny's influential *Changing Course* (1992), suggests that this connection is positive and environment enhancing. That is, higher standards of corporate environmental performance can lead to stronger international competitiveness. However, such a positive relationship is not necessarily 'normal' (always the case). This is as much an empirical question as it is a theoretical question that needs to be assessed in different circumstances.[8] This observed positive relationship depends on the specialised nature of inter-firm competition in the industry and the fact that buyers and sellers of Australian minerals have developed long-term contractual relationships, benefiting from buyers' expanding shares of global product markets. Incumbent firms seem to be operating within what Baumol el al. (1988) would describe as a 'sustainable industry configuration' characterised by three conditions: (1) a close approximation between demand and supply; (2) a market price regime that covers at least the costs of production; and (3) no apparent opportunities for new entrants to the market given the prices of incumbent firms.

Basically, costs of production in the industry are driven by two sets of related factors: one set is particular to the industry while the other set is particular to the market. The industry factors are easily identified as comparative advantage, the scale of production, and the intensity of capital use. By the nature of Australian minerals deposits, their type, quality and accessibility, producers have a significant competitive advantage relative to international producers and the needs of buyers. The most successful projects in the industry are those that offer increasing returns to scale and a physical geographical configuration that enables long-term, continuous production. In these circumstances, it is widely believed that average costs decline with the level of output, and return on capital invested increases with the rate of capital utilisation (over a day, a week, and over the year). Labour costs are a trivial proportion of total costs although the rate of capital utilisation (a determinant of the rate of profit) is directly related to the ways in which labour is managed (Gibson 1990). Given these industry factors, the largest firms seek projects across the globe that promise the highest possible returns; perhaps even returns akin to a natural monopoly (see Carlton and Perloff 1990, 113–14).

A second set of factors, particular to the market but related to the industry, are also important in determining costs and prices. These factors are generally related to technological choice and change. Sustaining higher returns on investment depends on using the best available techniques of production (capital) while choosing (investing in) plant and equipment that allows for *in situ* expansion, enhancement of quality, and flexibility with respect to changes in demand. There are, clearly, considerable risks involved in technological choice. Chosen technology may not perform to its specified limits, firms may not make the best choice compared with other firms' choices, market conditions may change so radically that anticipated benefits are not realised. Not surprisingly, there is evidence of technological transfer among firms in the industry drawing on national and international experience. At the same time, the application of technology is often particular to the segment of the industry, even particular to the site of production. Interaction between the choice of technology and the application of technology in particular circumstances encourages firm-based innovation and competition. Indeed for the largest firms, production-oriented research and development is a vital component protecting their long-term market position (cf. Porter 1990).

In terms of firms' environmental performance, these two sets of industry and market factors interact in mutually reinforcing ways to encourage higher standards of performance. This is not just because of internal management cultures that promote engineering excellence (though such cultures have been encouraged as part of corporations' strategies of international competitiveness). Higher quality environmental performance is consistent with lower costs of production and long-term profitability. Competition between rival companies sustains this mix of incentives and rewards (and penalties) for superior performance. To illustrate this point, it is useful to take each of the factors noted above and identify their relationship with environmental performance.

*Industry Factors*

(i) *Comparative advantage*  The nature of Australian mineral production — the terrain and geomorphology of mineral deposits — has allowed incumbent firms to develop valuable environmental expertise that is quite distinctive. The interaction between available technology and the problems of local environmental management, coupled with internal management accountability for environmental performance, has created an internationally competitive industry. The current size of companies and their operating bases across the globe (including Asia, North America, Latin America and Africa) are a testament to their recent competitive success. This kind of interaction has also 'created' another, secondary, comparative advantage, notably a strong reputation for environmental management that has a market among first-world banks and institutions such as the World Bank and the Japanese Overseas Economic Cooperation Fund, which are heavily involved in financing third-world development.[9] This expertise has proved very valuable to multinational companies in their negotiations with other nations and in the development of offshore projects. Internally, recognising the long-term career implications of environmental expertise, site management (often distant from corporate management) has been willing to comply with company and public environmental standards.

(ii) *Scale economics*  The scale of domestic and international mineral projects has had two advantages for incumbent firms. First, given the industry configuration, increasing returns have allowed companies to finance higher environmental standards out of the profits of current projects. Second, the scale of production has brought together two otherwise separate concerns: occupational safety and environmental safety. Given the scale of production, an environmental catastrophe affecting the welfare of employees and community residents (even citizens of adjacent states and countries) is a real possibility. This possibility, coupled with a financial capacity to maintain and improve environmental standards, has also encouraged firms to play a significant research role in setting public (as well as internal) standards of performance. Company-specific knowledge of how to best manage and develop these kinds of projects given the environmental risks involved has, at times, been an asset in gaining access to new sites of production in other countries.

(iii) *Capital utilisation*  Scale economies are just one determinant of internationally competitive costs, prices and profits (cf. Krugman 1990). Capital utilisation is also very important. Some of the largest minerals companies now do not own their working capital. Separation of the ownership of working capital from its

utilisation has been prompted by two related strategic considerations: the discounting of financial risk associated with holding
equipment, and the re-focusing of management on production
rather than the management of asset value. Thus site managers
are required to maximise two conditional objectives: maximum
output subject to maximum capital utilisation. In this context,
achieving maximum profits depends on capital utilisation to its
feasible limits on a continuous basis without disruption. Poor
environmental performance (accidents, spills, long-term degradation
etc.) may actually decrease the rate of profit as disruptions to
production decrease the rate of capital utilisation. By virtue of the
economic benefits of continuous production, management has a
strong incentive to make environmental performance an integral
part of the production process.

*Market Factors*

(i) *Product differentiation* This is a common and important
means of establishing and maintaining a distinctive market
position. While there is evidence that markets are increasingly
sensitive to environmental considerations (witness the importance
of eco-labelling), buyers of mineral products are not as sensitive
to such considerations as First World middle-class consumers. On
the other hand, buyers of mineral products are very sensitive to
the quality and reliability (delivery time) of products. In this
respect, the mineral market is quite segmented, favouring, on the
one hand, producer firms that can deliver on time quality products with long-term contracts while, on the other hand, forcing
into open competition producers who cannot perform according
to these requirements. Quality and reliability are heavily dependent on the technological sophistication of production. In this
sense, high environmental standards and controls are essential to
the continuity of contractual relationships. Again, the economic
incentives related to competition encourage higher quality
environmental performance.

(ii) *Flexibility* Being able to respond to, and even anticipate,
shifts in market demand is an essential component of international competitiveness. For many larger minerals companies,
enhancement of the flexibility of production has meant scrapping
or selling facilities that are too risky or too expensive to operate at
their design limits. Rather than radically retro-fitting existing
production facilities and restructuring mining sites in accordance
with higher standards of environmental performance, large
companies have sought new ventures (in Australia and overseas)
that can allow for the integration of new production methods with
new techniques of environmental controls. This strategy has been

conceived in order to realise development opportunities that can accommodate expected increased environmental standards (public and private), particularly in Third World countries that have been hosts to foreign producers, and potential needs for increased capacity and improvements in the quality of products produced at those facilities.

(iii) *Environmental services*    There is an emerging and important international market for environmental expertise. The largest companies have developed environmental consulting groups based within their own companies and subsidiaries. More recently they have extended beyond the originating companies into other sectors and countries. The market value of these services derives, in part, from the experience, management capacity and reputation of the companies. This kind of market value is rarely or even necessarily patented; it is embodied within the corporation and is difficult for others to replicate. But market value also derives from the technical procedures and research base of these companies — aspects of value that can be sold on the international market just as these companies buy other companies' research products. The potential international value of environmental services is so significant to incumbent companies that they have sought both to maintain and protect their reputations while limiting the transfer of knowledge and technology to potential new market rivals. These competitive strategies have been aided by close collaboration and the formation of alliances between the research groups of the largest companies.

By this assessment, it would appear that Australian minerals companies are engaged in a 'race to the top' in terms of relative environmental performance, driven by attributes of the industry and the markets for their products. This is not a domestic 'race to the top'. Given the international scope of minerals firms, it would appear that the 'race to the top' has had a significant positive relationship to their international competitiveness. In this respect, firms' international competitiveness is more than an issue of relative costs and prices. While important in the short-run (Snape 1992), the expected (public and private) costs of environmental control for these firms are accommodated, in part, by the choice of the site of production and the choice of production methods and technology. With the appropriate configuration of production, even additional pollution taxes and charges (for example) may be accommodated by increasing output, thereby moving down the average (per unit produced) cost curve. The international competitiveness of such firms seems more complex than standard tools of economic analysis would imply.

# Incentives and the 'Race to the Bottom'

On the basis of the preceding overview of the scope and nature of environment-enhancing economic incentives, there is insufficient evidence to accept, as a working hypothesis, the existence of an inter-firm 'race to the top' in the Australian minerals industry. Nonetheless, the previous analysis could be read as an exercise in idealism. Like Schmidheiny's (1992) report on global business and sustainable development, the previous analysis could be accused of ignoring the full range of firms' actions and the experience of green groups who have found the mineral industry unwilling to negotiate over environmental quality. The analysis could be read as naive or, worse, quite misleading. There is a risk that advocates of market-based solutions to environmental problems could read the analysis as further evidence of the putative environmental efficiency of the market.[10] To balance the analysis, it is important to recognise that the working hypothesis is limited in a number of ways. Here, I will emphasise five issues; the first pair are industry oriented, the second pair are market oriented. The fifth issue is related to management control down through the corporate hierarchy.

## *Size of Firm*
Large companies seem more able (and willing) than small ones to capitalise on the existence of environment-enhancing economic incentives in the industry. While large companies do not control their markets, there being intense competition between large multi-national companies for market contracts, the close relationships between large producers and consumers of mineral products are such that long-term issues dominate corporate planning.

By comparison, small firms are more oriented towards the short term. Small firms, more than large ones, depend on the spot-market for sale of their products. This part of the market is notoriously unstable, being very vulnerable to the raiding, dumping, and predatory pricing practices of larger companies. Consequently, the flow of revenue to small firms is very unstable. This affects both their ability to develop new projects and make long-term investments in environmental quality. These firms, more than large firms, are very dependent on existing sites of production, including those abandoned by the larger firms. If small firms rely on natural comparative advantage for their market position, they have neither the virtues of scale economies nor the capacity comprehensively to control the rate of capital utilisation. Not surprisingly, small firms are very sensitive to short-term price fluctuations. Inevitably, they have a vital interest in minimising the costs of production even if this means discounting environmental quality. For small firms, the imperatives of economic survival can easily degenerate into a 'race to the bottom'.

## Sunk Costs

Most firms' costs of production are dominated by the enormous initial, non-recoverable expenditures on infrastructure, environmental controls and equipment. For many firms in the industry, long-term profitability depends on maximising production levels and rates of utilisation until sunk costs are fully accounted for. By implication, all things being equal, higher than average profits are a function of extending the life of a production site beyond the accounting life of sunk costs. The significance of sunk costs to large and small firms alike can have two very important effects on environmental quality.

First, even if higher quality environment-enhancing production methods and techniques become available, companies have a strong economic interest in continuing to operate sites of production using existing capital. Innovation in environmental control at existing sites of production may be limited to just the extra standards imposed by public agencies. Absent increased environmental standards, the environment may pay a high price. Second, given the significance of sunk costs, companies have an economic interest in shifting the burden of those costs to others. Minimising their exposure to sunk costs enables companies to shift responsibility for initial and long-term environmental quality to agents or partners who are not part of the ownership or management of the corporation. In some countries, governments are willing to assume the sunk costs of production (especially those associated with long-term environmental quality) as an inducement to small investors. In effect, sunk costs may delay environmental enhancement, and even encourage a 'race to the bottom' between jurisdictions.

## Market Instability

The argument about the existence and significance of environment-enhancing incentives depends on the continuing stability of the existing industry configuration. If it is disrupted by a significant mismatch between supply and demand, a radical shift in relative costs and prices, or new entrants with a different set of comparative advantages, the higher environmental standards of incumbent companies may not be economically sustainable. This is entirely possible given the current global recession and declining levels of metals production in Japan and Korea, the impact on global commodity prices of Russian and Kazakhstanian minerals exports, and the likely shift of buyers to lower quality (lower price) minerals (the consequence of new metals production technology) (see Lieven 1992). What happens will depend, in part, on the access of multinational minerals companies to development sites in Russia as well as the response of companies to those new opportunities. It is possible that multinational companies could leave behind existing sites in favour of new sites, taking with them environmental techniques developed under the previous industry configuration. By this strategy, multinational companies may retain their market share but set-off a ruinous 'race to the bottom' among nations like Australia and Brazil concerned to maintain the competitiveness of their locally based minerals industries.

## Product Quality

Lower quality mineral products, produced at sites using inferior environmental methods, are a real danger to the continuity of the virtuous path of investment, competitiveness and environmental enhancement. It is entirely plausible that mineral consumers will develop technologies that can accommodate lower quality inputs without sacrificing the quality of output. Unfortunately, the market for steel and other similar metal products is not particularly sensitive to the environmental quality of the methods of production of inputs. By contrast, the pulp and paper industry is very sensitive to how the market understands or perceives the environmental quality of inputs. While the recent history of that industry could be interpreted along the lines of that suggested here for the Australian minerals industry (a virtuous path of investment, international competitiveness and environmental enhancement), a crucial difference exists. That is, the market is willing and able to discriminate between the environmental quality of factor inputs. Consumer preferences for recycled paper products coupled with production processes that are now totally self-contained have made a significant difference to the competitiveness of individual companies. At present, fabricated metal industries' markets are not so sophisticated. Indeed, it might be reasonably argued that new entrants to the industry from foreign-currency-starved countries depend on final consumers' inability to discriminate between competing products on the basis of the environmental quality of inputs. If the industry is to avoid a 'race to the bottom', consumer preferences for higher environmental quality must be integrated into the industry in one form or another.

## Corporate Control

It is tempting to treat large and small firms as unitary agents that simply and only reflect the aims and objectives of owners. But, in fact, this is hardly ever the case for large firms. In the previous analysis, it was argued that one necessary condition for a virtuous path of investment and environmental enhancement is the willingness of site managers to comply with company objectives. Companies at the leading edge of innovation and environmental enhancement in the industry seem to share a common set of values. These values can be thought to derive from shared cultural and professional backgrounds, as well as shared experiences inside and outside the companies. For many managers, career promotion depends on their industry reputations; the small numbers of workers in the industry contribute to a sense of shared identity. However, what if economic incentives dictated an exploitative stance with respect to the environment — would professional commitment to environmental quality survive? In small firms dominated by owner-managers there are reasons to be sceptical of the internal resilience of a pro-environmental culture. The putative micro-economic efficiency of combining the principal (owner) and the agent (manager) may translate into an over-whelming personal interest in maximising short-term income and maximising long-term wealth. For owner-managers, individual wealth may be dependent on the exploitation of the environment.

The issue of corporate control, and the possible environmental effects of separating or combining ownership with management, are too complex to consider in any further detail here. It is a vital issue, albeit under-researched. It is rarely considered when arguments are made about firms' long-term environmental interests. Rose-Ackerman (1991) argues that managers are more risk-averse than owners (concerning US firms' solvency and bankruptcy). The available evidence tends to support an analogous claim that managers in large minerals corporations are similarly risk-averse when it comes to choosing between investment options that carry a range of environmental risks (and pay-offs). With respect to Australian multinational minerals companies, I would argue that at present incentives for the 'race to the top' dominate incentives for the 'race to the bottom'. With respect to smaller locally based private companies, I am less confident that a similar set of incentives may be found.

## Rethinking Domestic and International Environmental Policy

So far, little has been said of the role of domestic environmental policy in promoting the 'race to the top'. The analysis of companies' incentives could be read as being sufficient to explain the development of higher and higher standards of performance. Even so, it could be argued that relatively high state-by-state domestic environmental standards, coincident with an economically sustainable industry configuration, prompted companies' initial investment in environmental performance. It is equally plausible that, notwithstanding occasional state-by-state competitive discounting of standards, the evolving nature of Australian environmental standards and the strength of the green movement has encouraged companies to see environmental performance as an escalating process. This process can only be efficiently accommodated by successive rounds of investment in new sites of production, technology and methods of environmental control. If this has been an effect of domestic environmental policy, it was not obviously intended (cf. Porter 1991).

Most Australian states' environmental policies are aimed at the end of industrial production processes. The licensing, monitoring and control of pollution from existing production facilities are the common tasks of state environmental authorities. There can be no doubt that this regulatory strategy is also very common in the OECD, and is increasingly common in developing countries. To the extent that pollution charges and taxes go beyond recouping the administrative costs associated with regulation, it is often supposed (in Australia, at least) that charges should be a marginal addition to production costs. As a matter of public policy, charges are rarely, if ever, so high that they threaten the economic viability of production. In most states, environmental laws require regulatory agencies to balance what are believed to be conflicting interests — environmental values and economic development. This is a conflict that is often amplified by political and legal contests of power between environmental and business groups over setting the balance.[11] Analytically, setting nominal charges is justified by reference to neoclassical economic assumptions about the virtues of competition and assumed marginal pricing practices.

However, most states have not made the prevention of pollution a central task, nor have they deliberately encouraged environment-enhancing, production-oriented technological change. It is as if the states subscribe to the common working hypothesis that high environmental standards reduce competitiveness. Equally plausible, it seems that most states have been basically concerned with maintaining the vitality of small mineral companies. Yet, if the alternative hypothesis is taken seriously, the logic of domestic environmental regulation ought to be redesigned. At the very least, economic incentives that promote higher environmental standards should be acknowledged and deliberately encouraged. Moreover, it should be recognised that companies in some industries are unlikely to change their behaviour in response to output-based marginal pollution charges. A rather different environmental policy regime is needed: one that can accommodate a range of economic worlds — being sensitive to the existence of very different industry-based incentives, disincentives and competitive circumstances.

A policy regime based on minimising short-term environmental damage and maximising long-term environmental quality might be general enough to provide authorities with the bureaucratic scope for tailored regulation in particular industries while accommodating the interests of environmental quality and competitiveness. To implement such a policy regime would require much more coordination of environmental policy between the states and the Federal Government than is currently the case. National industry plans may be needed to link short-term environmental damage control with long-term investment in environment-enhancing production. One recent step towards the integration of industry-specific short-term control and long-term investment strategies has been the National Strategy for Ecologically Sustainable Development (ESDSC 1992), which draws on the recommendations of a range of industry working groups set up by the Department of Prime Minister and Cabinet. To give effect to such initiatives, a wide range of policy instruments may have to be contemplated, including larger penalties for short-term environmental damage and long-term contracts between companies and regulatory agencies regarding the introduction of environment-enhancing technology. Such penalties and contracts would presumably be administered at the state level but would require federal involvement. Indeed, given the Federal Government's stake in international competitiveness, there may (for example) be scope for linking federal investment policies with states' environment-enhancing contracts.

If there is a mutually reinforcing relationship between international competitiveness and environmental quality, then all nations' peoples have an interest in fostering the conditions that make this virtuous relationship possible. However obvious this claim, as a practical matter its achievement is threatened by all kinds of specific national interests. For instance, nations that are not competitive in certain sectors and industries have an interest in limiting the geographical scope of international competition. Other nations that lack sufficient resources or material wealth may have an interest in discounting local environmental standards so as to gain market share and foreign currency reserves. Even the beneficiaries of international trade may use the environment issue to argue for protection if the existing industry configuration comes under attack by new competitors. There are many, many examples of national interests competing with the global interest in ecological sustainable development. This is the global commons problem, which is sometimes characterised as a problem of ill-defined property rights — the fact that '[c]ertain environmental assets [like ecosystems] may be owned by nations and yet be considered by some people as belonging to the world at large as part of the global commons' (Secretariat 1992, 5).

Clearly, a positive relationship between international competitiveness and environmental quality is not sufficient to deter a 'race to the bottom' if nations place sectional interests ahead of global interests in ecologically sustainable development. On the other hand, the fact there may be a positive relationship between competitiveness and environmental quality suggests that trade and the environment may also not be so opposed as often imagined. In fact, the integration of international trade and environmental policy making may be a vital first step away from a 'race to the bottom'. For nations confident of the competitiveness of their environment-enhancing industries, a liberalised international trade regime is a necessary element in any comprehensive national environment and development strategy. In this context, of course, barriers to international trade such as limited access to markets, subsidies, tariffs and quotas, national product standards, and policies that allow local competitors to avoid the full costs of their actions are also barriers to an enhanced global environment. Just as important, however, are trade-equity issues, particularly those relating to the access of non-aligned nations to the emerging supra-regional trading blocs and technological transfer between nations.

How an international integrated trade and environment policy-making process would be developed and managed is unclear. In part, the extent of integration will depend on whether there is a sufficient constituency to tackle environmental issues among member nations to the GATT and the new World Trade Organisation. Effective management would also require developing mechanisms to monitor and ensure the compliance of nations and their companies with existing international environmental agreements. At present, it appears that these mechanisms are inadequate.[12] An integrated trade and environmental policy-making process also depends on a reassessment of the meaning and application of OECD Guiding Principles related to nations' environmental policies (Stevens 1993b). Notwithstanding doubts about the effectiveness of economic incentives, the experience of the Australian minerals industry raises legitimate questions about the scope of each of the OECD's environmental principles. Of special interest are the Polluter Pays Principle, the Harmonisation

Principle, the National Treatment and Non-Discrimination Principle, the Compensating Import Levies and Export Rebates Principle and the Precautionary Principle.

The Polluter Pays Principle requires that companies bear the full environmental costs of their actions, denying the legitimacy of national policies that, in effect, subsidise production. A number of exceptions are allowed, including government assistance to industry during phase-in periods of more stringent environmental programs, the development of new pollution control technologies and the achievement of other important goals. If Australian governments were to shift to a new environmental policy regime that focused on long-term environment-enhancing investment in particular industry sectors, would the allowed exceptions be sufficient to accommodate such a policy regime? Perhaps. It depends on the accepted interpretation of the scope and intent of the principle. It could be argued that the Polluter Pays Principle is more concerned with trade than it is with the environment. In particular, it seems preoccupied with the trade implications of the short-term relative costs of production rather than the long-term quality of the environment. It could be also argued that the allowed exceptions ought to be the object of the principle. By this argument, the Polluter Pays Principle is only relevant to the extent that it can be shown to be an efficient means to the desired end — the development of new environment-enhancing technologies that can be traded on the international market.

The Harmonisation Principle requires nations to seek ways of increasing the compatibility between environmental policies, especially where local standards and regulations might be disguised barriers to trade. Provision was made for exceptions, particularly if local standards can be shown to have valid economic or ecological reasons for their existence. For instance, differences in nations' ecological assimilative capacity have been posited as a legitimate exception. In fact, as Stevens (1993b) notes, in practice harmonisation as a goal has evolved considerably over the past two decades, now being focused on the compatibility and comparability of nations' environmental policy instruments. Here, an important issue is the extent to which a new policy regime focused on encouraging long-term environment-enhancing development would be consistent with harmonisation if nations' policies differed in accordance with their particular natural comparative advantages (and disadvantages). What if a uniform tax regime, such as a carbon tax — imposed in the interests of harmonisation — were to stymie the development of national comparative advantage in particular environmental technologies? Clearly, harmonisation needs to be balanced against the heterogeneity of national circumstances, the basis of recent innovations in environment-enhancing technology.

The National Treatment and Non-Discrimination Principle requires that, with respect to environmental standards and regulations, imported products be treated by policy as similar to domestically produced products. This is a vital, yet remarkably vague, principle that could have very important implications for fostering the international market for environment-enhancing technology. What if a country were able to produce a good, like minerals, at a comparable price to other competing nations using a more efficient process or using facilities that had lower environmental costs? Would that country be able to discriminate in favour of the environment by discriminating against comparable imported goods that were produced using inferior technologies? At present, it appears the answer would be no. What if a nation discriminated against imported products so as to encourage the long-term development of local, superior environment-enhancing technology? Would these actions contravene the non-discrimination principle? At present, the answer would appear to be yes. The value of these answers for the environment (as opposed to trade) deserve more scrutiny, given the prospect of a national environmental policy regime that combines an interest in minimising short-term environmental damage while maximising long-term environmental quality.

The Compensating Import Levies and Export Rebates Principle requires member nations to refrain from imposing levies on imports or subsidising exports so as to off-set the higher costs of domestic environmental policies. Again, this principle is largely a trade-oriented device, a means of forestalling short-run distortions to trade when member nations implement higher environmental standards relative to other nations. It is believed that the need for this principle has been limited by the adherence of nations to the Polluter Pays Principle. Even so, it is worth speculating on the applicability of this principle when environmental policy regimes are focused on enhancing long-term environmental quality. To imagine it in operation is to presume a high degree of policy equivalence and comparability; how else could officials determine if a policy was or was not a countervailing trade measure? In fact, policies may be very different if nations encourage the development of environmental technology based on natural comparative advantage and economies of scale. Presumably the principle should not inhibit such developments. So what is its relevance in a world of experience-related paths of capital accumulation?

Finally, we might also ask how the introduction of a new principle, like the Precautionary Principle, might fit with OECD principles and the development of nation-specific and industry-specific environmental standards. In summary terms, the Precautionary Principle requires decision makers always to prevent serious or irreversible environmental harm, even if the activity or substance at issue can not be conclusively shown to cause harm. The burden of proof is not on regulators but on industry (Cameron and Abouchar 1991). At first sight, such a principle would not necessarily be antagonistic with a policy regime that sought to minimise short-term damage and maximise long-term quality. But what if application of the principle denied experimentation in the interests of long-term quality? How would such a principle fit with OECD principles that seem so concerned with trade? What if the application of the principle meant that international trade in toxic materials was found to be illegitimate?

These questions relating to the Precautionary Principle and the other OECD principles require further analysis and consultation. It would be naive and premature to suggest answers to these questions. At the very least, greater interest needs to be shown in an international environment and trade regime that can accommodate both short-term considerations relating to minimising environmental harm and our common, global interest in maximising long-term environmental quality.

## Conclusions

In this chapter, the recent experience of large Australian minerals companies served as a reference point for an analysis of international competitiveness and environmental quality. The analysis was framed in terms of companies' competitive strategies, their circumstances and choices. I argued that there is a positive relationship between companies' international competitiveness and high environmental standards. In particular, there appear to be economic incentives in the industry, and its markets, that enhance environmental quality, which in turn enhances companies' international competitiveness. In this context, domestic environmental policy was shown to have been less relevant to the industry than many might have imagined. Indeed, given the intricacies of comparative advantage and scale economies in the industry, as well as differentiation of the market with respect to product quality and delivery-time, domestic environmental policy seems to have been quite removed from these issues. I have also suggested that the design and implementation of international environmental policy should be re-thought given the plausible existence of such economic incentives in other sectors.

With respect to state-by-state domestic environmental policy making, at least, there may be few overlapping interests between policy makers and these kinds of firms. Even at the national level, policy makers may have to be more careful designing and implementing environmental policies. For example, policies such as pollution taxes and charges on output and production run the risk in the short term of being irrelevant to the economic incentives faced by companies that enjoy significant scale economies, just as they run the risk of irrelevance over the long term if these companies have options (inside and outside of the policy jurisdiction) for new sites of development. It is also possible that environmental policy makers, by following a conventional neoclassical cost–price approach to firm decision making, may not design policies that attach to the most relevant economic incentives of companies. Worst of all, policy instruments may be used that disrupt the virtuous relationship between competitiveness and enhanced environmental quality.

At the same time, there is a chance that policy makers may initiate a 'race to the bottom' by mistaking or ignoring the true incentives faced by these companies. Such 'races to the bottom' may only provide short-term advantage to companies unwilling or unable to develop the kinds of environmental expertise necessary to be internationally competitive.

In developing these arguments, I made several assumptions about large, multinational minerals companies that may not be readily apparent to the reader. First, it was assumed that these companies are very sensitive to longer term financial and market considerations relating to the development of sites of production. In fact, it was supposed that they are more sensitive to these issues than they are to short-term opportunities for wind-fall profits. This implies at least the existence of management cultures within companies that are finely tuned to the long-term survival of the organisations (and the future of individual managers in these organisations). Here, I suggested that companies' management have overlapping interests in competitiveness and environmental quality. The existence of these overlapping interests are clearly vital, motivating factors linking the interests of senior management through to the interests of site management. However, not all minerals companies are like this; not all companies have such well-developed cultures. A second, and related, assumption was that these companies are not especially loyal to any particular jurisdiction. Over the long term, it is commonly believed that the success of these companies depends on their being able to exploit market-relevant opportunities wherever their locations. In the end, these are global corporations whose future depends on minimising the costs of an adverse change in the existing industry configuration.

It is also important to acknowledge that my argument about environmental quality and international competitiveness is somewhat at odds with standard assumptions about the primacy of inter-firm perfect (or near perfect) competition. While competition between Australian minerals companies does exist, because of a considerable risk that the existing industry configuration will be destroyed by new entrants or radically altered by new competitive circumstances much of the analysis treated firms apart from other firms. In doing so, the focus was on the options and strategic choices of individual companies whose competitive interests are relatively well known, at least in the short term. To treat companies in this manner goes against conventional assumptions about the inescapable logic of competition. This analysis assumes that firm-specific knowledge, combined with its particular path of capital accumulation, can be an effective way of forestalling competition in the short term and an effective way of developing international competitiveness over the long term.

Consistent with Paul Romer (1986, 1990), we can suppose that increasing returns to scale, combined with firm-specific knowledge, can increase the rate of return on capital invested, prompting further rounds of environment-enhancing investment and growth. It is possible, of course, that companies can be so self-centered or myopic as to work themselves into 'blind-alleys' — paths of technical change and innovation that turn out to be less than industry-related best practice. Thus it is also important to recognise the potential role and significance of collaboration between near-rival companies on matters like environmental management and technology, even if technological transfer between countries remains elusive (witness Agenda 21). In part, this is why larger, multinational companies appear to be less interested in policy-induced short-term environmental windfalls. For a firm in the industry to move away from the development of internal or industry-based environmental expertise is to signal to rivals and investors alike that the firm can not sustain its place in the industry. In these circumstances, the environment may have to pay the price of a failed knowledge-based development strategy.

Finally, it is also important to acknowledge that this approach to the issue of international competitiveness and enhanced environmental quality is consistent with other developments in the invigorated and combined area of trade and growth theory. Following Grossman and Helpman (1990), it is assumed that having an initial natural comparative advantage in the production of a good can translate into nation-specific specialised knowledge that can not be exactly replicated. This carries the premise, of course, that firms' activities spill over into their host or originating nations. While this is the case in the Australian minerals sector, such beneficial spill overs may not be the rule. When this kind of comparative advantage is combined with the growing integration of the world economy, it should be apparent how and why free trade may enhance environmental quality: local, non-replicable expertise relating to environmental services and technology has a global market. At the same time, the internationalisation of minerals firms and their competition for development sites around the world may also encourage the application of high-quality environmental practices in countries that do not have the local expertise to go beyond simply exploiting the environment.

It is a fine line, nonetheless, between the virtues of environment-enhancing foreign investment and neocolonialism. Sovereignty issues remain important, especially in Eastern Europe and the newly established (and re-established) states of the old Soviet Union. Likewise, whatever the promised benefits of an international market for environmental quality, this analysis is offered as a working hypothesis. There are reasons to be sceptical of the scope of the hypothesis, especially with regard to the extent to which it replaces the common working hypothesis — that firms located in countries with high environmental standards are economically disadvantaged with respect to firms located in countries with low environmental standards. More empirical work on companies' investment choices is needed to 'flesh out' the limits of this alternative hypothesis.

# Endnotes

1. For instance, the development of supra-regional free trade blocs, like the North American Free Trade Agreement, have raised related concerns about the potential environmental impacts of capital mobility within blocs. In a recent report by the US General Accounting Office (GAO) (1992a), it was shown that Mexican environmental policies were hardly ever complied with by US owned companies operating in the *maquiladora* program. Non-compliance and, by implication non-enforcement, of local environmental policies is widespread. This is the case despite the fact that Mexican requirements are now comprehensive and more technically sophisticated than ever before (aided by the World Bank and international consultants).

2. This issue is of great concern to economic policy makers, companies and the green movement. While there is no doubt that all groups would like to reduce greenhouse gas emissions, the reliance of Australia on mineral exports is such that any substantial reduction

would have profound structural consequences for the Australian economy. The green movement has argued that a comprehensive structural policy conceived and implemented by the Federal Government is vital if Australia is to implement such agreements (see papers in the February 1992 issue of *Habitat* published by the Australian Conservation Foundation).

3. Key federal interventions include the 'saving' of the Gordon-below-Franklin river from a hydroelectric power scheme in Tasmania, the preservation of Queensland's wet tropical rainforests, the halting of the Wesley Vale pulp mill in Tasmania, the moratorium on logging in the southern forests of Tasmania and the prevention of mining in Kakadu National Park in the Northern Territory.

4. Although established as the Commonwealth Environmental Protection Agency (CEPA), the word 'Commonwealth' has since been dropped from the title. NEPC was originally established as the National Environmental Protection Authority (NEPA) (IGAE 1992, 23); however, this title was changed in 1994 to properly reflect the status of the body as a ministerial council.

5. See Littlewood's (1992) speech at the American Mining Congress's earth summit 'postscript'. Perceptions are very difficult to demonstrate in fact, or refute. The recent (1992) *Mabo* decision of the High Court of Australia (which recognised that Aboriginals and Torres Strait Islanders could claim common law native title in certain circumstances) has been pilloried by major mining companies; they fear that the *Mabo* decision encourages the formation of anti-development coalitions combining the interests of conservation groups with native land rights groups. But it is equally clear that green groups believe they have been quite unable to influence the path of development projects. While there have been instances of cooperation between green groups and Aboriginal groups, it is also possible that the *Mabo* decision will convert Aboriginal land title holders into project partners with the mining companies.

6. The urban middle-class are also very much concerned about the environment, particularly development projects that involve an interplay between Aboriginal land rights and heritage conservation. Success in federal politics (being elected and re-elected) is all about representing and managing that conflict in ways that appear to sustain both interests at the same time.

7. Compare Williamson (1985) with Bebchuk (1992) on the theory behind such a distinction.

8. Compare, for example, Stiglitz (1976) with Gaudet and Lassere (1988).

9. There has been increasing close cooperation between the World Bank and the OECF on environment and development issues. In the past few years, the OECF has made environmental quality an essential part of project evaluation in their funding process.

10. For a more general analysis of the problems of international trade and the environment, see Stevens (1993a). Stevens analyses how and why market failures can lead to undesirable environmental con-

sequences, and how and why government policies may hinder, and sometimes exacerbate, market failures related to environmental quality.
11. On the US experience, see Tietenberg 1993.
12. Two recent reports of the US General Accounting Office (GAO) (1992b,c) have noted that most of the nearly 170 international environmental agreements in which the United States participates do not impose sanctions for non-compliance. There are few useful ways to assess countries' implementation, and most agreements do not have adequate resources to even monitor countries' (and firms') actions.

# References

ABARE. (1990) *Submission to the Industry Commission. Mining and Minerals Processing: Industry Assistance, Taxation and the Environment*, Australian Bureau of Agricultural and Resource Economics, Canberra.

ANZECC. (1991) *A National Approach to Environmental Impact Assessment in Australia*, Australian and New Zealand Environment and Conservation Council, Canberra.

Baumol, W.J., Panzar, J.C. and Willig, R.D. (1988) *Contestable Markets and the Theory of Market Structure*, 2nd edn, Harcourt Brace Jovanovich, New York.

Bebchuk, L. (1992) 'Federalism and the Corporation: The Desirable Limits on State Competition in Corporate Law', *Harvard Law Review* 105, 1437–510.

Birdsall, N. and Wheeler, D. (1991) *Openness Reduces Industrial Pollution in Latin America: The Missing Pollution Haven Effect*, Symposium Paper, International Trade Division, World Bank, Washington DC.

Cameron, J. and Abouchar, J. (1991) 'The Precautionary Principle: A Fundamental Principle of Law and Policy for the Protection of the Global Environment', *Boston College International and Comparative Law Review* 14, 1–27.

Carlton, D. and Perloff, J. (1990) *Modern Industrial Organisation*, Scott Foresman/Little Brown, Glenview, Illinois.

Cary, W.L. (1974) 'Federalism and Corporate Law: Reflections Upon Delaware', *Yale Law Journal* 83, 663–705.

Clark, G.L. (1994) 'Strategy and Structure: Corporate Restructuring and the Scope and Characteristics of Sunk Costs', *Environment and Planning* A26, 9–32.

Ecologically Sustainable Development Steering Committee (ESDSC). (1992) *National Strategy for Ecologically Sustainable Development*, Australian Government Publishing Service, Canberra.

Edley, C. (1990) *Administrative Law: Rethinking Judicial Control of Bureaucracy*, Yale University Press, New Haven.

Fischel, D. (1982) 'The "Race to the Bottom" Revisited: Reflections on Recent Developments in Delaware's Corporation Law', *Northwestern University Law Review* 76, 913–45.

General Accounting Office (GAO). (1992a) *US–Mexico Trade. Assessment of Mexico's Environmental Controls for New Companies*, GGD-92-113, General Accounting Office, Washington DC.

GAO. (1992b) *International Environment. International Agreements are Not Well Monitored*, RCED-92-43, General Accounting Office, Washington DC.

GAO.(1992c) *International Environment. Strengthening the Implementation of Environmental Agreements*, RCED-92-188, General Accounting Office, Washington DC.

GATT. (1992) *International Trade 90–91*, Volume 1, General Agreement on Tariffs and Trade, Geneva.

Gaudet, G. and Lassere, P. (1988) 'On Comparing Monopoly and Competition in Exhaustible Resource Exploitation', *Journal of Environmental Economics and Management* 15, 412–18.

Gibson, K. (1990) 'Australian Coal in the Global Context: A Paradox of Efficiency and Crisis', *Environment and Planning* 22, 629–46.

Grossman, G. and Helpman, E. (1990) 'Trade, Innovation and Growth', *American Economic Review* 80(2), 86–91.

Hahn, R. and Stavins, R. (1991) *Economic Incentives for Environmental Protection: Integrating Theory and Practice*, CSIA Discussion Paper 91–15, John F. Kennedy School of Government, Harvard University, Cambridge.

Hilly, S. (1989) 'Trends in Steel Making Technology and Australia's Mineral Exports', *Agricultural and Resources Quarterly* 1, 48–58.

*Intergovernmental Agreement on the Environment* (IGAE). (1992) Department of Arts, Sport, Environment and Territories, February.

Kennedy, D. (1991) 'Turning to Market Democracy: A Tale of Two Architectures', *Harvard International Law Journal* 32, 373–96.

Krugman, P. (1990) *Rethinking International Trade*, MIT Press, Cambridge, Massachusetts.

Lieven, D.C.B. (1992) *Another Winter of Discontent: Continued Analysis of the Changes in East-Central Europe and Russia*, IDS Fund Management, 69 Old Broad St, London.

Littlewood, G. (1992) 'RIO: A Postscript for the Mining Industry', Paper presented to the American Mining Congress, Las Vegas, Nevada.

Lloyd, P. (1991) 'Domestic Processing, Value Added and Globalisation' in C. Hamilton (ed.), *The Economic Dynamics of Australian Industry*, Allen and Unwin, Sydney.

London Economics. (1992) *The Impact of Global Warming Control Policies on Australian Industry*, 91 New Cavendish St, London.

Moran, A., Chisholm, A. and Porter, M. (eds). (1991) *Markets, Resources and the Environment*, Allen and Unwin, Sydney.

Office of Technology Assessment (1992) *Trade and Environment: Conflicts and Opportunities*, US Congress, Washington DC.

Porter, M. (1990) *The Competitive Advantage of Nations*, Free Press, New York.

Porter, M. (1991) 'America's Green Strategy', *Scientific American* 264(4), 96.

Romano, R. (1990) 'The State Competition Debate in Corporate Law' in L. Bebchuk (ed.), *Corporate Law and Economic Analysis*, Cambridge University Press, Cambridge.

Romer, P. (1986) 'Increasing Returns and Long-run Growth', *Journal of Political Economy* 94, 1002–37.

Rose-Ackerman, S. (1991) 'Risk Taking and Ruin: Bankruptcy and Investment Choice', *Journal of Legal Studies* 20, 277–310.

Schmidheiny, S. with the Business Council for Sustainable Development. (1992) *Changing Course: A Global Business Perspective on Development and the Environment*, MIT Press, Cambridge, Massachusetts.

Secretariat. (1992) *Joint Session of Trade and Environment Experts*, Synthesis Report: The Environmental Effects of Trade, Environment Directorate, OECD, Paris.

Snape, R. (1992) 'The Environment, International Trade and Competitiveness' in K. Anderson and R. Blackhurst (eds), *The Greening of World Trade Issues*, Harvester–Wheatsheaf, Hemel Hempstead.

Stein, A.A. (1990) *Why Nations Cooperate: Circumstance and Choice in International Relations*, Cornell University Press, Ithaca.

Stevens, C. (1993a) 'The Environmental Effects of Trade', *World Economy* 16(4), 439–51.

Stevens, C. (1993b) 'The OECD Guiding Principles Revisited', *Environmental Law* 23(2), 607–19.

Stiglitz, J. (1976) 'Monopoly and the Rate of Extraction of Exhaustible Resources', *American Economic Review* 66, 655–61.

Tietenberg, T.H. (1993) 'Using Economic Incentives to Maintain Our Environment' in H. Daly and K. Townsend (eds), *Valuing the Earth: Economics, Ecology, Ethics*, MIT Press, Cambridge, Massachusetts.

Williamson, O. (1985) *The Economic Institutions of Capitalism*, Free Press, New York.

# Part V

# *Environmental Compliance, Justice and Democracy*

# 10

# *Changing Corporate Environmental Behaviour: Criminal Prosecutions as a Tool of Environmental Policy*

## Susan L. Smith[1]

How effective are criminal prosecutions as a tool of environmental policy? In answering this question, which applies equally to traditional and market-based schemes, I will be drawing primarily on the experience in the United States with federal prosecution of corporations and corporate managers for environmental crimes.

The United States experience over the past decade suggests that we have an extraordinarily powerful tool for changing corporate environmental behaviour, namely, criminal prosecution of corporate managers and directors for environmental crimes. Corporate officials are typically pillars of their community. They cannot conceive of being handcuffed, fingerprinted, photographed and thrown in a detention cell, much less sentenced to years in a federal penitentiary where fine wine, gourmet food and classical music are in relatively short supply and where brutal assaults are an every day occurrence. Yet, if a corporate manager is convicted of the garden variety environmental offence in the US — for example knowingly discharging toxic water pollutants in violation of permit conditions — he or she faces the real prospect of being sentenced to a term of one to two years in federal prison, without possibility of probation or parole.[2]

This fact, broadly disseminated by federal environmental prosecutors as well as corporate defence counsel, has proven to be a powerful engine for changing corporate behaviour. Through effective criminal prosecutions, the United States has captured what I call the 'command attention' of corporate boards and management (Smith 1991, 7). Corporate managers are now eager to design internal environmental compliance systems that prevent environmental violations from occurring. They are also willing, however begrudgingly, to spend the corporate dollars necessary to ensure compliance.

## Factors Creating An Effective Environmental Prosecution Program

Three primary factors have made the federal environmental criminal prosecution program effective. First, in general, environmental offences in the United States are statutorily graded by severity of harm created by the regulatory violation and by moral culpability.[3] The most severe maximum prison sentences, up to 15 years in prison, are reserved for regulatory violations that are knowing and that place someone in imminent danger of death or serious bodily injury. Severe felony maximum prison sentences, of two to five years, are reserved for intentional or knowing violations. Lesser misdemeanor sentences of one year in prison or less are available for negligent violations.

This statutory grading scheme has been refined by federal sentencing guidelines that limit the discretion of the federal courts in imposing sentences for most federal crimes, including environmental crimes. Federal courts *must* impose a sentence within a presumptive range established on the basis of the characteristics of the offence and the criminal history of the offender. The court can depart from that range only based on aggravating or mitigating factors not considered in formulating the sentencing guidelines and only if it specifically finds reasons for departure, which is a considerable disincentive against departures.

Under the sentencing guidelines, the presumptive sentence for a first offender committing a knowing endangerment crime is approximately five years, without possibility of probation or parole. The presumptive sentence for a first offender committing other knowing violations of environmental regulations can range from no jail time to over 10 years depending on a variety of factors.[4]

It should be noted that the presumptive sentences provided in the sentencing guidelines assume a knowing mental state. In the event that the crime was the product of criminal negligence rather than a culpable mental state, the guidelines indicate that the court may consider a downward departure from the presumptive sentencing range.[5]

This statutory grading scheme, and the sentencing guidelines, allow prosecutors to prosecute vigorously, content that they are serving justice and acting consistently with fundamental public values that regard corporate pollution, particularly pollution involving hazardous or toxic substances, as an extremely serious offence. The sentencing guidelines also prevent the exercise of judicial discretion in favour of white collar criminals who commit serious offences, including environmental criminals. As a result of the guidelines, environmental criminals will be treated far less leniently than in the past.

Second, federal prosecutorial policies are stringent. Apparent violations are reviewed first as potential criminal prosecutions. Prosecutors seek to punish not only blatant midnight dumpers, but also corporate 'sins of omission', which lead just as inevitably to environmental violations.[6] Most importantly, there is a policy of prosecuting the highest truly responsible corporate officer in addition to lower level employees who may have committed the criminal act.[7] Subsequent administrations have expanded the environmental criminal enforcement program and have continued a commitment to prosecute responsible corporate officers (see Marzulla and Kappel 1991). Thus, the typical corporate prosecution has three or more individual co-defendants, two-thirds of whom are corporate managers.[8]

Third, federal environmental criminal prosecutors are zealous. There are dozens of specialised environmental criminal prosecutors located in the Environmental Crimes Section of the US Department of Justice. These prosecutors have available the additional criminal prosecution resources of the US attorneys offices, the Federal Bureau of Investigation, specialised environmental criminal investigators located in the regional offices of the US Environmental Protection Agency (EPA), and the National Environmental Investigation Center. These prosecutors also have available to them the additional environmental enforcement expertise of the EPA regional enforcement lawyers and the EPA Office of Enforcement. This organisational structure creates a large cadre of dedicated individuals devoted to nothing other than environmental criminal prosecutions, who possess the necessary expertise and who have been given the investigative resources to conduct these admittedly difficult prosecutions.

In addition, the responsibility for investigating criminal matters does not fall on compliance inspectors in the field, but rather is assigned to regional enforcement lawyers and specialised criminal investigators. This permits field inspectors to maintain co-operative, working relationships with regulated parties, while matters appropriate for criminal prosecution are handled by other groups within the agency. This reduces the opportunity for co-option of field inspectors. It also circumvents the tendency of field inspectors to be concerned about securing compliance from an individual company (i.e. specific deterrence), rather than sending a message to the larger regulated community (i.e. general deterrence). Finally, it avoids the natural inclination of over-worked field inspectors to take less resource-intensive enforcement options.

# Evaluating The Results of an Effective Environmental Criminal Prosecution Program

As a result of a strong federal environmental criminal enforcement program, more than 150 individuals were sentenced to serve 365 years of prison in the eight years from Fiscal Year (FY) 83 to FY 91; 162 years had actually been served by the end of FY 91.[9] And, with the advent of the sentencing guidelines, the aggregate amount of prison time sentenced and served will increase dramatically as the percentage of individuals sentenced to jail increases from 30 per cent between FY 83 and FY 91 to virtually 100 per cent. The power of those statistics lies not in the impact of conviction on those individuals, but on the general deterrent effect of those convictions on every corporate manager and director, in the impact of those convictions on the effectiveness of the entire environmental enforcement system, and ultimately in the ability of criminal prosecutions to shape public preferences.

While no hard empirical data are available to verify the general deterrent effect of environmental criminal prosecutions, every scrap of anecdotal evidence suggests a very substantial effect. First, my own experience defending federal facilities accused of environmental violations indicated that the prospect of possible criminal prosecution of military base commanders and Department of Energy facility managers dramatically elevated the level of attention being paid to environmental compliance problems (see Smith 1991). Second, corporate managers, government enforcement personnel, environmental consultants and corporate defence counsel in both the United States and Australia have pointed to criminal prosecution with the potential of jail time as the primary motivation for the development of strong internal compliance and auditing systems.[10] Third, when the US Environmental Protection Agency conducted a study that attempted to establish the deterrent value of the Superfund liability system, it concluded that the *Resource Conservation and Recovery Act* (RCRA) regulatory system had a greater deterrent effect (United States Environmental Protection Agency 192). While the Agency did not evaluate what aspect of the RCRA regulatory program was so effective, that regulatory program does stress criminal prosecution — generating more criminal cases than any other environmental regulatory program (Cohen 1992, 1073).

In addition, once a violation has occurred, the credible threat of criminal prosecution makes the remainder of the enforcement system, administrative and civil, far more effective. In the United States, the vast bulk of enforcement takes the form of administrative or civil enforcement. Administrative enforcement involves direct imposition by the US Environmental Protection Agency of a variety of informal and formal sanctions, including oral or written warnings, administrative compliance orders, and administrative penalty orders (including penalties up to $200 000 under the *Clean Air Act*). Civil enforcement involves a civil suit brought in the federal district court to secure injunctive relief and civil penalties (including penalties up to $50 000 per day of violation). Civil penalties secured through civil enforcement in the United States routinely exceed $1 million for significant violations by large organisations, whether they are municipal sewage authorities or Fortune 500 corporations.

The availability of criminal prosecution of corporate officers with the realistic prospect of significant prison sentences makes violators far more cooperative with administrative or civil enforcement efforts. In many cases, the violator in essence faces the Hobson's choice between settling an administrative or civil enforcement action quickly with a rapid compliance schedule, stringent conditions, and stiff financial penalties or being deemed a recalcitrant by the EPA, which makes subsequent criminal prosecution far more likely.

Finally, while the criminal penalty structure reflects fundamental public values, it also shapes them by labelling environmental violations as 'crimes', not mere regulatory errors. It thus reinforces the stigma attached to corporate pollution and increases public support for stringent measures to reduce pollution.

# The Role of Criminal Prosecution in Enforcing Market Incentive Approaches to Environmental Regulation

While criminal prosecution has typically been used in the United States to enforce compliance with command-and-control regulation, criminal prosecution has an equally significant role to play in enforcing compliance with regulation based on market incentive approaches.

Marc Roberts noted nearly two decades ago that the need for enforcement remains in marketable rights and emission fee schemes (Roberts and Farrell 1978). Corporations and corporate managers must face a penalty function that makes it more attractive to comply with the rules of the game — whether those rules are a regulatory standard, an administratively determined permit, a requirement to secure sufficient marketable rights to cover the amount of pollution produced, or an emission fee — than to circumvent those rules. Moreover, the penalties for breaking the rules must be far greater than the savings from non-compliance because the likelohood of successfully detecting and sanctioning the violator is relatively small.

The role of criminal prosecution in enforcing market incentive approaches to environmental regulation is similar to that of the role played in more traditional regulatory systems: the possibility of criminal prosecutions makes it far more attractive to play by the rules. Although theoretically it is possible to impose substantial enough fines through civil or administrative enforcement schemes to create appropriate incentives for corporations and corporate managers to comply (Posner 1980), criminal enforcement has the critical advantage of prison time as a sanction, which has the value of a virtually infinite financial incentive. Inadvertant failures to pay appropriate emission charges or to secure adequate marketable rights may be appropriately sanctioned through administrative or civil penalties. However, certain behaviours will still be worthy of criminal sanctions such as intentional or knowing failures to pay appropriate emission charges or to secure adequate marketable rights. In addition, just as the criminal sanction is currently imposed for acts that impair the integrity of the traditional regulatory system, such as tampering with monitoring equipment or false recordkeeping or reporting, criminal sanctions will be necessary to prevent similar attacks on the integrity of monitoring, recordkeeping, and reporting systems associated with market incentives approaches.

# Enforcement Problems Uniquely Associated with Market Incentive Approaches

Advocates of market incentive approaches have either optimistically predicted that enforcement in market incentive regulatory regimes may be easier or assumed that enforcement problems disappear altogether (see Kneese and Schultze 1975; Friedlaender 1978 and Breyer 1982). For example, some commentators have suggested that policing emission fee schemes would be easier because corporations would resist findings of non-compliance more than they would resist paying a flat price for a certain amount of emissions (Ackerman et al. 1974).

Of scholars writing generally about market incentive approaches to environmental regulation, Breyer (1982) has probably considered relative enforcement problems in the most detail. Breyer conceded (unnecessarily) that monitoring compliance may be simpler under traditional command-and-control regulatory systems, but argued that voluntary compliance under market incentives approaches will be higher because firms know precisely what they are supposed to do, that firms will not have available the excuse that they must await a compliance schedule, the firms will pay for the extra emissions during a court battle, and that courts will not face the tough choice of allowing the pollution or forcing the firm to close down. However, Breyer's analysis seems somewhat off target. First, contrary to Breyer's analysis, command-and-control regulation usually specifies more precisely what the firm should do. Indeed, that is a frequent criticism of traditional regulatory systems — that they do not allow firms sufficient flexibility to adopt the most cost-effective means of achieving an environmental standard. Furthermore, flexibility is not always what firms do (or should) desire. It may be simpler (and less consumptive of the firm's analytic resources) to comply with regulations than to ponder what is the optimal level of pollution for the firm. Confronting environmental regulations as a constraint within which the firm seeks to maximise profit may be analytically easier than confronting market incentives that make environmental costs a production cost variable. Second, arguments that compliance with a regulatory standard is impracticable will simply be replaced by arguments that payment of an impossibly large fee or securing marketable rights is impracticable. Third, enforcement of command-and-control regulatory systems can include the use of non-compliance penalties to discourage delaying tactics. Fourth, considering the fact that emission fees or the cost of marketable rights may be sufficiently large to make a marginal firm insolvent, courts will continue to face the problem of giving the firm leeway or closing down the firm. I would argue that where the court is facing that choice, it is critical that the court view the problem as a choice between 'allowing unacceptable pollution' or 'closing down the firm' rather than as a choice between 'decreasing costs for fees or marketable rights paid by the firm' or 'closing down the firm'.

I see no grounds for optimism that enforcement will be easier under market incentive approaches to pollution control. Both marketable rights and emission fee systems will require monitoring, ideally, continuous emissions monitoring. (Indeed, one of the significant gains that environmental groups secured through the 1990 *Clean Air Act* amendments was employment of continuous emissions monitoring as part of the Title IV acid rain program, the most ambitious marketable rights program enacted to date; for a more detailed discussion, see Hahn in this volume). Both will require inspections to ensure that corporations have purchased sufficient marketable rights or have paid sufficient fees, that no one has tampered with monitoring equipment, and that records and reports are accurate.[11] Both will require that enforcement action be taken when rules are violated.

Indeed, the limited experience with these approaches in the United States suggests that market incentive approaches may have certain *additional* enforcement problems. For example, when marketable rights are sold between private parties, the government may become embroiled in the private disputes between buyer and seller in order to protect the integrity of the market. Such a market enforcement problem arose in what is perhaps the most successful United States experiment with marketable rights implemented to date: the lead phase-down program. Under that program, gasoline refineries faced gradually more stringent standards for lead content in gasoline. Firms that reduced the lead content in their gasoline below the standard earned lead credits that were available for sale to firms with gasoline above the standard. In *Farmers Union Central Exchange, Inc. (CENEX) v. EPA*, 881 F.2d 757 (9th Cir. 1989), the marketing of lead credits created some unusual enforcement problems. In the *CENEX* case, Associated Fuel Distributors (AFD) allegedly agreed to sell 25 million grams of lead credits to CENEX. In reports to the US Environmental Protection Agency, CENEX reported the sale, but AFD did not. AFD had in fact sold those credits to three other lead refiners. CENEX then sued the government to allow it to use the lead credits that AFD had allegedly agreed to sell to CENEX. The district court allowed CENEX to use the lead credits — even though the same lead credits had already been used by the other three lead refiners — with the net result that the environment lost.[12] One would hope that the district court's willingness to enforce a contractual bargain at the expense of the environment was idiosyncratic. However, it is clear that marketable rights schemes will face enforcement problems ranging from ordinary contractual disputes to more difficult anti-trust claims.

Another enforcement problem that looms for emission fee approaches is the difficulty of effective enforcement where the value at stake appears to be 'just money'. The recently revised criminal penalty structure of the *Clean Air Act* dramatically and neatly foreshadows this problem.

The criminal penalty structure of the Act provides that knowing violations of permits and standards are punishable by felony prison terms of five years, knowing violations of the monitoring and recordkeeping systems that make permits and standards effective are punishable by felony prison terms of two years, and knowing failures to pay fees are punishable by misdemeanor jail terms up to one year.

Thus, even where an emission fee may be the key to achieving the desired level of pollution control, Congress has predictably treated failure to pay a fee as just a matter of money — not to be subject to the severe felony penalties that would result from violations of permit conditions. This is an illustration of the danger that, once the enforcement of environmental quality is reduced to a matter of mere monetary payments, the failure to pay, even though critical to achieving environmental quality, will not be treated as a crime worthy of severe sanctions and therefore may be deemed unworthy of serious prosecutorial attention. Fees tend to sever the social disapprobation usually attached to corporate non-compliance with environmental regulations, rendering effective enforcement through the criminal sanction substantially more difficult.

## Enforcement Advantages of Market Incentive Approaches

There is one area where use of market incentive approaches may drastically reduce enforcement probems, namely, the regulation of multiple, small sources or diffuse sources. For example, much of the contamination of our waterways may be linked to agricultural contamination from literally millions of sources. Similarly, the congestion of our landfills is due to decisions made by millions of sources. Finally, the global warming problem attributed to greenhouse gases is caused at least in part by the energy utilisation decisions made by billions of people. Interestingly, these are three of the problems that Congressional leaders have considered appropriate targets for use of market incentives (Project 88, 1988).

To the extent that we attempt command-and-control regulation to deal with pollution problems caused by a multitude of diffuse sources, enforcement of such regulation can be extraordinarily difficult due to the enforcement costs associated with monitoring, inspecting, and taking enforcement action against such an enormous number of sources. At any reasonable level of enforcement effort, each source would face an infinitisimally small probability of detection, which would then require extraordinarily large penalties to make compliance rational. Governments are obviously most unlikely to impose such penalties on what are frequently small firms and individuals.

However, if those same minor sources face price signals in the form of a tax placed on pesticides or fertilisers responsible for contamination of waterways, a high waste disposal fee, or higher electricity costs, then the enforcement costs are drastically reduced because we need only ensure that the relatively few manufacturers of those pesticides or fertilisers, waste disposal companies, or utilities pay the tax. The market then ensures reduction in the amount of pesticides used, waste disposed of, or electricity consumed. Thus, as we move from the relatively easy task of securing compliance from major industrial point sources to the relatively difficult task of securing compliance from the multitudinous minor sources, market incentives approaches may be increasingly attractive.

## Conclusion

The reservations expressed in this paper about enforcement of market incentive approaches to environmental regulation should not be construed to suggest that we should not use market incentives. Rather, we must understand that in implementing market incentives, we will face a host of enforcement problems that we have barely begun to imagine. And, the ultimate criminal sanction — jail time — will continue to be an important tool in ensuring that everyone plays by the rules of the game, even if those rules include a market incentive approach to environmental regulation.

# Endnotes

1. Professor Smith was able to attend the Workshop on Beaucracy, Markets and the Environment, which gave rise to this anthology, due to a Fulbright Senior Scholar award from the Australian–American Educational Foundation and wishes to acknowledge the Foundation's kind assistance.

2. The US sentencing guidelines provide a narrow presumptive sentence range based on criminal history and the offence level. The presumptive sentencing range for a first offender who knowingly violated a water discharge permit by discharging a toxic pollutant in excess of the permit would involve a 10–16 month sentence, with no possibility of probation. But, if the violation was repetitive or ongoing, as are most corporate water pollution violations, the presumptive sentence would be 21–27 months, again with no possibility of probation (§ 2Q1.2).

3. This paper substantially oversimplifies the US environmental criminal laws, which are contained in more than a dozen separate environmental statutes. For example, the federal criminal laws concerning toxic or hazardous substances include: § 3008 of the *Resource Conservation and Recovery Act* (RCRA), 42 USC § 6928 (hazardous wastes); § 103 of the *Comprehensive Environmental Response, Compensation and Liability Act* (CERCLA), 42 USC § 9603 (failure to report release of hazardous substances); § 113 of the *Clean Air Act* (CAA), 42 USC § 7413 (including hazardous air pollutants and extremely hazardous substances); § 309 of the *Clean Water Act* (CWA), 33 USC § 1319 (toxic pollutants regulated under § 307); § 325 of the *Emergency Planning and Community Right-To-Know Act* (EPCRTKA), 42 USC § 11045 (failure to report release of extremely hazardous substances); § 14 of the *Federal Insecticide, Fungicide, and Rodenticide Act* (FIFRA), 7 USC § 1361 (pesticides); § 16 of the *Toxic Substances Control Act* (TSCA), 15 USC § 2615 (principally polychlorinated biphenyls [PCBs], fully halogenated chlorofluoroalkanes, and asbestos); § 105 of the *Marine Protection, Research, and Sanctuaries Act* (MPRSA), 33 USC § 1415 (ocean dumping of waste); the *Deepwater Ports Act*, 33 USC § 1517(b) (failure to report release of oil); the *Outer Continental Shelf Lands Act*, 43 USC § 1816(a) (failure to report release of oil); the *Safe Drinking Water Act* (SDWA), 42 USC § 300h-2 (control of underground injection control of toxic and hazardous substances), and the *Demonstration Medical Waste Tracking Program*, 42 USC 6992d (medical waste). In addition, there are other laws not implemented by the US Environmental Protection Agency that deal with hazardous materials such as the *Hazardous Materials Transportation Act* and the *Occupational Health and Safety Act*. Many of these laws also deal with pollutants other than toxic and hazardous substances.

4. The guidelines then distinguish between crimes involving toxic and hazardous substances and those involving other pollutants. A crime involving a toxic or hazardous substance has a base sentencing range

of two to eight months. A crime involving other pollutants has a base sentencing range of zero to six months. The court must then consider whether certain enhancement factors are present, including: (1) whether the offence involved a toxic or hazardous substance; (2) whether it resulted in repetitive releases to the environment; (3) whether there was a substantial likelihood of death or serious bodily injury; (4) whether it resulted in substantial cleanup expenditures or other community disruption, and (5) whether it involved failure to obtain a permit. If an offence involved all of the enhancement factors, the presumptive sentencing range would increase to 108–135 months. If it involved all of the enhancement factors other than a substantial likelihood of death or serious bodily injury, the presumptive sentencing range would increase to 41–51 months.

5. See the official commentary accompanying §§ 2Q1.2 and 2Q1.3 of the US Sentencing Guidelines.
6. See Locke (1991), citing the 8 March 1991 remarks of then Assistant Attorney General Richard Stewart.
7. The Justice Department's emphasis on prosecuting corporate officers dates back at least to 1980 when Attorney General Civiletti under President Carter pledged to prosecute corporate officials in order to deter illegal disposal of hazardous wastes. (See McMurry and Ramsey 1986).
8. During the period 1983 to 1990, when corporations were indicted for environmental crimes, individual co-defendants were also indicted 70 per cent of the time; 35 per cent of those indicted co-defendants were the president or owners of the business, 17 per cent were vice-presidents, directors, or corporate officers, 14 per cent were middle management, 15 per cent were supervisors, and 19 per cent were non-supervisory personnel. (See Cohen 1992).
9. From Fiscal Year (FY) 83 to FY 91, there were 810 indictments for environmental crimes, resulting in 592 convictions, over $72 million in fines, and imposition of 365 years of prison time of which 165 years have actually been served (received through *Freedom of Information Act* request).
10. Corporate managers, corporate defence counsel and corporate environmental consultants are apt to candidly disclose this point privately rather than publicly, and they have done so in numerous discussions with the author. One corporate environmental consultant, R.F. McCotter, recently pointed publicly to the changes in New South Wales and Victorian environmental legislation, which added stiff criminal penalties up to seven years imprisonment for certain environmental offences, as the primary reason for a five-fold increase in environmental auditing business (McCotter 1992). Similarly, the literature generated by former government enforcement personnel is replete with suggestions that corporations are responding to the threat of criminal prosecution by developing sound environmental compliance systems (Kris and Vannelli 1991; Marzulla and Kappel 1991). Mr Marzulla was Assistant Attorney General of the Lands and Natural Resources Division of the US Justice Department, the political officer responsible for federal prosecutions of environmental

crimes. Ms Kris was the Assistant US Attorney in charge of the Environmental Enforcement unit in the US Attorney's Office of the Southern District of New York, one of the largest and most expert environmental prosecution offices.

11. One of the additional practical problems associated with market incentive approaches is the difficulty of sampling to establish non-compliance. In a command-and-control regulatory system, the permit authority can write a permit that contains a 'never to be exceeded' emissions limit. With such a limit, an inspector can take a single grab sample and establish a violation of the permit. However, under emissions fee schemes, it is more difficult for an inspector to take a single grab sample and establish that the firm is failing to pay the appropriate emissions fees. Similarly, under a marketable rights scheme, it may be difficult for an inspector to take a single grab sample and determine instantaneously whether the firm possesses adequate marketable rights. Market incentive approaches will be most effective when the emissions goal is a mean emissions goal over a reasonably long length of time, rather than an emissions goal that is never to be exceeded or based on acute health effects.

12. When the district court granted summary judgment to CENEX requiring the EPA to recognise the AFD sale to CENEX, CENEX quickly sold the lead credits to other parties. The Ninth Circuit ultimately vacated the district court's injunction and remanded the case to be dismissed for lack of jurisdiction. However, the damage to the environment had already been done.

# References

Ackerman, B., Ackerman, S., Sawyer, J. and Henderson, D. (1974) *The Uncertain Search for Environmental Quality*, The Free Press, New York.

Breyer, S.G. (1982) *Regulation and its Reform*, Harvard University Press, Cambridge, Massachusetts.

Cohen, M.A. (1922) 'Environmental Crime and Punishment: Legal/Economic Theory and Empirical Evidence on Enforcement on Federal Environmental Statutes', *Journal of Criminal Law and Criminology* 82, 1054–108.

Friedlaender, A.F. (ed.). (1978) *Approaches to Controlling Air Pollution*, MIT Press, Cambridge, Massachusetts.

Kneese, A.V. and Schultze, C.L. (1975) *Pollution, Prices, and Public Policy*, Brookings Institution, Washington, DC.

Kris, M.E. and Vannelli, G.L. (1991) 'Today's Criminal Enforcement Program: Why You May be Vulnerable and Why You Should Guard Against Prosecution Through an Environmental Audit', *Columbia Journal of Environmental Law* 16, 227–51.

Locke, R.C. (1991) 'Environmental Crimes: The Absence of "Intent" and the Complexities of Compliance', *Columbia Journal of Environmental Law* 16, 311–31.

Marzulla, R.J. and Kappel, B.G. (1991) 'Nowhere to Run, Nowhere to Hide: Criminal Liability for Violations of Environmental Statutes in the 1990s', *Columbia Journal of Environmental Law* 16, 201–27.

McCotter, R.F. (1992) Address delivered at the *National Environmental Law Association Conference*, Perth, Western Australia, 22 September.

McMurry, R.I. and Ramsey, S.D. (1986) 'Environmental Crime: The Use of Criminal Sanctions in Enforcing Environmental Laws', *Loyola L.A. Law Review* 19, 1133–70.

Posner, R.A. (1980) 'Optimal Sentences for White Collar Criminals', *American Criminal Law Review* 17, 409–18.

Project 88. (1988) *Harnessing Market Forces to Protect Our Environment: Initiatives for the New President*, Washington, DC.

Roberts, M. and Farrell, S. (1978) 'The Political Economy of Implementation: The Clean Air Act and Stationary Sources' in A.F. Friedlaender (ed.), *Approaches to Control Air Pollution*, MIT Press, Cambridge, Massachusetts.

Smith, S.L. (1991) 'Shields for the King's Men: Official Immunity and Other Obstacles to Effective Prosecution of Federal Officers for Environmental Crimes', *Columbia Journal of Environmental Law* 16, 1–72.

United States Environmental Protection Agency. (1992) *Interim Report on Indirect Effects of the Superfund Program*, Office of Policy, Planning & Evaluation, 20 May.

## Statutes

| | |
|---|---|
| 42 USC § 6928 (1993) | : *Resource Conservation and Recovery Act* |
| 42 USC § 7413 (1993) | : *Clean Air Act* |
| 42 USC § 9603 (1993) | : *Comprehensive Environmental Response, Compensation and Liability Act* |
| 33 USC § 1319 (1993) | : *Clean Water Act* |
| 42 USC § 11045 (1993) | : *Emergency Planning and Community Right to Know Act* |
| 7 USC § 1361 (1993) | : *Federal Insecticide, Fungicide and Rodenticide Act* |
| 15 USC § 2615 (1993) | : *Toxic Substances Control Act* |
| 33 USC § 1415 (1993) | : *Marine Protection, Research, and Sanctuaries Act* |
| 33 USC § 1517(b) (1993) | : *Deepwater Ports Act* |
| 43 USC § 1816(a) (1993) | : *Outer Continental Shelf Lands Act* |
| 42 USC § 300h–2 (1993) | : *Safe Drinking Water Act* |
| 42 USC § 6922d (1993) | : *Demonstration Medical Waste Tracking Program* |
| 49 USC Appx § 1801 (1993) | : *Hazardous Materials Transportation Act* |
| 29 USC § 651 (1993) | : *Occupational Health and Safety Act* |

11

# Sustainability, Justice and Market Relations

## Janna Thompson

## What Justice Requires

Policies that impose extra burdens on the least well off members
of a society are contrary to the requirements of justice, as most of
us understand them. Rawls' theory of justice (Rawls 1972), which
is supposed to be based on our ideas of fairness, insists that
inequalities can only be justified if they provide maximum benefits
to the least well off, and even rival conceptions of justice that are
less egalitarian would rule out measures that benefit the wealthy
at the expense of the poor or that disadvantage the least well off in
a disproportionate way.[1]

Measures for reducing harm to the environment are often bad
news for the least well off people of a society. This is so whether
such measures are market based or bureaucratically administered.
For example, regulations that require industries to install anti-
pollution devices are likely to lead to higher prices for consumer
goods, which hurt those on lower incomes more than those on
higher incomes. However, taxes, licences and other devices for
encouraging industries to clean up their act are likely to have the
same effect, depending on the economic situation of firms and the
amount of competition between them.

Are such inequalities really unfair? It might be argued that it is
the least well off who benefit most from many environmental
reforms, for it is they who are most likely to live in polluted and

degraded environments. Since they receive more benefits from a cleaner environment, why not regard it as reasonable to make them bear a greater share of the cost? Or it might be argued that it is justifiable to put greater burdens on some people for the sake of the greater good of the whole society in this generation or the next. A utilitarian would not be so concerned about who bears the burden as long as the common good is maximised. Or it might be argued that burdens imposed by the market are immune from criticism since they result from everyone freely pursuing his or her own good.

None of these three arguments are convincing. The least well off may benefit more from some environmental improvements, just as they have from some public health measures, but it is not their fault that they live and work in degraded and polluted environments. They are not responsible, or are less responsible, for this degradation and should not bear the greater burden for cleaning it up. In any case, many environmental measures are not aimed at improving the well-being of the least well off. Those with wealth and power have usually not been very concerned with the environmental problems that especially affect people who live in slums or work in dangerous or polluted factories. Enzensberger remarks that 'the ecological movement has only come into being since the districts which the bourgeoisie inhabit and their living conditions have been exposed to those environmental burdens that industrialization brings with it' (1974, 10). This point, even if true, does not discredit environmental concerns. But it is a good reason for wanting to ensure that environmental policymakers do not overlook the importance of social equity.

The utilitarian position is also unsatisfactory. It is true that if environmental reforms are effective, then in the future both the least well off and the wealthier members of society will be much better off. It may also be justifiable to require that people bear heavier burdens now for the sake of their own future good (as in the case of forced contributions to superannuation funds). However, if one group of people is being required to suffer disproportionally for the sake of the general good, then there is reason for regarding the policy as unjust. Utilitarians are notoriously weak on matters of justice.

The idea that suffering inflicted by market forces does not count as injustice is also unconvincing. National governments do have some control over their economic affairs. Whether goods are distributed by the market or by more regulated means is a matter for choice, and this choice, and its consequences, can be assessed on moral grounds. It may be immoral not to interfere with the operation of the market if 'free' exchanges systematically disadvantage a part of the population.[2] On the other hand, justice does not require that a government ensure equal outcomes. A system that rations scarce resources so that everyone receives an equal share may in theory be the most equitable arrangement. However, it seems likely in a society like ours that rationing, especially if carried on for a long time, will lead to loss of efficiency, bureaucratic rigidity, corruption and an increase in other crimes. These negative effects are likely to place the heaviest burdens on the least well off, and may also get in the way of achieving the desired environmental goals. There are thus good reasons, from the point of view of justice, in Rawls' sense, as well as efficiency, for relying on the market to distribute some goods. But this does not justify all of the inequitable consequences that a market can produce. Nor does it justify the idea that governments should not interfere with markets for the sake of justice.

## Justice and Environmental Policy

What environmental policies are just? The justice or injustice of a policy depends, first of all, on whether or not it results in a greater burden being imposed on the least well off, and also on how easy or difficult it is for the least well off to reduce or avoid the burden. There are some taxes and charges that are likely to affect the rich more than the poor. An energy tax that makes cars more expensive to run may be justifiable since wealthier people are the ones likely to have more than one car, and to use their cars more frequently (Jacobs 1991, 173). However, whether such a tax is really just depends on the circumstances. If the least well off live in remote areas and have no access to public transport, or if most goods are transported by road, then such a tax becomes regressive. For not only will the poor pay proportionally more than the rich, but the poor are also not in a position to reduce their reliance on motor vehicles without great inconvenience or discomfort. A government decision (as was taken recently in Australia) to increase the price of leaded petrol also places a greater burden on the least well off, since they are more likely to have older cars that require lead. These considerations do not mean that no tax should be imposed (something like this may be necessary for environmental reasons), but it is reasonable to demand that the government alleviate regressive effects by such measures as improving public transport, providing subsidies to rural people and ensuring that cheap means are available for converting car engines.

A tax or restriction on the use of domestic fuels is even more likely to have a detrimental effect on the least well off (Jacobs

1991, 173). The poor are likely to have to pay a proportionally greater amount on something necessary for survival, especially in cold climates. Since the least well off people of a society are more likely to live in rented houses, or less able to afford the cost of better insulation or more efficient means of heating, they have a limited ability to reduce consumption. Once again, justice requires measures to alleviate the regressive effects of the tax: subsidies for insulating dwellings and reduced rates for the unemployed, pensioners and others on a low income.

On the other hand, a measure that requires that the charge for garbage disposal be proportional to the amount generated by each household is more acceptable on the grounds of equity. It is true that this measure is likely to have the immediate effect of making the poor pay more proportionally than the rich. However, in this case there are likely to be ways in which the poor can substantially reduce their expenses, provided the council provides information about recycling and convenient means of practising it. Some inequity still remains, particularly for large families, but this burden might be alleviated by rebates or in other ways.

What measures are justified also depends on how poor the least well off members of a society are. In a wealthy society it is generally reasonable to ask every member of a society, rich or poor, to take on some of the burden of solving environmental problems. But for people in extreme poverty any extra expense is a serious threat to their comfort or survival. For pensioners in a cold climate extra charges for fuel can result in hypothermia and death (Jacobs 1991, 174). For some people, an increase in the cost of food means malnutrition. Justice obviously requires that governments be able to identify those on whom environment reforms impose an unacceptable burden and provide compensation and assistance.

Measures that require compensation from those responsible for environmental damage are also justifiable. Environmentally negligent behaviour ought to be punished. However, in an interdependent, market society responsibility is often difficult to assign. Factories that dump wastes in rivers or in the atmosphere may simply be doing what seems to be necessary in order to cut their costs and stay in business. Fining them may be less productive, and less just, than paying them to change their ways.[3] Similarly, people who drive cars may have little practical choice about how they get from place to place, and should be provided with alternatives rather than be made to feel guilty for causing pollution.

What measures are justifiable also depends on the consequences of imposing them. As I earlier argued, the ideal of equality has to be weighed against other considerations. Because of its likely bad consequences, rationing scarce consumer goods is likely to be a less acceptable measure than other policies. A similar point can be made about proposals for reducing population growth. There is no doubt that many of the proposed measures would have inequitable consequences. For example, a policy that taxes people for having more than a specified number of children or increases the expenses of having children will put more burdens on the poor than the wealthy. The wealthy can still afford to have extra children without great sacrifice. The poor cannot. Robert Young (1980) argues that compulsory measures for reducing population growth (such as laws that limit the number of children a couple may have) are preferable to incentive and disincentive schemes both on grounds of equity and effectiveness. However, the Chinese example shows that such measures can be problematic. Compulsory programs are likely to be strongly resisted, especially in countries where extra children are an asset or where sons are strongly desired for cultural reasons. As a result, there will be problems with compliance, and officials who administer the program will be subject to pressure or corruption. Draconian measures will probably become necessary in order to ensure that people obey. A system of incentives and disincentives thus seems to be a more desirable means of reducing population growth in spite of their inequitable effects.

Consequences depend on the motivations of individuals and what kind of society they live in. If people were more aware of the environmental damage caused by their behaviour, if they were more inclined to make sacrifices for the general good and for each other, then more equitable policies would be possible. Rationing and regulations limiting family size might be a viable option in a society of environmentally concerned citizens. Environmentalists rightly urge the creation of a society in which both sustainability and justice are easier to achieve. The fact remains that we have to be practical and frame policies designed for the world in which we now live.

Given social conditions as they are, the egalitarian ideal is sometimes outweighed by other considerations. However, this point should not be misunderstood. It does not mean that justice is merely one more thing that we have to consider in making an environmental policy — together with efficiency, increasing the general good, and the freedom of individuals. Whether and when we should depart from the egalitarian ideal is itself a matter of justice. Rawls incorporates this requirement into his theory of justice when he insists that a departure from equal treatment must be justified by showing that it will increase the well-being of the least well off (more than any other alternative measure).[4] If an egalitarian policy results in crime, corruption and inefficiency then justice requires that something be done, for these undesirable consequences tend to have the worst effect on those who are least well off.

The environmental crisis, it might be argued, gives us a good reason for ignoring or over-riding principles of justice. For the sake of our survival, environmental problems must be solved, and if it turns out that the only way we can be saved is through draconian and inequitable policies, then this is what we will have to choose. The problem with this idea is that if the environmental crisis is really as serious as that, then there are likely to be no adequate policies, equitable or inequitable, just or unjust, that can be successfully adopted and carried out, at least in currently existing liberal democratic societies. If saving the planet requires that we put enormous taxes on industry or make stringent and difficult to achieve demands on producers and consumers, then we will face the collapse of our economic system, and with it the breakdown of the political compromises that make a society like ours possible. If the environmental crisis is really so serious that just policies cannot deal with it, then we should be talking about alternative societies rather than policy options.

In a wealthy liberal democratic society like Australia it seems reasonable to believe that we can achieve a sustainable economy without violating any of the requirements of justice. The main issue is whether we have the will to do so. However, many environmental problems are global problems. How, if at all, can just environmental policies, and our views about what is just, be applied to the world as a whole?

## Global Environmental Justice

The least well off people of the world are not generally found in Australia or the developed countries of the Western world. They are living in the *favelas* of Rio de Janeiro or the deserts of North Africa and increasingly in the blighted industrial slums of the former Soviet Union. The World Bank estimates that one billion people in the world live below a poverty line of $370 per year (World Bank 1990). The worst forms of environmental degradation and the worst effects of industrial development are also found in these developing or under-developed parts of the world. The problems of poverty and environmental degradation are closely associated. Impoverished people are more likely to exploit marginal lands, to tolerate unsafe and polluting industries, or to allow their land to be stripped of natural resources.

Moreover, poor countries can often not afford environmental reforms. Susan George argues (1977, 312–17) that poor countries are not in the position to phase out the use of pesticides, since people depend too much on the extra productivity that they make possible. Even a temporary setback would be a disaster for many people. Nor can many Third World governments afford to meet the terms of agreements to cut down on the emission of greenhouse gases. Forcing them to do so by threatening to withhold aid or trade is likely to result in making the poorest part of the population even worse off.

Not all environmental programs are bad news for the poorest people of the world. Aid given to villagers to improve their farming methods, conservation projects that employ local people, education programs aimed at women and the development of environmentally sound local industries and cooperatives can have the effect of restoring degraded environments, slowing down population growth and at the same time improving the lot of the least well off. Nevertheless, it is unlikely that such projects by themselves are an answer to Third World poverty and environmental degradation.

To most people it seems obvious that the development of industry and the economies of Third World countries is the only feasible solution to the problem of poverty. The United Nations declares that the people of the world have a 'right to development', which it defines as 'a comprehensive economic, social, cultural and political process, which aims at the constant improvement of the well-being of the entire population and of all its individuals on the basis of their active, free and meaningful participation in the development and in the fair distribution of benefits resulting therefrom' (United Nations 1986). Environmentalists will add that this development must lead to environmental sustainability, both nationally and internationally. The two goals, it seems, should go together. People who are better off are also in the position to protect their environment better.[5]

Some environmentalists are sceptical about the very possibility of achieving development, equity and sustainability for everybody. Rudolf Bahro, for example, does not regard the dream of development as feasible: 'On a world scale industrialisation cannot be achieved any longer, for the earth will not yield the material consumption of the North American middle class for the 10 to 15 billion people of the next century' (1982, 130–31). The right of development does not require that everyone in the world achieve the standard of living of the North American middle class. But it is hard to imagine that sustainable development can be achieved in an equitable way unless the countries of the developed world are prepared to transfer some of their wealth to the poor of the world. Do we, the relatively rich, have a duty of justice to the impoverished people of the world, and if so, what is required of us?

The wealthy people of the world bear a large part of the responsibility for poverty and environmental destruction in the Third World. Apart from the colonial legacy, which still adversely affects some areas of the world, the world market operates in a way that disadvantages the poor. Industrialised countries, as Jacobs remarks, 'export unsustainability' (1991, 34–38). Simply because they are wealthy, they can often avoid the externalities of their economic activity and thrust them onto people in the Third World. They can afford to buy up scarce resources, determine where and how goods should be produced, and export their waste products elsewhere. Their demands for food and fibre result in lands being deforested to grow commercial crops and local people being denied basic goods.

Since the activities of the wealthy substantially contribute to the plight of the poor and the destruction of Third World environments, it seems that justice demands that the wealthy take responsibility for undoing the harm. Jacobs suggests that we have a moral duty to compensate Third World people for the damage we have done. We could, for example, discharge the debts owed by many Third World governments to international banks (Jacobs 1991, 182). However, there are a number of problems with compensation, whatever form it takes. One of them is that Third World governments would not necessarily use the benefits received either to improve the lot of the least well off or to make environmental reforms. Some governments and aid organisations insist that recipient governments use money for particular projects, but as Jacobs notes, attaching strings to the use of compensation payments does not accord very well with the idea that these payments are not aid, but what we owe to those we have harmed. In any case, it might be difficult to ensure that governments do use benefits in an environmentally sound way once they have received them.

There are more serious problems with the idea that justice demands that the wealthy compensate the poor. Who, exactly, owes benefits to whom? Much of the damage to people and environments has been done not by individuals or even states but by multinational companies. Governments and citizens have only limited control over what these organisations do. In fact, it is difficult to determine whom to hold responsible for what is simply the normal operation of the international market. Governments have a limited control over their domestic economy and can thus be held responsible for regulating economic affairs so that the least well off are not disadvantaged, but individual states or companies have virtually no control over the operation of the international market. Even the power of the USA over world economic affairs has diminished significantly in the past two decades, and though some multinationals have a powerful position in Third World countries, they must still do what is necessary to survive in an increasingly competitive international market. But if agents, whether individuals, companies or states, are simply doing what is necessary for their own viability in a world economic system, then it is more difficult to regard anyone in particular as being morally responsible for the export of unsustainability, and there is not much point in singling out particular agents for punishment.[6] This does not mean that appeals to justice are meaningless or pointless in world society, or that we have no duties to the least well off. Rather, the problem of assigning responsibility to particular agents suggests that what is needed is a collective global strategy for solving the related problems of poverty and environmental degradation. Our primary duty of justice is to do what we can to implement this strategy.

## The Global Economy: 'Free' or Regulated?

Let us consider two opposing ideas about how a sustainable and more just world order could be created.

The first is favoured by those who think that a free market can solve most social and environmental difficulties.[7] They point out that restrictions on trade tend to advantage the rich and penalise the poor. Agricultural subsidies and tariffs that most developed countries retain, penalise primary producers in Third World countries. Similarly, the quotas or tariffs that developed countries impose on industrial products prevent Third World countries from getting an advantage out of their lower labour costs. So it is arguable that if world trade became more free then the situation of Third World people would improve, and so would their ability to protect themselves and their environment. The aim of such a strategy would be a world system in which resources were efficiently used and distributed by the market, and where all people, including the least well off, had an opportunity to share in the wealth created by this world market.

However, it is unlikely that free trade would prevent the export of unsustainability. For one thing, externalities will not go away. The invisible hand of the market will not conjure away phenomena like acid rain and the greenhouse effect. Some international regulation seems necessary to deal with these problems. Moreover, in a world without tariff barriers, most of the natural resources are still likely to be monopolised by a few large companies based in the developed world. Free trade is not going to be much of a help to Third World people who have lost the ability to control their own resources; nor will it save them from environmental degradation. More important, free trade is not going to help people who, because of over-population, or lack of natural resources or industry in their own country, have limited opportunities to improve their life chances. As long as there are restrictions on immigration and residency rights, free trade is not likely to have its desired equitable consequence. However, few proponents of free trade are prepared to advocate the lifting of politically imposed restrictions on the movement of people, even though the logic of their argument seems to require this. Is it possible or desirable to aim for a world society in which such restrictions do not exist?

The dismantling of all forms of protection of domestic industries is also likely to lead to an immediate deterioration of the standard of living of the least well off in developed countries. They will face unemployment or a drop in real wages in a situation in which their governments may not be able to afford to make compensations. The conflict between a government's responsibility to protect its own citizens and wider duties of justice will become critical. Even if it is true that the market in the long run will produce better results for most people, it is not clear that this overall good consequence (which is, in any case, not assured) can justify the suffering caused in the short term.

For these and other reasons strategies that rely wholly or heavily on market forces to save the environment and make the world more just are likely to be inadequate and morally undesirable. The alternative world strategy is to supplement and sometimes replace market relations with more effective forms of regulation capable of ensuring that the environment can be protected in a way that promotes equity. This means that there will have to be international bodies that not only make policy but also have the power to enforce it. These bodies will have to be able to protect and compensate the least well off people for whatever inequities or dislocations are caused by world environmental programs, just as domestic governments are supposed to do in the case of their own citizens. To ensure that people really do have the goods necessary for a decent life, it may be necessary for world organisations to transfer in a systematic way wealth from the rich of the world to the poor.

Any proposal for the establishment of international regulatory bodies, especially ones that are supposed to have considerable power, is likely to be met with scepticism or outrage. To whom would such international bodies be responsible, and how could they be made accountable? What is to prevent them from becoming corrupt, authoritarian, inefficient and wasteful? How are they going to exercise their authority? Effective regulation of environmental activity and enforcement of measures that are supposed to secure equity seem to require a considerable amount of interference in the internal affairs of national states. The practical difficulty of obtaining compliance from states that desire to remain independent, and from citizens who may have their own ideas of what justice requires, would be difficult to surmount. And the question remains whether such drastic international interference in the affairs of governments and citizens can really be justified. Philosophical as well as practical issues are at stake. Strategies for achieving sustainability and equity raise questions about the nature and limits of our obligations to those outside our borders and about the justification of the entitlements associated with national sovereignty. Closely associated with these moral issues are political questions about the feasibility of proposed changes in international society.

Perhaps we can avoid having to debate such daunting issues. Michael Jacobs argues (1991, 186–87) that we have good prudential reasons for making sacrifices to help people in Third World countries solve their environmental problems. Since many environmental problems are global, we have to obtain the co-operation of people in Third World countries, which means giving them the aid and technology that will enable them to comply with environmental programs without sacrificing their development goals. `It is certainly unlikely that Third World countries will agree to any international convention on global warming unless very substantial aid is provided to enable them to comply' (1991, 187). Moreover, there are generally good pragmatic reasons to help impoverished people solve their own environmental problems. Desperate people do desperate things. Even if they cannot succeed in threatening us directly, they are likely to devastate their environment, devastate their forests, wipe out essential species and create international tension. To protect ourselves, we must give them help.

However, these prudential reasons for giving aid to developing countries do not take us far enough. Developed countries tend to have a stronger bargaining position. It might be possible to force compliance with a greenhouse treaty by threatening a boycott of needed goods. We might be able to protect ourselves from the depredations of needy people by invasion or threats. In any case, not every Third World country has resources that need to be preserved. What is to prevent us from following Garrett Hardin's advice and leaving those who are most needy and helpless to starve?[8] The debate about what justice requires cannot be avoided.

Moreover, as the above discussion suggests, environmental crises require that we reflect on the nature of world political organisation. We need to ask whether the political and economic structures that now exist are adequate to solve environmental problems, as well as to satisfy people's needs, and what developments are possible and desirable. Our ideas about what a just world order would be like are obviously central to these reflections.

## What is a Just World Society?

I will briefly consider two opposing views about world justice, the advantages and problems associated with each of them and, in particular, what implications they have for the ideal of environmental sustainability.

The first view takes it as basic that all human individuals (and perhaps some animal individuals) have an equal entitlement to respect and moral concern. United Nations declarations of human rights make this assumption about universal moral equality. Philosophers who advocate this position give various justifications for the idea that individuals are all equal from the point of view of morality. Utilitarians stress that all individuals have needs and wants and can suffer harm. Neo-Kantians argue that all human individuals are owed respect because of their status as rational, moral legislators. But whatever the justification, the implications of moral egalitarianism are cosmopolitan: we have the same duties of justice to everyone, whether fellow citizens or distant strangers. Though it may be easier to carry out these duties with respect to fellow citizens (which is why United Nation declarations of human rights are largely promissory notes), the fact remains that we do have an obligation to do what we can to promote a just order where everyone is able to have his or her rights protected and basic needs satisfied.

Beitz (1979) argues that Rawls' principles of justice ought to apply to everyone in the world. We ought to adopt the policies that are most likely to improve the lot of the least well off people of the world, wherever they happen to live. He insists that we, the citizens of wealthy countries, are not entitled to keep our resources for ourselves and our fellow citizens. Similarly Brian Barry (1982) and Onora O'Neill (1986) argue that we have an obligation to help all individuals who are in need, wherever they are.

What kind of world order is implied by the cosmopolitan idea of justice? Neither Beitz nor Barry nor O'Neill are advocating new political structures. Nevertheless, it seems likely that in a world that is already economically interdependent, their idea of justice will work best in a society where international institutions can distribute goods much as national governments do in our world. Markets will be able to operate without artificially imposed barriers; the opportunity of individuals will not be limited by national borders; and the rights, freedoms and security of every individual can be promoted and protected through institutions that have the power to tax and regulate. Cosmopolitanism thus seems to require that we do what we can to bring such a world order into existence.

The cosmopolitan world society seems in some respects to answer to the needs of environmentalism. World organisations capable of regulating a world economy and distributing goods and services would also, it seems, be capable of achieving an environmentally sustainable world society. Or would they? Some environmentalists believe that protecting the environment requires people to develop a sense of place — an identification with a community that is bonded to a particular location. Bioregionalism, for example, is a movement that encourages people to appreciate and identify with their location in an environment and take responsibility for its well-being.[9] Cosmopolitanism, with its emphasis on interdependence and individualism, may not be compatible with the development of this sense of place. If a cosmopolitan economy encourages mobility and consumerism, it may lead to further destruction of the environment. The existence of the political means for achieving sustainability does not necessarily mean that sustainability will actually be achieved.

The second conception of justice places a much greater emphasis on the centrality of community. Walzer (1983) does not deny that all individuals deserve respect, but he believes that we have special moral obligations to members of our own community — to people with whom we share 'a common life'. We have a duty to share our resources with other members of our community and ensure that their needs are met. To people outside our community, our moral duties are not so demanding. We have a duty to help them if they are in dire need (if they are starving or suffering from oppression); we are obligated to do our share to take in refugees, and we owe a special concern to those people who for historical or ethnic reasons have a special relation to us. But beyond this, we are not obliged to share our resources with outsiders. Furthermore, we are justified in defending our common life from enemies who attempt to destroy it, and presumably also from international market forces that are undermining our autonomy and traditions.

Walzer's conception of justice comes much closer to ordinary views about the limits of obligation and the entitlements associated with national sovereignty. Most people believe that they have a greater obligation to help members of their own society than outsiders, and think that it is legitimate to keep most of their collective resources for their own use. There is some justification for this idea. In a community where caring relationships are encouraged, people are likely to be happier and better off than they would be in a world where they count only as free individuals. Moreover, a political society, particularly a democratic society, needs to have some scope to determine its own destiny, which includes determining how its own resources are used. Walzer's position is likely to be attractive to environmentalists who believe that community is a necessary basis for a responsible attitude to the environment. Though he is concerned with states and the relations of citizens, his view about the moral importance of community could be applied to communities that environmentalists find more viable and congenial, including bioregions. However, Walzer's conception of a just world order has little to contribute to a solution of the related problems of Third World poverty and environmental degradation. Not everyone has a community in which their needs can be satisfied; some groups of people do not have many resources to distribute among themselves, and are too poor to avoid damaging the environment. In any case, we live in a world where communities are not independent economically or politically. Some form of international regulation has to exist in order to prevent harm being done to people and environments, whether this harm is deliberate or simply the result of the operation of the international economy.

Neither Beitz's nor Walzer's conception of a just world order is adequate for the solution of the twin problems of poverty and environmental destruction. Is there a way of combining their desirable features: promoting community relationships and at the same time the incentive and ability to solve global environmental problems and to provide goods and services to the least well off? There are a number of possibilities worth exploring. One common idea is a hierarchy of communities based on territory, with appropriate responsibilities and decision-making powers at each level (such as a world consisting of local communities, national states, regional states and international organisations). The European Community is an attempt to realise this idea at a regional level. Freedom of trade and free movement of people is possible within the member states. Environmental and other inter-community matters are decided at a regional level, but at the same time states and some smaller communities are allowed a sphere of autonomy. However, the European attempt to balance regional decision making with national and local autonomy is precarious, and the future of the European Community is far from certain. In any case, it is a model of doubtful value for the world as a whole, in which diversity of culture and the disparity between rich and poor seem to rule out political union.

A more radical, but less developed, idea for a new world order is to promote and build on forms of association that are not based exclusively on territory and that unite people across national and regional boundaries, particularly associations that bring together people from the wealthy and the poor areas of the world.[10] Some associations like this already exist, though their ability to unite people and achieve their ends is now constrained by existing boundary restrictions. They include religious, ethnic and cultural groups, political and trade union links, international and regional pressure groups — including environmental associations. More of these regional and international associations are likely to be brought into existence or be encouraged by interdependence between national societies, the operation of the world economy, the growth of communications networks, and the need of people in different communities to solve common problems.

Communities that cross existing boundaries may help to over-come some of the difficulties of balancing local autonomy with international institutions, and market freedom with regulation. By forming such associations, particularly those that unite the rich and the poor of the world, people are in a position to develop the understandings, loyalties and relations of care that make a more cosmopolitan idea of justice practical. At the same time, the people of each association will value their own customs and ideals and will want to gain more control over matters they regard as important. We can imagine that in a future world society some of these associations may take on the responsibility of redistributing goods among members according to their own idea of what is just. But since most people will belong to a number of associations, they will not be inclined to develop exclusive, uncompromising or inward looking loyalties. They will be recep-tive to the idea that all individuals and the communities they value deserve respect, and that international regulation is needed in order to ensure that the needs of all individuals can be fulfilled, to preserve the network of inter-related communities that indivi-duals value and to overcome problems that communities cannot adequately deal with by themselves. They will welcome the new opportunities for freedom of action and association that economic interdependence and markets make possible; but they will also be able to develop and preserve communities and relationships that are meaningful to them. Cosmopolitan freedom and communitarian values will both be realisable in a world system of diverse, inter-connected communities.

Could environmental sustainability be promoted in such a world? I have suggested that the development of new bonds between individuals and communities are necessary to create relations of justice between people who now regard each other as distant strangers. Similarly, it seems likely that the needs of the environment will only be fulfilled in a world where people can develop an expanded sense of place — where they are concerned not just with the well-being of the environment they happen to live in, but are also willing to combine with people all over the world to preserve and protect other environments, including environments in Third World countries. The ability of people to identify with the fate of an environment somewhere else in the world is demonstrated by rain forest action groups and other international environmental pressure groups. In a world society where associations of people from different countries and regions become common, international environmental organisations that include as members people from both wealthy and poor countries could become more prevalent and more able to put effective pressure on national governments, multinational companies and international institutions. Their actions, and the alliances they make with other associations, could give rise to international regulatory measures that are universally accepted and effective.

Speculation about the nature of a world order that is just, environmentally sustainable, allows scope for market freedom, but is amenable to regulation, has a limited value. There is no model that can guarantee these good results, and no obviously right answer to the question of what is a desirable international society.[11] What does seem obvious is that national boundaries have become problematic in a world where the economy is increasingly international and crises are global. We need to think more about how new communities and relationships can be formed among people in different parts of the world and what they might mean, as far as justice and sustainability are concerned.

# Endnotes

1. In what follows I simply assume that Rawls' account of justice, or something like it, is basically sound. There have been some radical challenges to Rawls' theory, especially Nozick's `economic rationalist' critique (1974). For an attempt to apply economic rationalist ideas of justice to problems of the environment, see Machin (1984).

2. Those who defend markets sometimes argue that truly free exchanges cannot be inequitable. However, in the real world exchanges are never completely free, and therefore inequity is a real possibility.

3. This is the point that Passmore is making when he says that we should not assume that the polluter should always be the one who pays (1974, 70ff).

4. Rawls also regards individual freedom as the first requirement of justice. Oppressive means of bringing about equality, even if effective, would not be justified.

5. For some discussions on how development and sustainability can be combined see the contributions by Dower, Hunt and Attfield in Attfield and Wilkins (1992).

6. This is not to deny that sometimes individuals and companies are clearly morally responsible for the harm done to Third World people. Nothing excuses the negligence that resulted in the Bhopal disaster.

7. P.T. Bauer (1971, 1981) is one of the most vociferous advocates of this position.

8. Hardin argues in *Promethean Ethics* (1980) and elsewhere that in providing aid, developed countries ought to institute a system of triage. Only those countries who are willing to adopt birth control measures and have some capability of solving their own problems should be helped. Those who are better off do not need our help, and the poorest should be left to fend for themselves as best they can.

9. See Sale (1985) and, for a discussion and criticism of bioregionalism, Eckersley (1992, 167–70).

10. There is an increasing number of suggestions along this line. John Burnheim (1986) makes an interesting attempt to envision a world order based on organisations that perform a particular function, such as protecting an environment or managing a communication system. These organisations are predisposed to cooperate for the sake of achieving what each wants, and thus systematic solution of problems is supposed to be possible without world government. I have developed a more conventional idea of an interlocking system of communities in *Justice and World Order* (1992).

11. I have not considered in this chapter anarchist ideas about social organisation, or, more generally, the views of those who believe that the forces that are creating an international market and an international society ought to be resisted — that we need a revolutionary change in the way we live and govern ourselves.

# References

Attfield, R. and Wilkins, B. eds. (1992) *International Justice and the Third World*, Routledge, London.

Attfield, R. (1992) 'Development and Environmentalism' in R. Attfield and B. Wilkins (eds), *International Justice and the Third World*, Routledge, London.

Bahro, R. (1982) *Socialism and Survival*, Heretic, London.

Bauer, P.T. (1971) *Dissent on Development*, Weidenfeld and Nicolson, London.

Bauer, P.T. (1981) *Equality, the Third World and Economic Delusion*, Weidenfeld and Nicolson, London.

Barry, B. (1982) 'Humanity and Justice in a Global Perspective' in J. Pennock and J. Chapman (eds), *Nomos XXIV: Ethics, Economics and the Law*, New York University Press, New York.

Beitz, C. (1979) *Political Theory and International Relations*, Princeton University Press, Princeton.

Burnheim, J. (1986) 'Democracy, Nation States and the World System' in D. Held and C. Pollitt (eds), *New Forms of Democracy*, Sage, London.

Dower, N. (1992) 'Sustainability and the Right to Development' in R. Attfield and B. Wilkins (eds), *International Justice and the Third World*, Routledge, London.

Eckersley, R. (1992) *Enviromentalism and Political Theory: Toward an Ecocentric Approach*, UCL Press, London.

Enzensberger, H. (1974) 'A Critique of Polical Ecology', *New Left Review* 84, 3–31.

George, S. (1977) *How the Other Half Dies: The Real Reason for World Hunger*, Penguin, Harmondsworth.

Hardin, G. (1980) *Promethean Ethics*, University of Washington Press, Seattle.

Hunt, G. (1992) 'Is there a Conflict Between Environmental Protection and the Development of the Third World' in R. Attfield and B. Wilkins (eds), *International Justice and the Third World*, Routledge, London.

Jacobs, M. (1991) *The Green Economy*, Pluto Press, London.

Machin, T. (1984) 'Pollution and Political Theory' in T. Regan (ed.), *Earthbound: New Introductory Essays in Environmental Philosophy*, Random House, London.

Nozick, R. (1974) *Anarchy, State and Utopia*, Blackwell, London.

O'Neill, O. (1986) *Faces of Hunger: An Essay on Poverty, Justice and Development*, Allen and Unwin, London.

Passmore, J. (1974) *Man's Responsibility for Nature*, Duckworth, London.

Rawls, J. (1972) *A Theory of Justice*, Oxford University Press, Oxford.

Sale, K. (1985) *Dwellers in the Land: The Bioregional Vision*, Sierra Club Books, San Francisco.

Thompson, J. (1992) *Justice and World Order: A Philosophical Enquiry*, Routledge, London.

United Nations. (1986) *Declaration on the Right to Development*, 41/125.

Walzer, M. (1983) *Spheres of Justice: A Defence of Pluralism and Equality*, Martin Robertson, Oxford.

World Bank. (1990) *World Development Report*, Oxford University Press, Oxford.

Young, R. (1980) 'Population Problems, Coercion and Morality' in D.S. Mannison, M.A. McRobbie and R. Routley (eds), *Environmental Philosophy*, Dept of Philosophy, RSSS, Monograph Series 2, Canberra, Australia.

## 12

# *Democracy and Environmental Policy Instruments*

## John S. Dryzek

To what extent can we hope to secure effective democratic control in environmental policy? This issue can be unpacked into two more precise questions. The first is a 'macro' one: can *any* more effective shaping of environmental policy be undertaken by democratic means in contemporary liberal capitalist societies? The second question is more 'micro', and contingent on some degree of affirmative answer to the first: can the choice of environmental policy instruments affect the prospects for democratic control? In keeping with the focus of this collection, I shall approach the second question through reference to regulatory and quasi-market orientations to anti-pollution policy.

## Environmental Democracy and State Imperatives

To begin with the first, larger, question, there are reasons to doubt that either extended democratic control or any deeper commitment to environmental values is possible in existing capitalist democracies. If so, then obviously any measures that promise both a deepening of democracy *and* a greater commitment to environmental protection are likely to be doubly difficult. These reasons stem from the fact that contemporary liberal democratic states have been structured to respond to some powerful forces emanating from the capitalist economy. Environmental concerns are but a recent addendum to the state's agenda. In the 25 years or so in which their importance has been recognised in most industrial societies, environmental issues have not achieved the centrality of these more established forces, and they may yet fail to do so. The prospects here stand irrespective of the extent of popular commitment to environmental protection, which opinion polls indicate is consistently high in all industrial societies. There is, then, an inherent conflict between democratic pressure on behalf of environmental values and the structural constraints on states. To see why, consider the main imperatives facing states in capitalist societies.

States in these societies must perform three essential maintaining tasks. First, and arguably foremost, they must secure economic stability and growth. If they fail in this task, then they are 'punished' by both falling tax revenues for any projects that state officials might want to pursue, and by unpopularity in the eyes of their populations. If the latter can vote, then there is the danger of electoral defeat; if voting is not an option, then other channels of political protest, both peaceful and violent, are available for the expression of popular discontent. Neo-Marxists (for example Offe 1984; O'Connor 1987) refer to this as the accumulation imperative, though one does not have to be a Marxist to recognise its importance (see, for example, Lindblom 1977 and 1982 for a liberal recognition of this imperative). One way to ensure economic downturn is to pursue policies with a negative impact on the confidence of capitalist investors. The latter may respond with 'disinvestment' to policies that redistribute income, regulate private corporations more closely, or increase taxation rates. Democracy, too, can be bad for business, if it leads to an increase in demands on the state for financial resources to be redirected toward previously excluded or unrepresented groups. Such was, for example, the fear of the ungovernability theorists prominent in the late 1970s, who recommended restricted democracy for the sake of the political and economic survival of liberal democracies (see, for example, Crozier, Huntington and Watanuki 1975). The new right's political program in the 1980s, especially in the United States and the United Kingdom, was in part a response to such concerns. Whatever else that program accomplished, it was certainly effective in breaking the power of unions and other organisations capable of making political demands on behalf of the less prosperous members of society.

The second maintaining function that states must perform is the keeping of order in societies. In large part this task involves legitimating the prevailing political–economic system in the eyes of the population, and it is easy to interpret the growth of the welfare state in such terms (Offe 1984). For the welfare state provides a cushion for those who would otherwise suffer mightily from the instability inherent in capitalist economies. However, the welfare state is not a simple political–economic necessity, for political repression can substitute for it in the keeping of political order (again, as the experience of Britain in the 1980s illustrates). The 'disinvestment' and 'social order' constraints can sometimes pull the state in different directions, especially when it comes to the question of determining the most functional size and scope of the welfare state.

The third maintaining function facing all states involves staying afloat in a hostile world, constituted by other states and by the international political economy. The national security or military aspect of this constraint is increasingly less of an issue for the states in North America, Western Europe, East Asia, and Australasia lucky enough to be in the prosperous 'core' of the global political economy; these states appear to have now given up on the idea of ever fighting one another. But staying afloat economically mostly means abiding by the dictates of international regimes for trade and finance, and this requirement constrains both core and peripheral states. These regimes increasingly feature an emphasis on the free movement of goods, services, and capital across national boundaries, and increasingly limit the freedom of national policy makers to undertake policies that would restrict the operation of international markets.

The implications of these three constraints for democracy are quite obvious: if democratic pressure, be it on behalf of environmental values or anything else, gets in the way of any one of them, then it is democracy and the demands it generates that must normally give way. The implications for the environment are equally major, though less easily summarised. Clearly, if environmental protection is bad for business confidence (which is often, although not always, the case; see Grabosky and Clark in this volume), then states will be punished to the extent they pursue it — despite the level of expressed public support for environmental values, and democratic pressure on their behalf. Anti-pollution policy can, of course, make life more expensive and less profitable for private business, which can respond either by not investing or by moving its investments elsewhere. Movement of the latter sort is facilitated by the emerging global free trade regime, and by the negotiation of regional free trade agreements. Thus the *maquiladora* industries in Northern Mexico, which produce for the United States market and are mostly owned by US based or multinational corporations, can and do produce levels of pollution that would be unacceptable north of the border. Mexico, for its part, is now precluded from following ecologically sound, sustainable development strategies because it is so thoroughly enmeshed in the free trade regime that it must pursue export-oriented production in both manufacturing and agriculture, whatever the environmental and social costs. The environmental side-agreements negotiated prior to the ratification of the North American Free Trade Agreement (NAFTA) between Canada, the United States, and Mexico in 1993 speak to the issue of polluting industry in Mexico (though not to barriers facing ecologically sustainable development). However, Mexico already has many anti-pollution laws that go unenforced, and there is little reason to suppose the side-agreements will make much difference in this respect. The system of free trade in which Mexico is enmeshed extends beyond Canada and the United States, and it continues to generate powerful incentives not to implement anti-pollution laws.

The principles of free trade intrude upon environmental policy in still more insidious ways. For example, restrictions on pesticide content in imported food, or on the ways in which imported fish can be caught (to protect marine mammals) can constitute violations of the General Agreement on Trade and Tariffs (GATT), as can government subsidies for pollution control equipment.

There can also be a conflict between the second imperative, involving the need for states to maintain internal order, and environmental priorities. For inasmuch as environmental protection involves spending public funds (I recognise this will not always be true), then the money so expended is money not available for 'legitimating' welfare state expenditure. This conflict will of course be especially acute in times of fiscal stress.

In the light of these constraints on states, what are the prospects for effective state pursuit of environmental objectives? It should be clear that it is not very easy for states to take on commitments in support of any set of priorities that conflict with the three established imperatives. There are two possibilities for overcoming this problem here, each of which involves the assimilation of environmental protection to a more established imperative.

The first such possibility would connect environmental protection to the legitimation imperative. If public opinion were to become more strongly environmentalist then legitimation of the prevailing political–economic order in the eyes of the public might have to involve more in the way of governmental effort on behalf of the environment. However, for this change in public opinion to have the desired effect it would have to be so strong that it could act as a counterweight to the economic imperative. The latter would remain ready to automatically punish governments for any environmental measures that damaged business confidence. It is noteworthy that the cause of environmental conservation does not prosper during economic recessions. Moreover, the shift in public opinion would have to be truly massive to make much of a difference here. It should be noted that public opinion in most countries already seeks levels of environmental protection greater than governments currently provide (though public opinion polls are not very good at measuring the intensity of this kind of commitment). Throughout the Western world, there was a wave of environmentalism that crested in 1990. But unlike the previous wave two decades previously, this second wave did not produce much in the way of public policy legacies at the national level in most countries, although it did produce a lot of pro-environmental rhetoric on the part of politicians and corporate public relations departments. The second wave was perhaps more influential at the international level, especially in terms of the agreements on biodiversity reached at the 1992 Earth Summit in Rio and earlier agreements on ozone layer protection.

The second possibility for engaging states in the effective pursuit of environmental objectives would involve tacking them on to the 'accumulation' imperative. In other words, if environmental protection were demonstrably *good* for economic growth, or at least for recession-avoidance, then its pursuit would be facilitated. This situation might arise if the environment is so degraded that economic production suffers (Gorz 1980).

The evidence to date is that environmental degradation that has affected the agricultural productivity of land has met with mostly piecemeal and limited responses, in the form of (for example) government-subsidised soil conservation measures in a number of countries. When it comes to manufacturing industry, it should be remembered that air and water can constitute inputs to production processes, and thus impairment to their quality can be bad for the profitability of business. For example, polluted air may corrode the physical plant of a factory or make its workers less healthy and therefore less productive. Polluted water will have to be cleaned (expensively) before it can be used as a material input for production. This degree of environmental degradation would describe the situation in the industrial areas of much of the former Soviet bloc, where it seems that environmental recovery should be an integral part of economic recovery.

The situation is not quite so dire in most of the world's capitalist democracies, however bad it might be in some localities, and some industries. In these countries it may therefore prove a less straightforward matter to assimilate environmental protection in economic growth. But it is not necessarily impossible. For a clean and attractive environment can be a factor in enticing industry, other than that of the 'heavy' polluting kind. This has certainly been a factor in the economic growth of the Pacific Northwest of the United States, where I resided (until recently). The high-technology industries, which are increasingly prominent in the economy of that region, can tout the 'second paycheck' that they offer workers, in the form of mountains, rivers, coastline, and forests. As a result, these industries often taken pro-environmental positions on at least some policy issues. The lesson has yet to sink in fully in state and federal politics; so there are parts of the region that look like Brazil's Rodonia from the air, as the clearcutting of old growth forests still proceeds.

The moral here may be that the fact that environmental protection can actually help to avoid disinvestment and economic recession is not of itself sufficient to ensure that governments will recognise the fact and act on it. A degree of 'new thinking' may be required. Weale (1992, 75–88) suggests that this kind of ideology, which he terms 'ecological modernisation', has caught on in Germany more than anywhere else. On Weale's account, ecological modernisation involves the redesign of production processes with minimisation of environmental impact in mind, as opposed to 'end of pipe' specifications for pollutants. This ideology also recognises that what seems like avoidance of pollution control costs may in fact involve the displacement of these costs somewhere else in space (to whoever suffers the costs where the pollution eventually ends up) or in time (as the damage will have to be cleaned up, possibly at greater expense, in the future). Weale attributes Germany's lead over other countries here to the fact that the legal-constitutional influence in public policy making is sufficient to ensure that the goals specified in environmental statutes get taken seriously (which they generally do not else-where), and to the threat to the established parties provided by the Greens. If Weale is right on this last point, it would be ironic indeed if the major impact of the German Greens were to render German capitalism, and German economic growth, more ecologically sustainable — and less in need of a green critique.

Broad commitment to this kind of ecological modernisation ideology in a political system probably requires an ability to take a long-term view. In the short term, conflicts between business profitability and economic growth, on the one hand, and environmental protection, on the other, are far more apparent.

Thus a great deal turns on the time horizons embedded in political and economic systems. Horizons are likely to be short in times of economic crisis (which may explain why ecological modernisation as an ideology has not caught on in Eastern

Europe, despite the dire state of its environment); and of course electoral politics introduces its own kind of myopia.

In short, the established constraints faced by states in capitalist societies do not totally preclude effective policy commitment to environmental protection. But there remain good structural reasons why the environmental struggle is and will remain an uphill one, despite the degree of subscription to environmental values on the part of public opinion. This conclusion should be more than a little disturbing, not just for environmentalists, but also for anyone else interested in democratic control in political life.

## Environmental Democracy and the Choice of Policy Instruments

My analysis has so far proceeded at a fairly abstract and 'macro' level, focusing on the possibilities of general commitment to environmental values in political life and public policy. And I have concluded that democratic control in an environmental context is very hard to achieve, not because there is any conflict between environmental values and democratic ones (I believe there is not), but because state-related imperatives emanating from the capitalist political economy and international system stand ready to frustrate democratic pressures on behalf of environmental values. But a more 'micro'-level focus can be equally instructive, so now I turn to a contemplation of alternative policy instruments for pollution control. To put it crudely, the foregoing analysis suggested that democracy in environmental policy needs all the help it can get. So the micro-question becomes: do the broad strategies for pollution control that governments pursue have implications for the degree of democracy that can prevail? Or, in other words, can the content of environmental policy help to produce more, or less, in the way of effective democracy? I shall argue that different policy instruments are indeed conducive to different levels of democratic control, and that in particular we should be wary of the anti-democratic effects of quasi-market instruments.

At first glance, it might seem that the choice among policy instruments here has little or no implication for democracy. For both regulatory and quasi-market mechanisms are things that can be chosen by legislatures and then implemented by bureaucratic agencies. If one abides by time-worn ideas about the separation of politics and administration, and so sees democracy as something that could only exist during the 'politics' phase of instrument adoption, then the degree of democracy prevailing in policy choice would be independent of the content of that choice.

However, matters are not quite that simple. For the broad kind of policy strategy in operation can have substantial impact on the content of policy processes (see Lowi 1964). Such processes are not just a matter of legislation and its associated debates, but of more complex interactions of elected and unelected public officials, institutions, private interests, and perhaps even ordinary citizens. Moreover, politics pervades administration, which is never mere neutral policy execution. Thus every choice of a policy instrument helps to constitute a particular kind of politics. Let me turn now to the kind of political world that regulatory instruments help to create.

*Regulation*
On one (highly stylised) account, a regulatory strategy can only be bad for democracy on the grounds that the agencies entrusted with administering regulations can normally expect to be captured by the very interests they are supposed to be regulating. Stigler (1971) goes so far as to suggest that regulation is typically sought and maintained by and on behalf of the regulated industry, mainly to increase its profits and protect it against competition. These kinds of arguments have been developed by American social scientists observing the operations of self-interested political actors in the United States political system. According to the capture argument, individual members of the public who are the notional beneficiaries of regulation have little time, little information, and little at stake. The regulated industry, in contrast, has a great deal in the way of political resources, and a great deal at stake. Thus its corporate members have every incentive to keep close watch on, influence, and infiltrate the agency in question. The result is a very close relationship between industry and agency, culminating in a 'revolving door' for career paths that move between the two sides. In the United States, this kind of pattern can be found in the regulation of interstate transport, food and drugs, nuclear energy, and (before deregulation) air transportation. To the extent that this pattern applies, the consequence is a conspiracy between agency and industry against the public — and against democracy.

But the pattern does not apply to environmental policy. Even in the United States, the home of the theory and practice of regulatory capture, the federal Environmental Protection Agency (EPA) and its state-level counterparts have avoided this fate. And even when the Reagan White House tried to hand the United States EPA over to polluting industry in the early 1980s, the move eventually failed in the face of massive resistance from Congress, the courts, environmentalists, and public opinion. The agency was crippled — but it was not captured.

The reason for this resistance is that environmental protection falls into what Wilson (1974) calls the 'entrepreneurial' category of regulation. Wilson formulated this category in response to free-market economists like Stigler who argued that regulation would always succumb to industry capture. Political entrepreneurs such as elected officials and leaders of environmental groups can act as counterweights to industry here. Even if they act on purely self-interested motives (as economists always aver), political entre-preneurs can further their own careers by acting as visible advocates for diffuse interests, thus balancing industry opposition to environmental regulation. So while it is true that the benefits of regulation are diffuse, spread across broad publics, while the costs are concentrated upon polluting industry, political entrepreneur-ship ensures that industry interests do not always prevail.

In fact, as environmental regulation has grown over the past two or more decades it has been accompanied, at least in North America, by *increased* democracy in policy making (Paehlke 1988). Far from being characterised by deals between regulators and polluters behind closed doors, environmental policy has featured a variety of process innovations designed to increase the level of informed public participation in policy making. Examples include right-to-know legislation, public hearings of various kinds, and impact assessment procedures that specify opportunities for public comments on written documents and submissions to formal hearings. The environmental movement itself constitutes not only a public interest lobby but also a channel for the participation in politics of large numbers of people motivated by something other than material self-interest. Environmental policy in North America has also been home to a variety of process innovations that involve conflict resolution, and sometimes even policy making, through free discussion among the parties to a dispute oriented toward consensus, usually under the auspices of some third party acting as a facilitator. These innovations can be called 'discursive designs' for short (Dryzek 1990, 43–48). Environmental mediation, policy dialogue, and regulatory negotiation fall into this last category. Such innovative forms of political interaction constitute something of a growth industry in both the real world of policy making and the academic world (Harvard University has an inter-disciplinary Negotiation Project concerned with such forms as they operate in both domestic and international settings).

Not all of this democratic activity relates directly to the regu-latory side of environmental policy. For example, the impact assess-ment process mandated under the 1970 US *National Environ-mental Policy Act* applies only to projects planned by or with the financial support of federal government agencies. However, some of this activity does relate to regulation. Environmental mediation has occurred in connection with some site-specific air pollution problems. And most obviously, regulatory negotiation brings together polluters, public interest groups, and regulatory agency representatives in face-to-face dialogue (see Harter 1982). So far, this kind of negotiation has been restricted to just a few experiments, and certainly does not characterise the bulk of environmental regulation. And it is not always a paragon of democratic participation in that it is restricted to a relatively small number of parties, some of whom may, at worst, be the victims of attempted co-option on the part of corporations or government agencies. Nevertheless, the style of political interaction involved relates directly to the 'deliberative' ideal stressed by many democratic theorists (see Miller 1992). These procedures should not be confused with the European — and especially British — tradition in anti-pollution policy, which involves quiet and exclusive dialogue between government and industry representatives. The very existence of these discursive designs is a concession on the part of state officials to the principle that legitimate decisions require public dialogue and consent.

In short, a regulatory approach to environmental policy does seem to allow for a degree of democracy, and democratisation, in the formulation of regulations. There is of course nothing intrinsic to that approach that automatically leads to any degree of democratic participation, for regulation can also proceed by administrative fiat or by secret and exclusive negotiations among regulators and polluters. In environmental regulation, no less than elsewhere, the price of democracy is vigilance on the part of democrats.

*Quasi-market Schemes*

When it comes to assessing the impact of quasi-market schemes on the degree of democracy in environmental policy making there is far less in the way of experience to draw on. Obviously these schemes are far less prevalent than regulation in just about every country that has taken anti-pollution policy seriously (as the surveys of Jacobs, Hahn and Christoff in Part III of this volume confirm). And I am aware of no policy process innovations that have occurred in connection with the introduction or administration of quasi-market mechanisms. Instead, the few schemes that have been set up seem to have been established through public administration as usual. Thus any account of their implications for democracy has to proceed at a slightly more rarefied level than my discussion of regulation.

It is conceivable that market-type mechanisms may have positive implications for democracy, at least if the objectives of policy are set by public decision (in terms of Michael Jacobs' taxonomy in chapter 2, this implication cannot therefore apply to what he calls the 'property rights' approach). The argument here would be that regulation is inevitably characterised by continuous 'street level' decisions by regulatory bureaucrats, who must interpret regulations in particular cases, and decide whether or not a process is in compliance with particular specifications. A process that involves a continuous stream of low-level decisions is probably going to be skewed toward the regulated industry, which has the opportunities, the resources, and the financial incentives to attend closely to the actions of the street level bureaucrats. In contrast, setting the level of charges for particular pollutants or determining the total number of units of pollution allowable for (say) a lake could be high-visibility decisions with more of a 'once and for all' character, in which case there would be more of an opportunity for public attention to and participation in the crucial stage of decision making.

Anderson et al. (1977, 188) argue along these lines for a centralised regional or even national approach to charge setting, in part because 'Charge setting depends less than direct regulation on finely accurate abatement performance information because the consequences of being somewhat inaccurate are not as severe for the polluter or the pollution control agency'. Charges can and should be geographically uniform; otherwise, there would be an incentive for polluters to move to low-charge jurisdictions. And if charges are uniform, debate over their content can take place 'in a centralised and open decision making forum', which 'means that the resources of the opposing sides are likely to be more equalised, with environmental groups having a relatively greater influence on the final decision than they would on the effluent standard decision made by a multitude of jurisdictions' (Anderson et al. 1977, 189). Environmentalists stand to benefit politically here because 'such a change favors groups with fewer numbers and monetary resources but with competitive analytical skills' (189).

This argument is contingent on the details of particular schemes, as Anderson et al. admit. If, for example, charge levels are subject to continuous adjustment on the part of the supervising agency, or if they are subject to local variation, or if interpretation is needed in particular cases, or if compliance and monitoring remain problematic, then the kinds of interactions between agency officials and polluting firms are not going to be any less frequent, or any more visible to the public, than under regulatory procedures. Thus any argument to the effect that quasi-market schemes automatically have positive implications for democracy is false; it all depends on the details of the scheme in question.

The negative implications of such schemes for democracy are not entirely obvious, but I believe they are significant and important. Now, some kinds of quasi-market approaches would see policy design as a purely technical matter, in which economic reasoning would predominate. The 'property rights' approach would fall into this category. Presumably the establishment of any scheme along these lines would be a matter for rationalistic design alone, and any subsequent interactions would be the province of markets and the courts (to decide disputes over the content and meaning of rights). Democratic participation and deliberation would not enter.

Quasi-market approaches that allow for public decision on policy objectives are less easily criticised in this fashion, for they would seem to allow democratic deliberation at this objective-setting stage (if not subsequently). However, I believe that these approaches too are detrimental to democracy in environmental policy making. My reasoning begins with Kelman's (1981) observation that many environmentalists oppose incentive systems for pollution control because such systems fail to stigmatise pollution as morally wrong. Instead, pollution becomes something to which you have a right if you can afford to pay for it. This is true for 'standards and charges' schemes, but even more true for markets in pollution rights, where pollution is something that you cannot only pay government to do, but to which you also have a private property right, which, like any other private property right, can be sold to other parties. Goodin (1992) compares the selling of rights to pollute by government with the selling of indulgences by the medieval catholic church. In both cases, the authority in question is selling to sinners something not rightfully its to sell. Just as places in heaven are not for the church to sell, so the environment is not for government to sell.

Notice that the argument against quasi-market mechanisms here does not turn on the effectiveness or otherwise of incentive systems in reducing pollution and protecting the environment, but rather on the intrinsic morality of making pollution something that can be bought or sold. The moral implications are fairly clear; but what do they have to do with democracy?

The answer is that quasi-market incentive schemes reinforce and help to establish more firmly an economically rationalistic world, one populated by *homo economicus* rather than *homo civicus*. *Homo economicus* is motivated only by material self-interest, and calculates means to this end in an instrumentally rational fashion. *Homo civicus*, in contrast, is open to persuasion on the part of others in public debate, and is capable of taking the public good into account, rather than simple private interest. Of course, any one individual is probably going to feature some mix of these dispositions. In an environmental policy context, Sagoff (1988) argues that every individual has preferences as both consumer and citizen, and that these preferences may lead to directly opposed positions on particular issues. To use his own example, an individual may look forward as a consumer to enjoying the facilities of a ski resort, while as a citizen oppose construction of the resort on the grounds that it will destroy a valuable wilderness area.

*Homo economicus* is not good for democracy. At best, a world populated by his (and it is a model of man we have here, so 'or her' is not an appropriate qualifier) kind allows a democracy of consumer preference aggregation. This is the kind of democracy that is portrayed by attempts to apply micro-economic reasoning to politics in the public choice school of thought. But as public choice theory has itself shown, a democracy of economic men is an incoherent mess, subject to all kinds of paradoxes, cycles over collective decisions (as when policy A is preferred to B, B to C, and C to A), arbitrariness in collective choice, and subversion of the public good by self-interested politicians, bureaucrats, and private lobbyists (for a survey, see Dryzek 1992).

Thus the more public policies reinforce the standing of *homo economicus* in public life, then the more is democracy undermined. There becomes no place for active citizenship, democratic talk, and moral persuasion. Democracy of any sort requires reasoning, debate, preference adjustment, and some notion of the public good — in short, *homo civicus*.

This recognition of the subtle ways in which quasi-market schemes can undermine democracy in environmental policy should not be taken to imply that a regulatory approach actually enhances the standing of *homo civicus* and deliberative democracy in any straightforward way. To the degree that regulation reproduces bureaucratic hierarchy then it will arguably promote the standing of rule-conforming 'organisation man', *homo bureaucratis*, who is no better for democracy than *homo economicus*. But regulation in practice is far more complex than the militaristic hierarchy that the term 'command-and-control' connotes. Regulation is in fact a very loose category in terms of the kinds of political interactions it allows. Interpersonal interactions within and across legislatures, public agencies, interest groups, and industry may sometimes prove rigidly hierarchical under a regulatory regime (though probably quite rarely). But such interactions can also be competitive, strategic, cooperative, communicative, and persuasive. The mix will vary across time and place; sometimes interactions will be relatively open and democratic, sometimes they will not. Again, my argument is not that regulation promotes democracy, merely that a quasi-market approach introduces some additional impediments to democratic control.

## Conclusion

To the extent that market-type mechanisms have this negative effect on the prospects for democracy in environmental policy, then their more widespread adoption would constitute one more obstacle in what is an uphill struggle in any event. The fact that public opinion in Western countries is generally quite committed to environmental values might seem to suggest that a marriage between environmental policy and democratic control would be easy and happy. But as I have noted, powerful structural forces frustrate democratic pressures for environmental values. In the face of these forces, advocates of democracy in an environmental context have four options, which are not mutually exclusive. First, they can oppose market-type policy instruments, whose adoption would reduce still further the amount of effective democracy in environmental policy. Second, they can point to, and try to expand, the islands of democratic control that do exist (for example in connection with opportunities for public participation in impact assessment processes, or discursive designs more generally). Third, they can try to demonstrate that environmental protection is actually good for one or more of the imperatives facing states, in particular, the imperative to avoid disinvestment and economic recession. And finally, if all else fails they can join in democratic insurgency against a political economy that still fails to treat environmental values with the concern they deserve.

## References

Anderson, F.L, Kneese, A.V., Reed, P. D., Stevenson, R.B. and Taylor, S. (1977) *Environmental Improvement Through Economic Incentives*, Johns Hopkins University Press for Resources for the Future, Baltimore.

Crozier, M., Huntington, S. P. and Watanuki, J. (1975) *The Crisis of Democracy*, New York University Press, New York.

Dryzek, J. S. (1990) *Discursive Democracy: Politics, Policy, and Political Science*, Cambridge University Press, Cambridge.

Dryzek, J. S. (1992) 'How Far is it From Virginia and Rochester to Frankfurt? Public Choice as Critical Theory', *British Journal of Political Science* 22, 397-417.

Goodin, R.E. (1992) 'The Ethics of Selling Environmental Indulgences', Paper presented to the Australasian Philosophical Association Annual Conference, University of Queensland.

Gorz, A. (1980) *Ecology as Politics*, Pluto, London.

Harter, P. (1982) 'Negotiating Regulations: A Cure for Malaise', *Georgetown Law Journal* 71, 1–118.

Kelman, S. (1981) *What Price Incentives? Economists and the Environment*, Auburn House, Boston.

Lindblom, C.E. (1977) *Politics and Markets: The World's Political-Economic Systems*, Basic Books, New York.

Lindblom, C.E. (1982) 'The Market as Prison', *Journal of Politics* 44, 324–36.

Lowi, T.J. (1964) 'American Business, Public Policy, Case Studies, and Political Theory', *World Politics* 16, 677–715.

Miller, D. (1992) 'Deliberative Democracy and Social Choice', *Political Studies* 40 (Special Issue), 54-67.

O'Connor, J. (1987) *The Meaning of Crisis: A Theoretical Introduction*, Basil Blackwell, Oxford.

Offe, C. (1984) *Contradictions of the Welfare State*, MIT Press, Cambridge, Massachusetts.

Paehlke, R. (1988) 'Democracy, Bureaucracy, and Environmentalism', *Environmental Ethics* 10, 291–308.

Sagoff, M. (1988) *The Economy of the Earth*, Cambridge University Press, Cambridge.

Stigler, G.G. (1971) 'The Theory of Economic Regulation', *Bell Journal of Economics and Management Science* 2, 3–21.

Weale, A. (1992) *The New Politics of Pollution*, Manchester University Press, Manchester.

Wilson, J.Q. (1974) 'The Politics of Regulation' in J.W. McKie (ed.), *Social Responsibility and the Business Predicament*, Brookings Institute, Washington, DC.

# Index of Names

# Index of Subjects